SA'ADYAH GAON

THE LITTMAN LIBRARY OF
JEWISH CIVILIZATION

Dedicated to the memory of
LOUIS THOMAS SIDNEY LITTMAN
*who founded the Littman Library for the love of God
and as an act of charity in memory of his father*
JOSEPH AARON LITTMAN
and to the memory of
ROBERT JOSEPH LITTMAN
who continued what his father Louis had begun
יהא זכרם ברוך

*'Get wisdom, get understanding:
Forsake her not and she shall preserve thee'*
PROV. 4:5

*The Littman Library of Jewish Civilization is a registered UK charity
Registered charity no. 1000784*

SA'ADYAH GAON

ROBERT BRODY

Translated from the Hebrew by
BETSY ROSENBERG

Oxford · Portland, Oregon
The Littman Library of Jewish Civilization

The Littman Library of Jewish Civilization

Chief Executive Officer: Ludo Craddock
Managing Editor: Connie Webber

PO Box 645, Oxford OX2 OUJ, UK
www.littman.co.uk

———

Published in the United States and Canada by
The Littman Library of Jewish Civilization
c/o ISBS, 920 NE 58th Avenue, Suite 300
Portland, Oregon 97213-3786

First published in Hebrew © 2006 the Zalman Shazar Center for Jewish History
English translation © The Littman Library of Jewish Civilization 2013
First English translation published in hardback 2013
First published in paperback 2016

A catalogue record for this book is available from the British Library

Library of Congress cataloging-in-publication data
Brody, Robert, Dr.
[Rav Se'adyah Gaon. English]
Sa'adyah Gaon / Robert Brody ; translated by Betsy Rosenberg.
p. cm.
Includes bibliographical references and index.
1. Sa'adia ben Joseph, 882–942.   2. Rabbis—Iraq–Babylonia—Biography.
3. Jewish scholars—Iraq—Babylonia–Biography.   I. Title.
BM755.S2B6513 2006
296.092–dc23   [B]   2012031028
ISBN 978-1-906764-90-6

Publishing co-ordinator: Janet Moth
Copy-editing: Agnes Erdos
Proof-reading: Fern Seckbach
Production, design, and typesetting by Pete Russell, Faringdon, Oxon.
Printed in Great Britain on acid-free paper by
TJ International Ltd., Padstow, Cornwall

Preface and Acknowledgements

⁂

THE PRESENT BOOK aims to acquaint readers with one of the most colour-ful, original, and influential Jewish figures of all times. Rabbi Sa'adyah ben Joseph Gaon (882–942) inhabited a world as far removed from our own culturally and intellectually as it is in time. The age in which he lived, the era of the geonim, was an extraordinarily dynamic phase of Jewish history, thanks in part to broad contact with Muslim culture—and through it with the legacy of the classical world—and to the proliferation of cults and sects within Judaism itself. Because the decisive influence of this age on the later development of Judaism is so little known to contemporary readers, I have attempted in the first chapter to provide a brief sketch of the geonic era and the world in which Sa'adyah was active. The second chapter sets forth all the details known to us concerning Sa'adyah's life— far more than we know about the lives of most of his contemporaries but a great deal less than would be needed to write a standard biography. The remaining six chapters are devoted to Sa'adyah's spiritual and intellectual endeavours in the fields of theology, biblical exegesis, linguistics, poetry, halakhah, and polemics.

Such an arrangement does not do justice to Sa'adyah's distinctive modes of thinking and writing, which defy neat classification, but it is unavoidable if one wishes to set down the main facets of his work as clearly as possible against the background of his predecessors and contemporaries. I have also attempted to compensate for the inevitable separation of related discussions with a fair number of cross-references within the book. In addition to supplying references and some brief notes which were lacking in the original, I have made a few minor changes with the English reader in mind.

Numerous passages in the book have been translated from Judaeo-Arabic, as well as from texts originally written in Hebrew and Aramaic. Many of the Judaeo-Arabic passages have been translated into Hebrew by other writers; except in a few cases where the original no longer survives I have consulted their translations together with the original sources. I would like to take this opportunity to express my gratitude to Haggai Ben-Shammai, who helped me with the translation of a number of words and phrases. I have added explanations and clarifications as necessary, in square brackets, within some of the translated passages.

Quotations of biblical passages are based on the Jewish Publication Society translation of the Bible (corrected version of the 1917 edition, published in 1955).

I would like to thank the Zalman Shazar Center and its director, Zvi Yekutiel, for inviting me to participate in the series Great Jewish Intellectuals and Their Works, and the series editor, Professor Aviezer Ravitzky. I am deeply grateful to friends and colleagues who have read selected chapters in their areas of expertise, saved me from errors and suggested improvements: Menahem Ben Sasson (Chapter 2), Sarah Stroumsa (Chapter 3), Haggai Ben-Shammai (Chapter 4), Aharon Maman (Chapter 5), and Shulamit Elizur (Chapter 6). I would very much like to thank my talented translator, Betsy Rosenberg, and the various members of the Littman Library staff who were instrumental in producing the English version of this book, especially the managing editor Connie Webber, the copy-editor Agi Erdos, and the designer Pete Russell.

And last but by no means least I am grateful to the first readers of the book, my wife Cory and my friends Maurice Cohen and David Kazhdan. May they all be blessed.

Contents

❧

Contents

Note on Transliteration

Hebrew

The transliteration of Hebrew in this book reflects consideration of the type of book it is, in terms of its content, purpose, and readership. The system adopted therefore reflects a broad approach to transcription, rather than the narrower approaches found in the Encyclopaedia Judaica or other systems developed for text-based or linguistic studies. The aim has been to reflect the pronunciation prescribed for modern Hebrew, rather than the spelling or Hebrew word structure, and to do so using conventions that are generally familiar to the English-speaking reader.

In accordance with this approach, no attempt is made to indicate the distinctions between *alef* and *ayin*, *tet* and *taf*, *kaf* and *kuf*, *sin* and *samekh*, since these are not relevant to pronunciation; likewise, the *dagesh* is not indicated except where it affects pronunciation. Following the principle of using conventions familiar to the majority of readers, however, transcriptions that are well established have been retained even when they are not fully consistent with the transliteration system adopted. On similar grounds, the tsadi is rendered by 'tz' in such familiar words as barmitzvah. Likewise, the distinction between *ḥet* and *khaf* has been retained, using *ḥ* for the former and *kh* for the latter; the associated forms are generally familiar to readers, even if the distinction is not actually borne out in pronunciation, and for the same reason the final heh is indicated too. As in Hebrew, no capital letters are used, except that an initial capital has been retained in transliterating titles of published works (for example, *Shulḥan arukh*).

Since no distinction is made between alef and ayin, they are indicated by an apostrophe only in intervocalic positions where a failure to do so could lead an English-speaking reader to pronounce the vowel-cluster as a diphthong—as, for example, in *ha'ir*—or otherwise mispronounce the word.

The *sheva na* is indicated by an *e*—*perikat ol*, *reshut*—except, again, when established convention dictates otherwise.

The *yod* is represented by *i* when it occurs as a vowel (*bereshit*), by *y* when it occurs as a consonant (*yesodot*), and by *yi* when it occurs as both (*yisra'el*).

Names have generally been left in their familiar forms, even when this is inconsistent with the overall system.

Arabic

A simplified system has also been used for Arabic transliteration. *Hamza* and *ʿayn* are indicated by ' and ' respectively (apart from initial *hamza*, which is omitted), but otherwise no special signs are used. Long vowels are not indicated, and there is no differentiation in print between soft and hard *t*, breathed and unbreathed *h*, *sin* and *sad*, *dal* and *dad*, or *zayn* and *za'*. The letter *tha'* is indicated by *th*, *dhal* by *dh*, *kha'* by *kh*, and *shin* by *sh*. The definite article is represented throughout as *al-*, with no attempt to indicate elision, either following a vowel or preceding a sun letter. *Ta' marbuta* is indicated by a, except in the construct (*idafa*), when it is represented as *at*. All Arabic words, apart from proper names standing alone, are italicized. When proper names occur within a transliterated phrase, they are italicized and written with the initial letter in lower case.

Arabic sources listed in the references are cited with their full transliterated Arabic title following the English translation of the title. In the notes, they are referred to by this English translation (sometimes shortened), followed by (Arab.).

Titles of Arabic and Hebrew Works

Most of the works discussed in this book were originally written in Arabic and we do not always know the Arabic title. Some of these also have fairly well-established Hebrew titles and a few have established English titles. For consistency's sake, English titles have been used throughout for all the works originally in Arabic, while the works that were originally written in Hebrew—for example, the *Egron* and *Esa meshali*—are referred to in Hebrew transliteration. A table is provided below, with the Arabic and Hebrew equivalents, when known.

Arabic and Hebrew Titles of Works Referred to in English

✢

R. Sa'adyah Gaon

	Arabic	Hebrew
The Book of Bailments	*Kitab al-Wadi'a*	*Sefer hapikadon*
The Book of Beliefs and Opinions	*Kitab al-Amanat wa-al-I'tiqadat*	*Sefer ha'emunot vehade'ot*
The Book Collecting the Proofs for the Lamps	*Kitab Jam'at al-Hujja li-al-Suruj*	
The Book of Distinction	*Kitab al-Tamyiz*	
The Book of the Eloquence of the Language of the Hebrews	*Kitab Fasih Lughat al-'Ibraniyyin*	
The Book of Religious Law	*Kitab al-Fiqh*	
The Book of the Source of the Non-rational Commandments	*Kitab Tahsil al-Shara'i' al-Sama'iyya*	
The Book of Testimony and Legal Documents	*Kitab al-Shahada wa-al-Watha'iq*	*Sefer ha'edut vehashetarot*
Commentary on the Book of Creation	*Tafsir Kitab al-Mabadi'*	*Perush sefer yetsirah*
Commentary on Daniel	*Kitab al-Mamalik wa-al-Malahim ma Yakun fi 1386 Sana*	
Commentary on Isaiah	*Kitab al-Istislah*	
Commentary on Job	*Kitab al-Ta'dil*	
Commentary on the Pentateuch	*Kitab al-Azhar*	
Commentary on Proverbs	*Kitab Talab al-Hikma*	
Commentary on Psalms	*Kitab al-Tasbih*	
Explanation of the Seventy Isolated Biblical Words	*Tafsir al-Sab'in Lafza min Mufradat al-Qur'an*	
The Laws of Claims and Oaths	*Ahkam al-Mutalaba wa-al-Ayman*	

R. Saʾadyah Gaon (*cont.*)

	Arabic	Hebrew
The Laws of Succession	*Kitab al-Mawarith*	*Sefer hayerushot*
The Refutation of Anan	*Kitab al-Radd ʿala ʿAnan*	
The Refutation of Ben Asher	*Kitab al-Radd ʿala Ibn Asher*	
The Refutation of Ibn Saqawayh	*Kitab al-Radd ʿala Ibn Saqawayh*	
The Refutation of an Overbearing Aggressor	*Kitab al-Radd ʿala al-Mutahamil*	
Siddur	*Kitab Jamiʿ al-Salawat wa-al-Tasabih*	Siddur

R. Hai Gaon

	Arabic	Hebrew
The Book of Buying and Selling	*Kitab al-Shiraʾ wa-al-Buyuʿ*	*Sefer hamekaḥ vehamimkar*

CHAPTER ONE

✥

The Geonic Period and the Background of Sa'adyah Gaon's Activities

To COMPREHEND THE CHARACTER and achievement of Rabbi Sa'adyah ben Joseph, or, as he is better known, Sa'adyah Gaon, it will be necessary to gain some idea of the background of his age. In Sa'adyah's day, the vast majority of Jews viewed themselves as subject to the authority of one or another of the two ancient Jewish centres, Palestine and Babylonia, and sometimes both. The recognized spiritual leaders of these centres, known as geonim, headed the prestigious and internationally renowned academies of Sura and Pumbedita in Babylonia and the central academy in Palestine, which operated in different cities at different times, chiefly Tiberias and Jerusalem.[1] Despite the great importance of this era as a link in the chain of Jewish history, it is not very well known to readers, so I will outline it here in brief before going on to consider the unique figure of Sa'adyah Gaon.

The apparently simple question we must initially pose is one of chronological boundaries: when did the geonic period begin and end? The two transitional points are somewhat difficult to pin down, though for different reasons. If we approach the question of time from the perspective of rabbinic literature, we find that the age of the geonim was preceded by an even more obscure era, that of the *savora'im*. Available sources that might shed light on the period of the *savora'im* are scarce indeed, and the nature of their endeavours—or even the fact of their existence—remains a matter of controversy. What follows is based mainly on a unique source of tremendous importance for our knowledge of Jewish history in the first millennium CE, the famous *Epistle of Sherira Gaon*, written in 986. This epistle clearly belongs to the characteristic geonic genre known as responsa literature, consisting of questions, mostly on talmudic and halakhic issues, sent by Jews from communities around the world to the senior members of the academies headed by the geonim and the replies they received. Nevertheless, the *Epistle of Sherira Gaon* stands out as extremely atypical, both in content and in scope. It is, in

---

[1] The title 'gaon' (eminence; geonim in the plural form) is probably an abbreviation for 'leader of the academy which is the pride of Jacob'. The phrase *ge'on ya'akov*, meaning the pride or glory of Jacob, is from Ps. 47: 5.

fact, a small book containing R. Sherira's answers (and those of other sages in the academy who may have contributed to the composition) to queries sent by the sages of Qayrawan—an important Jewish centre of the day in what is now Tunisia—headed by a famous scholar, Jacob ben Nissim ibn Shahin. The queries concerned two main areas: the redaction of talmudic literature (particularly the Mishnah, the *baraitot*, and the Babylonian Talmud) and its place in the historical context of the Oral Law, and the continuation of the line of transmission of the rabbinic heritage after the period of the *amora'im*. The questions with regard to talmudic literature are numerous and relatively detailed, but there is only one question about the period of 500 years that preceded the questioners' own time, formulated in a quite general way: 'And how were the savoraic sages ordered after Ravina [one of the last *amora'im* who shaped the Babylonian Talmud], and who presided after them as the heads of the academies and how many years did they preside, from that time until today?'[2]

R. Sherira devotes a major portion of his famous responsum to this last question, and even expands the discussion to a subject the questioners never brought up, the history of the *amora'im*. In his words, 'We have seen fit to explain to you the main points of this topic and how the authority of Israel was in early times and how the two academies diverged, because there is some confusion concerning this matter.'[3] In other words, the questioners evidently felt that their knowledge of the amoraic period was sufficient and thus asked only about a later period, whereas the Gaon found it necessary to instruct them concerning the history of the amoraic period as well. R. Sherira's exposition in this epistle is the basis for our timeline of the savoraic and geonic periods and one of our main sources for the chronology of the amoraic period and the history of talmudic literature as a whole.

For our purposes, what is most important is what R. Sherira has to say about the savoraic period and the beginning of the geonic era. He treats the question of the savoraic period twice, first in his detailed discussion of the development of talmudic literature and of how authoritative instruction (*hora'ah*) accumulated over time until Ravina's generation, and later in his historical review. Ravina is cited in this context by the questioners and is referred to along with R. Ashi in a well-known talmudic dictum as marking 'the end of *hora'ah*'. R. Sherira writes thus:

And after this, although there was no further *hora'ah*, there were explanations and opinions approximating *hora'ah*, and these rabbis were called *rabanan savora'ei* [opining rabbis] and they explicated whatever had been left indeterminate [by the Talmud]—for example, R. Rahumi and Raba Yosi and R. Ahai of Behetim and R. Ravai of Rov . . . and these and the rabbis who succeeded them, such as R. Aina and R. Simuna, included several [of their] opinions in the Gemara [Talmud].[4]

---

[2] Lewin, *Epistle of Sherira Gaon* (Heb.), 6.   [3] Ibid. 72.   [4] Ibid. 69–71.

Sherira also furnishes several examples of the interpretations and opinions of these sages that are included in the Talmud. In other words, although the *savora'im* did not enjoy the authority and prestige of the *amora'im*, they played a role, albeit one difficult to determine precisely, in the elaboration and final redaction of the Babylonian Talmud. Although their opinions may not have merited inclusion in the most authoritative category of instruction or *hora'ah*, like those of the *amora'im*, they came 'close to *hora'ah*' and to a limited extent even gained entry into the Babylonian Talmud, the most influential work of all in rabbinic Judaism. It seems that the crucial difference between the *savora'im* and the geonim, at least as far as Sherira was concerned, was precisely this: the geonim were no longer occupied with the redaction of the Talmud but with its study, teaching, explication, and implementation in practice. For them it was an authoritative source that required interpretation but it had been sealed and was closed (in principle) to further additions and emendations.

Before I quote the second portion of the epistle devoted to the *savora'im*, I should point out that R. Sherira, like most oriental Jewish writers until recent times, reckons dates with reference to the Seleucid Era, which began in 312 BCE. Here in brief is R. Sherira's description of the period of the *savora'im* and of the transition to the era of the geonim:

And after him [R. Sama ben Rava] Rabah Yosi presided, and in his day *hora'ah* ended and the Talmud was sealed. And then came the savoraic rabbis and most of them died within a few years . . . And there were years of persecution and troubles at the end of the Persian [i.e. Sasanian] monarchy, and they were unable to establish *pirkei* [public lectures which attracted relatively broad audiences] and convene the academies and conduct the customs of the geonate for a number of years, and our rabbis came from Pumbedita to the neighbourhood of Nehardea, to the city of Piruz Shabur. And these are the names of the geonim who were in our city of Pumbedita after those events, at the end of the Persian monarchy, from the year 900 [= 588/9 CE]: Mar R. Hanan of Ashikiya, and after him reigned R. Mari our ancestor . . . and in his day there was in Sura Mar R. Mar ben Mar R. Huna Gaon.[5]

The transition from the savoraic to the geonic age, as reckoned by R. Sherira, almost certainly occurred during the mid-sixth century CE. There had been an interruption at this time in the normal functioning of the central academies in Babylonia—apparently lasting several decades—and when the Sages finally renewed their full range of activities and appointed new leaders, they no longer considered themselves as belonging to the savoraic period but to what later came to be known as the geonic era.

Other than the names listed in R. Sherira's epistle, our knowledge of the first 200 years of the geonic era is exceedingly limited, and prior to the mid-eighth

[5] Ibid. 97–100.

century very little is known about the Jews of Babylonia and Palestine or the
geonim and their academies. During these 'dark ages' the political and cultural
milieu of the Babylonian and Palestinian Jews underwent sweeping changes following the great wave of Islamic expansion in the seventh century. Up to that
time, the Jews of Babylonia had lived under the Sasanian dynasty, Iranian in origin
and Zoroastrian in religion, while the Jews of Palestine lived under Christian
Byzantine rule. With the astounding success of the Islamic conquests, a new situation emerged: 90 per cent of all the Jews of the world—including the Jews of
Babylonia, Persia, Palestine, Lebanon, Syria, and North Africa—now lived under
Islamic rule in a cultural milieu where the dominant language was Arabic.

The upheaval following the Muslim conquests brought with it numerous
opportunities and challenges. For example, the phenomenon of conversion became much more widespread under the new religion, which sought to include as
much of the populace as possible, than under highly particularistic religions such
as Zoroastrianism. In certain cases, converts to Islam acted out of a desire to
improve their personal lot, whether they aspired to high office or felt ill-treated
within the religious framework of Judaism (women, for example, who wished to
leave their husbands and were unable to obtain a *get* or divorce document). But
beyond such practical concerns, there is no doubt that the culture which evolved
in the Muslim world, to which important contributions were made by various
minorities, particularly the Christians, had a profound influence on large numbers
of Jews. Their exposure to a dynamic new culture with its universal aspirations—
a culture which also transmitted important elements of ancient Greek civilization through translations and adaptations of earlier works—greatly altered the
approaches and attitudes of Middle Eastern Jewry. Muslim society offered Jews
and other minority groups a host of opportunities for cultural enrichment, yet
it also presented a tremendous challenge to those within the Jewish elite who
remained loyal to their own religion and cultural tradition and sought a way to
integrate the two worlds without violating sacred Jewish values. These Jews also
took up a struggle for the souls of 'simpler' believers who were so powerfully drawn
to the prevailing culture that some of them had begun to doubt their own tradition
and developed feelings of inferiority amid the dazzling civilization of Islam.
The effort to meet these challenges was to become, as we shall later see, a salient
feature of the brilliant, wide-ranging activities of Sa'adyah Gaon.

A more technical implication of the Islamic conquests was the prospect of
strengthening ties among far-flung Jewish communities. Under Muslim rule,
communications between the Jews of the Middle East and North Africa became
easier and more efficient. This was so even when different dynasties came to
power in different regions, in contrast to earlier periods during which the Jews of
Babylonia and the Jews of Palestine had lived under rival empires. The benefits of
improved communications were greatest after the middle of the eighth century,

when the capital of the Muslim empire was transferred from Damascus to Baghdad (in 762 CE), close to the ancient centres of Jewish settlement in Babylonia. From this period onwards, we are witness to a rising tide of responsa linking the Babylonian centre with the outlying regions of the Muslim world. These responsa from the mid-eighth century and after provide far more information about Jewish life and culture in the East than we have with respect to prior centuries.

When we try to date the end of the geonic period and the transition to the age of the *rishonim*, or 'earlier authorities', we find vastly more material than for the beginning of the period, but the transition itself was gradual. This slow development did not occur within a given milieu—as it had during the transition from the savoraic to the geonic era—but rather reflects a shift in power relations between centre and periphery. A distinguishing feature of the geonic era, at least from the mid-eighth century onwards, was the acknowledged spiritual dependence of diaspora Jews on the ancient centres of Babylonia and Palestine. As time went by, other communities in North Africa and Europe gained in strength and became less dependent on the Eastern centres. There were, likewise, political and economic circumstances that contributed to the decline of the communities in Babylonia and Palestine, and impeded the maintenance of close ties with the Jews of the West. It is therefore difficult to assign a precise date to the end of the geonic era, which came about as the result of a lengthy process that the last geonim were able to retard but not prevent. The demise of R. Hai ben Sherira in 1038 is usually seen as a major turning point, but Hai was outlived by the gaon of Sura, R. Israel ben Samuel, and the academy of Pumbedita where he had served as gaon continued to function after his death, although its leader apparently no longer held the title of gaon.

The Geonic Academies: Continuity and Change

The two great academies of the geonic era, Sura and Pumbedita, saw and presented themselves as the successors of two central academies of the amoraic period in nearly unbroken continuity.[6] The Suran academy, also known as the academy of Mata Mehasya, was founded by the *amora* Rav during the first half of the third century CE, while another academy was founded in Nehardea by his contemporary Samuel, upon whose death the academy moved to Pumbedita. The academies were associated with the cities of their origin and are thus referred to as the academies of Sura (or Meḥasya) and Pumbedita (or Nehardea), even though both of them relocated to the capital, Baghdad, in the course of the geonic age. There is clear evidence concerning the time and background of the Pumbedita academy's move to Baghdad: 'And R. Hai Gaon son of R. David . . . had been a

---

[6] For a more detailed treatment of this topic see Brody, *The Geonim of Babylonia*, chs. 3 and 4.

judge in Baghdad for many years before his geonate [*c*.890–7] . . . and he was the first of the geonim who dwelt in Baghdad.'[7] Although we have no precise information about the date of the Suran academy's relocation, it evidently took place before Sa'adyah's appointment as gaon of the academy in 928.[8] The full impact of this relocation is difficult to gauge, but we can safely say that the move to Baghdad must have brought the scholars of the academies increased exposure to non-Jewish intellectual trends and easier access to government and court officials.

Some scholars view the existence of Babylonian academies in amoraic times with profound scepticism, claiming that teaching at the time was confined to small circles personally associated with one or another of the masters. The issue is beyond the scope of our discussion here, but it is certain that even if (as seems likely) there were functioning academies in amoraic Babylonia, their institutional framework was far less developed than that of the geonic academies, and our information about them is much more limited. The rise of the central academies during the geonic era is apparent in various ways, including the fact that we rarely hear mention of any other academies in Babylonia at this time. The two principal ones virtually filled the stage and held sway over the Jewish world to an extent undreamt of by their forerunners. They developed an elaborate hierarchy of functions, with offices obtained largely through family influence. A related phenomenon of some importance was the highly structured financial system that provided stipends for scholars and students, the details of which I shall presently set forth.

The geonic academies also pursued a curriculum far different to those of earlier scholars. The Babylonian Talmud, completed in the course of the savoraic period, was now accorded near-absolute authority. The freedom of manoeuvre of later scholars had been greatly circumscribed and their roles changed significantly. No longer permitted to offer independent opinions on questions already settled in the Talmud, they could only provide interpretations and draw practical conclusions. Of course, the need to interpret and apply talmudic halakhah offered the geonic sages a large purview, in addition to which new questions were constantly emerging and demanding their attention. Furthermore, earlier scholars had never been entirely free to offer their own opinions either, being constrained by the opinions of the great sages of previous generations. The difference lay in the proportional shift that took place during the geonic era between innovation and the elaboration of existing texts.

Another significant aspect of the age was the largely collective nature of the geonic academies and their mode of operation. For example, many traditions that were transmitted anonymously in academy circles seem to have enjoyed more

---

[7] The quotation is from a responsum republished in Lewin, *Geonic Thesaurus* (Heb.), vi: *Yoma, Responsa*, no. 121; for further details see Brody, *The Geonim of Babylonia*, 31 n. 47.

[8] See Sa'adyah's letter quoted on p. 28 below.

authority than those attributed to specific sages, including ones reported in the name of leading geonim. Moreover, as we have seen, the geonic 'responsa' were composed by groups of sages, under the direction of a particular gaon, rather than by individuals. Throughout most of the era, geonim did not engage in individual literary activity. Such literary activity, which began towards the end of the period in the wake of exposure to the surrounding non-Jewish culture, is associated primarily with Sa'adyah Gaon.

At the top of the academic pyramid stood the gaon, whose primary task was to instruct the members of the academy, as we shall presently see. He also filled the role—very important for his contemporaries—of presiding judge of a rabbinical court. The existence of this court is well documented, though we seldom hear of its decisions for the simple reason that the academies' archives and those of their affiliated institutions, if indeed such archives existed, have not survived; nor was there any reason, other than in special cases, to mention court decisions in a literary context. A better-known function of the gaon was to compose responsa to questions sent to the academy from all over the Jewish world or, to be more precise—as mentioned earlier—to serve as head of the panel of senior scholars which issued these responsa. Nevertheless, the officiating gaon's decisive contributions to the responsa of this period resulted in their attribution to him by name. Another responsibility of the gaon's office was the administration of the regions, known as *reshuyot*, which were subject to his academy (to this too we shall later return). Other tasks were less central or undertaken by only a few of the geonim. For example, the geonim rarely engaged in formal legislation—we have clear evidence of only two or three *takanot* (official enactments) throughout the period—although they had opportunities to introduce halakhic change in a less direct fashion. A few geonim from Sa'adyah's time onwards authored books on various topics, and we shall discuss Sa'adyah's pioneering role in this literary enterprise later on. Certain geonim are also known to have engaged with Muslim authorities on behalf of their co-religionists, and here, too, Sa'adyah stands out, as we shall see in the following chapter.

The gaon's vice principal was known as *av beit din* (father of the court) in Hebrew or *dayana dibava* (judge at the gate) in Aramaic. Both titles suggest that one of this sage's main functions was to head a court affiliated to the academy, alongside the court presided over by the gaon. Under the authority of the gaon and his vice principal were seventy scholars who were said to represent a kind of Great Sanhedrin, emphasizing the continuity of the geonic academies with earlier institutions and 'borrowing the glory' of ancient times. The scholars of this group sat facing the gaon in rows (seven according to one source, although it may be that they sat in three longer rows in the academy of Pumbedita). Each row was headed by a *resh kalah* (head of a row) or *aluf* (chief) who sat in the front row (though it should be noted that similar honorific titles were also bestowed on leading figures from outside the academies in appreciation of their personal achievements and their support of the academies).

Alongside these high offices, we find mention in geonic literature of a number of more technical positions sometimes filled from outside the Sanhedrin. Prominent among these were the *tana'im*, who specialized in the recitation of tannaitic literature; less frequently, we hear of the *amora'im*, presumably expert in reciting the Talmud. Lastly, we hear of the academy scribe, *sofer hayeshivah*, who took dictation from the gaon and was responsible for the official correspondence of the academy, including the actual writing of responsa. This position sometimes served as a stepping stone to higher office.

Presumably, academy appointments—including membership in the Sanhedrin —were left to the discretion of the gaon, although considerations of inheritance played a major role, according to the testimony of R. Nathan the Babylonian:

And the seven are called heads of rows. And it sometimes happens that others are greater than they in wisdom but are not appointed [instead of them] as heads of rows, [and those of lesser wisdom remain in place] not because of their excellence but because they have inherited their father's rank—for if one of the heads of rows has died and left a son capable of filling his place, he is appointed [to his father's place and occupies it]. And if one of the fellows is slightly greater in wisdom than the son, he is not promoted over him and it [i.e. the rank] is not removed from the son [of the deceased], and it is the prerogative of the head of the academy to appoint as head of the row whom he pleases . . . And if one of the members of the seven rows is greater than another in wisdom, he is not seated in his place—because he did not inherit it from his father—but he is given an increased allocation on account of his wisdom.[9]

It is unclear whether these considerations also prevailed in selecting the vice principal, but we know for certain that the position of gaon was not inherited. Only one case, Hai's replacement of Sherira, shows a gaon succeeding his father, but here exceptional circumstances had intervened. While it is true that a number of geonim were sons of geonim, they only acceded to this office after a period of many years. Sa'adyah's own son, R. Dosa, succeeded him seventy-one years after his death!

We do not know exactly how the gaon himself was selected. The consensus of the academy's scholars seems to have played a crucial role in this, although occasionally they were unable to reach an agreement and would temporarily split, each faction recognizing its own candidate as gaon. At times, as in the case of Sa'adyah, the exilarch himself took an active role in the appointment. However—except perhaps in the early period—the exilarch never attempted to impose his choice on the academy's scholars, and intervened only when they were unable to reach an

[9] This translation is based on the fragmentary Arabic original published in Ben-Sasson, 'The Story of Nathan Habavli' (Heb.), 194–5, supplemented by the Hebrew version published in Neubauer, *Mediaeval Jewish Chronicles*, ii. 87.

agreement or when it proved impossible to find a suitable candidate within their ranks and it became necessary to 'import' a gaon from elsewhere. In all likelihood, the choice was made on the basis of intellectual and spiritual distinction, though family influence added considerable weight. As we shall see in the case of Sa'adyah, the appointment of a gaon from outside the academy was considered exceptional and problematic.

In terms of the types of study which took place in the academy, we must distinguish between the two *kalah* months, Adar and Elul, and the remaining months of the year. During *kalah* months students who did not attend at other times would assemble in the academies, as described in detail by R. Nathan the Babylonian, who apparently witnessed a *kalah* session at the Sura academy in the early part of the tenth century:

And this is the manner of their seating: the gaon of the academy stands in front, and before him are ten scholars who are called 'the first row'... behind these are the next ten, and up to seven rows, all facing the head of the academy. And behind these sit the rest of the students, none of whom knows his place [i.e. they have no designated seats], but in the seven rows everyone knows his place and no one sits in the place of his fellow.[10]

Following this comes the description of a lesson taught by the head of the academy, with the active participation of its scholars and students:

And when the head of the academy wants to examine them concerning their study texts (*girsah*) they gather around him in the four sabbaths [i.e. weeks] of the month of Adar and he sits and the first row recites before him, and the other rows listen in silence. And when they reach a point which is obscure to them, they discuss it among themselves and the head of the academy listens to them and understands their words and then he reads and they are silent and they know he has understood their dispute ... and when he finishes his reading he recites and expounds the tractate which each of them recited at home during the winter and explains in the course of his exposition the point which the students have debated. And sometimes he asks them for an explanation of laws ... and each one speaks according to his wisdom. And he expatiates on the meaning of every law until all is clear to them. And when all is very clear to them, one [of the members of the first row] stands up and expounds it publicly ... and then the other students analyse it and investigate it and explicate it thoroughly; and this is what they did throughout the month.[11]

The *kalah* session ended with an examination by the head of the academy to determine the level of each scholar and the amount of the stipend he would receive:

And in the fourth sabbath [i.e. week] all the Sanhedrin and all the students read, and the head of the academy examines each of them and probes and tests them until he sees

---

[10] Neubauer, *Mediaeval Jewish Chronicles*, ii. 87. [11] Ibid. 87–8.

which one is of quicker intelligence than his fellow. And when he sees one whose Talmud is not well ordered in his mouth, he deals harshly with him and reduces his stipend and chides him with reprimands and informs him of the places where he has been lazy and negligent, and warns him that if he . . . fails again to pay attention to his Talmud, he will be given nothing. They therefore engage in their learning thoroughly and rigorously so that they will not stumble before him with respect to the law. And no row leaves him until they are informed which tractate to study at home; but the other students do not need to be informed [of this selection], as each of them is free to study the tractate of his choosing.[12]

R. Nathan's account conveys the impression that most activities at the academy were suspended throughout the remaining ten months of the year, with each of the permanent scholars studying the tractate announced by the gaon at the end of the *kalah* month in his own home during the ensuing five months, and everyone reconvening at the end of the 'semester' for another *kalah* month, at which time they reviewed the tractate they had studied. This description, however, is misleading, and other evidence suggests that regular studies took place in the academy between one *kalah* convocation and the next, though we know very little about the nature of these studies and the manner of instruction that was employed. R. Sherira gives the following description of the activities of his son R. Hai in one of his epistles: 'And furthermore our son Hai is diligent in teaching them [the students] and putting [the texts] in their mouths, and whosoever does not know how to ask, he teaches him the method of objection [*kushya*] and endears this method to him.'[13] In similar fashion, R. Sar Shalom Gaon offers the following praise of personalized instruction, apparently referring to study frameworks more intimate than the mass sessions held during the *kalah* months:

If you were before us it would be possible to explain them [i.e. the laws in question] very well and distinguish very well between one and another, like 'a word fitly spoken' [Prov. 25: 11], for when a student sits before his master and discusses a matter of law, his master perceives the trend of his thoughts and what he has overlooked and what is clear to him and what stubbornly eludes him, and explains to him until his eyes light up . . . but in writing how much is possible?[14]

We may reasonably suppose that between *kalah* months many of the Sanhedrin scholars as well as assistants such as the *tana'im* would have remained at the academy. This fits in well with the conclusion emerging from a number of sources that under normal circumstances scholars did not have to engage in outside work to support themselves.

A system which provided financial support for so many scholars must have

---

[12] Neubauer, *Mediaeval Jewish Chronicles*, ii. 88.

[13] This text was first published in Schechter, *Saadyana*, 118–21.

[14] For bibliographical details of this responsum see Brody, *Geonim of Babylonia*, 53 n. 2.

been quite costly to administer. The academies depended on three main sources of income: taxes collected from the Jews of the *reshut* (see below), voluntary donations, and revenues from lands owned by the academy—apparently purchased as an investment out of surplus funds. The three institutions of Jewish authority in Babylonia—the academies of Sura and Pumbedita and the exilarchate—divided the territories adjacent to Babylonia into *reshuyot* (areas of hegemony), and each authority bore responsibility for the administration of Jewish life within its purview. The relationship of the central institution to the area under its authority consisted mainly in the right to appoint judges (who supervised other functionaries) for the various communities, and in the levying of internal taxes to cover the expenses of the central institution as well as the judges' salaries. Here, too, R. Nathan the Babylonian provides ample data. For example, he estimates the annual revenue of the Suran academy at 1,500 gold coins (dinars), a sum apparently large enough to satisfy the needs of a few dozen households, and this 'in addition to pledges and donations'.[15] Such pledges and donations came in not only from areas officially linked to the academy but also—and perhaps mainly—from more remote regions which were not formally dependent on the Babylonian centre but recognized its authority and the importance of the geonic academies. We sometimes hear of people pledging sums in special circumstances and of occasional fund-raising drives conducted in different locales, but what deserves particular note is the custom of enclosing contributions along with the questions that were referred to the academies.

The Exilarchate

The geonic academies shared the leadership of Babylonian Jewry with another institution rooted in the distant past: the exilarchate.[16] The exilarch had been the designated representative of the Jewish minority since the Persian period, or at the latest since the rule of the Sasanian dynasty, founded in 226 CE. After the Muslim conquest, the new rulers of the empire adopted the former administrative system's practice of selecting an individual to represent each of the significant religious minorities. Since these representatives presumably filled similar roles, we may round out our knowledge of the Jewish exilarch using information concerning the Catholicos, or head of the Christian community. Of particular importance for our purposes are several writs of appointment to the office of Catholicos transmitted by Muslim authors. These documents date from a somewhat later period, yet they shed light on certain aspects of the geonic period, assuming there were no major changes in the interim. Such an assumption is reinforced by the language of the writs with their emphasis on the continuity of the office, endowing the newly

---

[15]   See Neubauer, *Mediaeval Jewish Chronicles*, ii. 86–7; Brody, *Geonim of Babylonia*, 39 n. 19.

[16]   For a more detailed presentation see ch. 5 of Brody, *Geonim of Babylonia*.

appointed Catholicos with the powers of his precursors. The writs attest to an important point implied in Jewish sources as well, though never explicitly stated: the minority representative had to be accepted both by his own religious community and by the Muslim authorities. Once elected by the leaders of his own people, the Catholicos required confirmation by the caliph, the Muslim ruler. There is, however, one important difference between the office of exilarch and that of the Catholicos: the exilarch was chosen from among the scions of a single family, believed to have descended from the Davidic dynasty, so that this office was seen by Jews as the last vestige of Jewish sovereignty. Such a view also explains the title by which the exilarch was often referred to in geonic times: *nasi*, or prince.

Although the parameters of the exilarch's office are not precisely defined, he undoubtedly held two sorts of privileges and responsibilities: towards the non-Jewish authorities and towards the Jewish people. As to contact with the central government, the exilarch was the main conduit for requests from his community, although we find no explicit references to this in the sources (nor even in those pertaining to the Catholicos). Nevertheless, there is one source that describes the exilarch's regal reception by the caliph (encouraged by gifts to courtiers), to whom he offered 'honeyed words until he granted his every request';[17] presumably these requests were not for himself alone but also—and perhaps mainly—on behalf of the Jewish community. It is often assumed that the exilarch was responsible for collecting taxes owed to the government by the Jewish community, but there is no real evidence for this. According to certain Muslim sources, the exilarch was also expected to present the case for Judaism at theological disputations that took place among the representatives of various religions. If these reports are correct, it seems that the exilarch was perceived—by Muslim authorities at any rate—not only as 'head of the Jews' in a political sense but as a significant religious figure as well.

As for the exilarch's functions within the Jewish community, the sources at our disposal are somewhat richer. These include two relatively detailed descriptions—one by R. Nathan the Babylonian, and the other by a Muslim author, al-Qasim ibn Ibrahim—as well as some scattered comments in various Jewish and Muslim sources. We have already touched on the system of *reshuyot*, which assigned specific territories to three spheres of influence: those of the exilarchate and of the geonates of Sura and Pumbedita. The relationship between the exilarch and his Jewish 'subjects' was more or less identical to that of the gaon and the Jewish residents of his *reshut*. It was expressed, as we have noted, mainly through the appointment of judges for local communities and the collection of internal taxes from members of the community. The exilarch may also have borne the additional responsibility of providing certain welfare services for the community as a whole.

---

[17] Neubauer, *Mediaeval Jewish Chronicles*, ii. 85.

According to the Muslim author mentioned above, the exilarch was responsible for raising children born to Jewish prostitutes, who were regarded as his servants when they reached maturity, but there is no real proof of this assertion.

The exilarch conducted a life of courtly splendour in the manner of the Muslim dignitaries among whom he served and, judging by our sources, the Jewish community took great pride in their grand leader—the social equal of the most important ministers and regarded as such even by non-Jewish authorities. I will illustrate this with a description of the exilarch by R. Nathan the Babylonian:

And from then on [i.e. from the time of his inauguration] he does not leave his house [even to attend the synagogue] and the people congregate and pray with him at all times—whether on weekdays, sabbaths or festivals. And if he wants to go out and pursue his needs he rides in a viceregal carriage like the carriage of the king's ministers, in splendid clothes, with up to fifteen people walking after him ... and when he passes a Jew they run up to him and seize him by the hand ... until there are fifty or sixty of them gathered about him, all the way to his destination. And he never goes out without a full retinue, and his progress resembles that of one of the king's ministers.[18]

Already in talmudic times the relationship between exilarchs and scholars had been complicated and highly fraught, and the situation remained essentially unchanged throughout the geonic period. As far as we can judge from available sources, the exilarchs and the geonim and their scholars were generally able to cooperate, as is shown by the fact that the geonim were involved in the selection of the exilarch and the latter participated in the appointment of geonim. Usually the gaon was chosen by the scholars of his academy and the participation of the exilarch was for the most part ceremonial, but on occasion the exilarch would play an active role in appointing, and even in deposing, a gaon. Thus, Sherira Gaon states in his *Epistle* that he is unable to provide full details of the geonim of Sura before the end of the seventh century CE, 'and there were also upheavals and dismissals by *nesi'im* [exilarchs], who deposed them and restored them to office'.[19]

Around the year 825 CE the power of the exilarchate declined considerably as a result of Caliph al-Ma'mun's decision to authorize any group comprised of ten or more members to form a separate faction and elect its own leader. The event made a huge impression and was seen as a milestone by Jewish and Christian writers alike. Nevertheless, a century later, in the first half of the tenth century, we hear of two serious altercations between exilarchs and geonim. In the first instance, the exilarch Ukba tried to appropriate funds normally set aside for academy scholars, but his attempt was foiled after some important Jewish bankers interceded on the scholars' behalf with the government authorities. The second controversy forms an important part of Sa'adyah Gaon's biography and will be discussed at length in the next chapter.

[18] Ibid. 84–5.

The Palestinian Centre and its Competition with Babylonia

A distinctive feature of the geonic era was the prolonged and often fierce rivalry that existed between the two ancient Jewish centres of Babylonia and Palestine.[20] As opposed to the amoraic period, when each had sought to influence the other, in the geonic era the two centres vied for spiritual dominance over the entire Jewish world. But before we delve further into that competition, let us survey what we know about the Palestinian centre in this period.

There is a certain amount of information in talmudic literature about the main rabbinic academies of Palestine during the tannaitic and amoraic periods, roughly 70–350 CE. After that, however, we lose sight of them until some time in the mid-eighth century, and even then there are only a few reliable sources on the subject. But we have ample evidence concerning the tenth and eleventh centuries, mainly from documentary items found in the Cairo Genizah, the attic of a synagogue where hundreds of thousands of pages had been preserved over the centuries. From the perspective of the Babylonian institutions of the time, the Palestinian academy combined the functions of the central academies and the exilarchate. The head of this academy was recognized by Muslim authorities as the official representative of the Jewish minority in the *reshut* comprising Palestine, Lebanon, Syria, and Egypt, and the documents found in the Genizah which concern the Palestinian academy refer mainly to these dimensions of its activity.

The Palestinian academy was dominated by a smaller number of families than its Babylonian counterpart, and in Palestine, unlike Babylonia, it was not unusual for a son to inherit his father's position as head of the academy, or for several members of the gaon's family to hold high positions in the academy simultaneously. The leadership structure of the Palestinian institution was also different in terms of its official positions. As in Babylonia, the two highest-ranking officials in Palestine were the gaon and the *av beit din*, but the lower-ranking scholars were given numerical titles: the third (in the academy), the fourth, and so on down to the seventh. Another title, comparable to the Babylonian *resh kalah* or *aluf*, was *ḥaver* (roughly 'colleague'), granted to prominent scholars outside the academy, whether these scholars were emissaries of the academy serving as heads of Jewish communities throughout its *reshut*, or eminent scholars with whom the academy sought to strengthen its ties. Connections with the diaspora were extremely important to both the academy and the communities it served. The scholars of the academy offered guidance to diaspora communities not only in halakhic matters but on a whole range of communal issues, and were at the same time largely dependent on the financial and political support provided by these communities. Ties were maintained beyond the official territories of the *reshut* and extended to

[19] Lewin, *Epistle of Sherira Gaon* (Heb.), 105.
[20] For a more detailed treatment of this topic see Brody, *The Geonim of Babylonia*, ch. 7.

regions such as Sicily and parts of Italy, which in an earlier age had belonged to the Byzantine empire together with Palestine. The most important ties, however, were the ones forged with the Jewish community of Egypt, which enjoyed both prosperity and proximity to the seat of power under the Fatimid caliphate.

The prestige of the Palestinian academy rested chiefly on its location in the Holy Land and its claim to continuity with the ancient institutions of Jewish self-governance. The academy was first situated in Tiberias, as it had been during the amoraic period. Towards the end of the tenth century, however, it relocated to Jerusalem, where an imposing ceremony was held each year, at least during the eleventh century: the annual convocation on the Mount of Olives on the last day of Sukkot (the day of Hoshana Rabah). On this occasion, official proclamations were made on matters such as the calendar, public appointments were announced, prayers and blessings were offered on behalf of the financial patrons of the academy, and curses were heaped on the Karaites.[21] The presence of many pilgrims at this season helped strengthen ties with the diaspora and facilitated the working out of communal issues. The gathering made a profound impression not only on the Jews but on their Christian and Muslim neighbours, as evidenced by the descriptions they left.

The Palestinian academy endured a series of severe leadership disputes in which both the sages and the important communities affiliated with them played a role. One can trace the rise and decline of diaspora centres in correlation to their influence on the heads of the academy. As the communities of the Maghreb in north-west Africa had risen to prominence by the late tenth century, so had two Mughrabi families which were contending for the leadership of the Palestinian academy. By the eleventh century many heads of the academy were descendants of these families. Throughout the eleventh century, particularly towards its final decades, the Egyptian centre rose in prominence at the expense of the Palestinian academy, which was forced by political and economic difficulties to move first to Tyre and later to Damascus. The waning of ties with the Holy Land was a severe blow to the academy's prestige and exposed it to harsh competition from abroad. A short while after the transfer of the academy to Tyre, an Egyptian scholar named David ben Daniel, whose father had served as head of the Palestinian academy a few decades earlier, set himself up as the leader of Palestinian Jewry. He was recognized as such for about ten years by a large segment of Egyptian Jewry and various important Palestinian communities until his deposition in 1094. Soon after that, the Palestinian academy disappeared altogether. At the beginning of the twelfth century its remnants moved to Fustat (Old Cairo) and became part of the Egyptian community.

[21] The Karaites represented the greatest sectarian challenge to rabbinic Judaism during (and after) the geonic period. See pp. 147–53 below.

The cultural and intellectual landscape of Palestinian Jewry differed significantly from that in Babylonia. Prior to Sa'adyah's ascension to the geonate, the Babylonian academies had occupied themselves almost exclusively with the study of the (Babylonian) Talmud and halakhah, while in the academy of Palestine the role of such studies in the curriculum appears to have been far more limited. One striking indication of this is the paucity of responsa from Palestinian geonim as opposed to hundreds of their epistles found in the Genizah that were devoted to administrative matters. Moreover, they appear to have played a less central role in cultural life than their Babylonian counterparts, judging by the scarcity of literary finds in the Genizah from this period that can be linked to them with any certainty. Furthermore, the Rabbanite Jews of Palestine (those who accepted the authority of the talmudic rabbis and their successors) had to contend with the intense opposition of the Karaites, who set up a centre in Jerusalem towards the end of the ninth century (see below) and began to overshadow Rabbanite activities, at least in certain areas.

An important outlet for creative expression in Palestine was liturgical poetry or *piyut* (*piyutim* in the plural; the word goes back to Greek *poiesis*, literally 'making', which is related to our English word 'poetry'). The genre originated in talmudic times but did not reach full flowering until the Byzantine era (fifth to seventh centuries CE). Up to and throughout this period, Palestine was the only centre where *piyut* was composed, as far as we know. Even during the later geonic era, by which time activity in this sphere had spread abroad, Palestine was still its leading centre; and even afterwards, when the major creative centres shifted to Europe, the Palestinian influence on *piyut* remained strong.

Early *piyutim* provide us with extremely important information about the spiritual and intellectual life of the Jews of Palestine during the Byzantine and geonic eras. They incorporate elements of halakhah and midrash in poetic paraphrase, especially those that relate to sabbath and festival readings from the Pentateuch and the Prophets or to the nature of the day. Our knowledge of early *piyut* has grown dramatically as a result of the discovery of the Cairo Genizah, and since then thousands of new liturgical poems have been published, clarifying some essential questions pertaining to their nature and evolution. Although in later times *piyutim* were considered adjuncts to the standard prayers, they were originally intended as replacements of central portions of the service, especially the precentor's repetition of the Amidah (standing prayer). Instead of hearing the same prayer they had just recited, congregants were treated to a new prayer that blended artistry and erudition with religious feeling and content.

Another area of literary creativity in Palestine was midrash, which supplied poets with many thematic elements as well as important literary devices. We have no precise information regarding the redaction of the classical collections of midrash, but the scholarly consensus is that these were compiled in Palestine during savoraic and geonic times.

The Jews of Palestine followed a variety of approaches in their diligent study of the Bible. A major phenomenon during this period was the activity of the Masoretic sages who established the Masoretic Text of the Bible with great precision, down to the finest nuances of vocalization and cantillation signs. These scholars, whose main centre was in Tiberias, engaged in their activities over a period that spanned many generations, culminating in the ninth and early tenth centuries with the work of the Ben Asher family, ultimately recognized as the outstanding authorities in this sphere. Scholars have long debated whether the Ben Asher family and other Masoretes were Rabbanite or Karaite Jews (see pp. 22–3, 151–4). Systematic biblical exegesis, on the other hand, was at first indisputably the domain of the Karaites, who based their entire approach on a return to the biblical text. The activity of Palestinian Karaite sages in this field goes back to the establishment of their Jerusalem centre, which coincided roughly with the activities of the Ben Asher family of Masoretic scholars. Another area of systematic study that developed about this time, both in Palestine and in neighbouring lands, was theology. Here, too, it is unclear whether those who engaged in this study identified themselves as Rabbanites or Karaites.

In the field of halakhah, so fervently pursued in the Babylonian academies, the productivity of Palestinian sages was far more modest. The redaction of the so-called 'minor tractates', made up for the most part of selected materials found in earlier Palestinian sources, is commonly attributed to Palestinian sages of this period, though no proof exists that the work was actually carried out in the academy of the Palestinian gaon. We know of only a few responsa written by Palestinian geonim, most of which were incorporated in collections devoted mainly to the responsa of Babylonian geonim under the heading *teshuvat erets yisra'el* (Palestinian responsum). These are distinguishable from the responsa of the Babylonian geonim by their Hebrew diction, unmixed with Aramaic, and by a number of stylistic features.

A small quantity of Palestinian fragments of halakhic codification have come down to us in the Genizah. Some of these come from a collection known as *Ma'asim livnei erets yisra'el* (Palestinian case decisions), the existence of which is first mentioned in a responsum of Hai ben Sherira Gaon. The fragments were not organized thematically but in sections, each starting with the term *ma'aseh* and describing a specific case along with its disposition, all in Hebrew with a sprinkling of Greek. The collection appears to have come from the archive of a central court, probably associated with the Palestinian geonic academy. Other fragments contain a mixture of Babylonian and Palestinian traditions, and appear to reflect the growing Babylonian influence in Palestine at the expense of the indigenous tradition. In a few other fragments we find an attempt at thematic codification of halakhic material on certain topics. The most prominent example is the collection known as *Terefot de'erets yisra'el* (discussing the laws of *terefah*, i.e. diseases or injuries that render an animal unfit for consumption, of the Palestinian Jews).

In addition to the halakhic literature discussed above, various other sources, particularly *piyutim*, contribute to our knowledge of Palestinian legal tradition. Also significant, though to a lesser degree, are the fragmentary prayer books and certain legal documents discovered in the Genizah. Though many of these date from a later era than that of the geonim and originate from outside Palestine, they retain some of the earlier Palestinian traditions. Another unique source of information is a work known by several names that exists in a number of versions, listing approximately fifty differences between Babylonian and Palestinian customs. The author provides short accounts of the distinctions, generally without indicating his own preferences. Many of these differences are recorded in other sources as well, though certain customs documented elsewhere are missing from the list in question for reasons that remain unclear. The sources and aims of the piece are not sufficiently clear either. It was often cited by Karaite writers to disparage Rabbanite Jews and impugn their alleged ancient tradition, arguing that if indeed the 'Oral Law' had been divinely transmitted to Moses at Sinai as they claimed, we should not find numerous discrepancies between the 'Oral Law' of one Rabbanite centre and another.

Our earliest source of information relating to the conflict between Babylonia and Palestine in the geonic era is an open letter written by a Babylonian sage named Pirkoi ben Baboi at the turn of the eighth and ninth centuries. The letter was addressed to members of the Jewish communities of Spain and Africa in an attempt to convince them that the Babylonian tradition is the one and only legitimate voice of Rabbanite Judaism. The Jews of Babylonia, Pirkoi argues, had enjoyed an atmosphere of tolerance and tranquillity dating back to the last days of the First Temple. This allowed them to preserve their ancient traditions without interruption, whereas the Jews of Palestine suffered such fierce persecution under Christian–Byzantine rule that their link to the early traditions had been broken and replaced with 'customs of persecution' (*minhagei shemad*) and other halakhic distortions. Pirkoi speaks of earlier attempts by Babylonian Jews to challenge Palestinian tradition even within the Holy Land. As an example of this, he cites a letter from Yehudai Gaon (head of the Sura academy in approximately 760 CE and a figure he greatly admired) to the community of Palestine concerning 'all the precepts in which they do not act in keeping with halakhah but according to customs of persecution', to which the Palestinian community responded: 'Custom overrides halakhah.'[22] Furthermore, Pirkoi relates that 'in Jerusalem and every other town where Babylonians lived, they created strife and controversy until they [the local Palestinian Jews] agreed to recite the Kedushah every day' in accordance with Babylonian custom.[23]

The efforts invested by the Babylonians apparently bore fruit even in Palestine, and this is attested in several ways, including the translation of Babylonian

---

[22] Ginzberg, *Ginzei Schechter* (Heb.), ii. 559–60.   [23] Ibid. 556.

literature into Hebrew, the language of halakhic writing in post-talmudic Palestine; in one case there are even indications that the translations were carried out in Palestine itself. The fact that Babylonian elements filtered into the halakhic literature of Palestine proves that the interest of the Palestinian sages in Babylonian literature was more than theoretical, and Babylonian influence on a variety of Palestinian customs is evident as well. For example, some communities worked out compromises between the Palestinian triennial cycle of Torah readings and the Babylonian practice of reading the entire Torah in a single year. One defining moment in this relentless struggle was the fierce calendrical dispute (see pp. 26–7, 154–6) in which Sa'adyah played a role that no doubt helped propel him to the Geonate. This was a last-ditch battle, and when it ended, the Babylonian triumph in halakhic matters was complete.

We find an indication of Palestinian 'surrender' to the talmudic and halakhic legacy of Babylonia in a letter written by Solomon ben Judah, an eleventh-century Palestinian gaon, in which he mentions that his son was studying at the Babylonian academy of Hai Gaon. It is hard to avoid the conclusion that the sages of Palestine acknowledged the superiority of the Babylonian rabbis in their traditional areas of expertise. The Babylonians' status was also recognized in a number of communities abroad with strong ties to Palestine, where Palestinian influence was still discernible beneath the surface during the Middle Ages. At a conscious level, diaspora sages everywhere declared their allegiance to the Babylonian Talmud, and some of them had to make great efforts to legitimize customs of Palestinian provenance.

Nevertheless, it would be overly simplistic to describe the geonic era as the age of Babylonian ascendancy over Palestinian tradition. Babylonian tradition itself witnessed not a few changes during this time, brought about largely by Palestinian influence. A striking example of this is the adoption of the practice of reciting *piyutim* by the synagogues of Babylonia as early as the beginning of the tenth century—a custom Pirkoi ben Baboi had once deplored. It was Sa'adyah, brought up in Egypt with its strong Palestinian orientation and educated in Palestine, who played the pivotal role in bringing Palestinian influence to the rabbinic elite of Babylonia, as we shall see throughout this book. The legacy that crystallized during the geonic age and would continue to dictate the development of Jewish culture in the Middle Ages was an amalgam of the two traditions: Babylonian expertise took precedence in matters of halakhah, while in other areas models created by the sages of Palestine were adapted and enhanced.

The Sectarian Challenge

A major challenge facing the geonim and their colleagues was the repeated sectarian attack on talmudic-rabbinic Judaism.[24] The main bone of contention was the Rabbanite claim that the Jewish religion is based not only on the Torah or Written Law, but on the equally authoritative Oral Law. The roots of this controversy over extra-biblical practices reach back to the Second Temple period, when other Jewish groups rejected the Pharisees' claim that the 'traditions of the fathers' are as binding as biblical laws. The dissenting groups faded out after the destruction of the Temple, and it is a long time before we hear again of any organized and systematic opposition to the pharisaic conception of Judaism, yet we should not infer from this that all the Jews of the world embraced it and lived their lives accordingly.

Despite the widespread revival of sectarian activity during the geonic era, our sources reveal little concerning most of the sects, their origins and circumstances, the activities they engaged in, or the positions they held. Certain general observations can be made: sectarian groups emerged mainly in the peripheries of the Jewish world, not in the centres of Babylonia and Palestine. They all had charismatic leaders, some of whom were also messianic pretenders, and what they held in common in terms of belief was an outright rejection of the authority of the extra-biblical tradition represented in their day by the geonim and the academies. A number of these sectarian movements appeared during the first half of the eighth century, at least two of them in Persia.

The second half of the eighth century was an important turning point marked by the activity of Anan ben David, sometimes described as the founder of the Karaite movement. Despite his great influence on succeeding generations, only a few clearly biased sources relating to his life have survived, and these—whether written by his admirers or his detractors—are of very dubious value. What we do know is that Anan was brought up in the milieu of the Jewish elite of Babylonia—according to some, he was descended from the exilarchic dynasty and one source even claimed that he was a leading contender for the position of exilarch—and that he diverged from Rabbanite Judaism in about 770. We have a great deal more information about his ideas than about his biography, chiefly from the Cairo Genizah, where substantial portions of his work *Sefer mitsvot* (The Book of Commandments) have been found. This work was written in an Aramaic idiom closely resembling that of the geonim, and the author was clearly well acquainted with the literature of the Talmud, its substance and dialectical character. Anan's methodology is also reminiscent in a general way of talmudic literature, yet he almost never agrees with the content of talmudic law, and it appears that he strove

---

[24] For a more detailed presentation see ch. 6 of Brody, *Geonim of Babylonia*.

to distance himself systematically from its halakhic conclusions. In contrast to talmudic literature, Anan does not present conflicting opinions or alternative approaches but only one dogmatic system of halakhah buttressed by numerous citations from biblical proof-texts. Another prominent difference is that the talmudic sages derive halakhah primarily, though not exclusively, from the Pentateuch, whereas according to Anan, all parts of the Bible stand on an equal footing.

A central question regarding Anan is how he conceived of his own authority: to what extent did he claim that his system was binding? The style of his work suggests that he believed he was establishing normative precedents. This also seems to have been the impression of Natronai ben Hilai Gaon, who quotes Anan as saying, 'Forsake the words of the Mishnah and Talmud, and I will compose for you a Talmud of my own.'[25] Yet Karaite authors themselves did not view Anan's beliefs and writings as binding. Some even quote him as having said, 'Search diligently in the Torah and do not rely on my opinion,' as if he himself had not intended for others to accept him as an authority but only to follow his example as a paradigm of dissent from Rabbanite authority while striving as individuals to fathom the depths of the Written Law. The authenticity of this saying attributed to Anan is quite dubious, and it may well have been promulgated in order to represent him as the founder or forerunner of the Karaite movement while retroactively legitimizing many Karaite departures from his specific positions.

Sectarian writers in the century after Anan do not appear to have regarded themselves as his disciples; they adopted his opinions on a selective basis, even criticizing him harshly on occasion. It was not until the late ninth or early tenth century that a Karaite movement with a fairly distinct identity took shape and a community of Karaites formed in Jerusalem, which became the spiritual centre of Karaism up to the time of the Crusades. As a rule, early Karaites enjoyed considerable leeway in their halakhic rulings. In the absence of a binding tradition or an institution empowered to issue decisions, every Karaite author was free to interpret the Bible in his own way and to disagree with others, and for this reason it is difficult to speak in this period of 'Karaite halakhah' as a well-defined entity. Only in later eras did the Karaites find ways to restrict the radical individualism of their rulings.

The most important controversies that took place between Karaites and Rabbanites did not involve abstract theological issues, though such arguments did occur, as when Karaites accused the talmudic sages of anthropomorphism. The main disagreement between them concerned the relationship between biblical law and extra-biblical tradition, both in principle and in relation to specific laws. As noted earlier, one of the tenets of Rabbanite Judaism is that the Oral Law, formulated in the writings of the Sages and later expounded by the geonim and the

[25] See Brody, *Responsa of Natronai Gaon* (Heb.), 258.

scholars of their academies, is equal to the Written Law in both authority and antiquity. In disputing with the Karaites, the Rabbanites could not base arguments on this tenet which their adversaries rejected out of hand. As a result, they had to provide fresh justifications derived from their common ground, principally the Bible. A central argument which the Rabbanites used against their opponents, as developed by Sa'adyah and repeated by his successors, was that the Bible itself presupposes the existence of external sources of knowledge, without which it is impossible to understand the Bible or to implement its precepts in many areas of halakhah. This idea appears in various formulations in the writings of Sa'adyah Gaon, and a number of typical examples will be given below.

The Karaites for their part argued that if, as written in Psalm 19: 8, 'The Torah of the Lord is perfect', then Scripture can and must be understood without reference to any outside source whatsoever. And if, for example, there is no specification in the Written Law of the quantity required for the performance of a given commandment, this does not imply (as Sa'adyah argues) that an outside authority must be brought in to decide the issue, but merely that there is no statutory minimum. The need to answer all questions without overstepping the bounds of Scripture led Karaite authors to treat the entire Bible in all its parts equally, basing the laws on the books of the Prophets and the Writings no less than on the Pentateuch. In addition, they stretched the limits of hermeneutics, particularly through the use of analogical proofs (Hebrew *hekesh*, Arabic *qiyas*) to resolve questions not answered in the Bible. When it was their turn to take the offensive, the Karaites strove to disprove the Rabbanites' claim that their halakhah is based on an Oral Law accurately transmitted over many generations. They pointed to numerous controversies among the Sages, to the inconsistency of custom in Rabbanite communities (particularly the centres of Babylonia and Palestine), and to the fact that talmudic sources themselves attribute many rabbinic laws to relatively late sages and describe historical developments in the halakhah that are difficult to reconcile with the claim of a faithfully preserved ancient tradition.

Let us also look briefly at some of the major disputes between Rabbanites and Karaites regarding normative halakhah. Several of these relate to the calendar and to fundamental concerns over how to determine it. Rabbanite Judaism had dropped the earlier method described in the Talmud according to which the new moon was only declared when it had been observed by two eye-witnesses, and various techniques were used to decide when an intercalated month was to be added so as to close the gap between the solar and lunar years. Even before the geonic period, rabbinic tradition had adopted a calendar based on astronomical calculations, while the Karaites insisted on maintaining the more ancient practice (even though it is not mentioned in the Bible). The Karaites (like many other sectarian movements in the history of Judaism) likewise contended that Shavuot must always be observed on a Sunday, in accordance with a literal reading of Leviticus

23: 15–16. Conflict over calendrical issues had long been held to demarcate rival Jewish groups, and so it continued.

With regard to worship, Anan and some of the early Karaites forbade the use of post-biblical liturgy and considered Psalms to be the only authorized book of prayers, although later Karaism introduced changes that aligned it more closely to the rabbinic tradition. In the sphere of ritual law (such as the laws of food purity, family purity, and the sabbath), the Karaites tended towards greater stringency than the Rabbanites, though there are several exceptions, such as their disregard for the regulations of *terefot*. They kept the sabbath far more strictly than Rabbanite Jews and famously extended the prohibition of kindling fire on the sabbath (Exod. 35: 3) to include lighting a fire on Friday that would continue to burn on the sabbath. As a result, they forbade the lighting of sabbath candles shortly before sunset—an obligatory practice according to rabbinic law. They also prohibited various ways of keeping food warm or reheating it on the sabbath that were permitted according to rabbinic law. As a result of these prohibitions, some rabbinic authors asserted that anyone who does not eat warm food on the sabbath should be suspected of heresy or *minut*—in other words, of belonging to the Karaite sect.

The early Karaites also took the prohibitions on incest far beyond those specified in the Talmud, not to mention the Bible. Consequently, within the limited populations of most Karaite communities it became extremely difficult to find a suitable mate, and this in time led to a modification of earlier Karaite law. Another major difference in lifestyle arose from the extreme approach of many Karaites to the destruction of the Temple. They expressed their deep sense of loss by various practices in daily life (such as avoiding meat), a tendency most conspicuous among the Karaites of Jerusalem, who were known collectively as *avelei tsiyon* (the mourners of Zion).

The attitude of Rabbanite Jewish leaders to the different sectarian movements—particularly the Karaites—was, naturally, quite negative. Yet the geonim before Sa'adyah seldom referred or responded to the Karaite challenge. Those who addressed questions to the sages do not seem to have been overly troubled by sectarian competition, whereas the geonim themselves had no direct contact with Karaite Judaism and their knowledge of it was quite limited. We find a striking illustration of this in a responsum of Natronai ben Hilai, the gaon of Sura in the mid-ninth century, concerning a peculiar version of the Passover Haggadah. This turns out to be a Palestinian Haggadah but the Gaon construed it as a Karaite text, even though it included selections from talmudic literature. The responsum offers some indication of the extent of the Gaon's knowledge on this point and reflects his attitude towards the Karaite movement:

These are sectarians who mock the words of the Sages and they are disciples of Anan, may his name rot . . . who said to all who strayed and went a-whoring after him, 'Forsake the words of the Mishnah and Talmud, and I will compose for you a Talmud of my own.' And they still maintain the error of their ways and have become as a separate nation, and he composed a Talmud of wickedness and injustice for himself.[26]

In this, as in many other matters, the turning point came with Sa'adyah, who had campaigned against sectarians since his early youth. In the course of his life he devoted a number of compositions to polemics attacking not only the Karaites but also other heretics, such as Hivi of Balkh (in today's Afghanistan). Polemics of this kind occupied an important place in his other writings as well, not only where one would expect to find them—for example, in his biblical commentaries or *The Book of Beliefs and Opinions*—but also in more surprising contexts, and sometimes only by implication (as we shall see further on, particularly in Chapter 8). The geonim who followed Sa'adyah were less vehement in their anti-Karaite polemics, but they were certainly more forceful than the geonim who had preceded him. Examples of these polemics can be found in the biblical exegesis of Samuel ben Hofni Gaon and in several responsa by Hai ben Sherira to questioners who were troubled by Karaite claims and sought the Gaon's help in defending the Rabbanite tradition.

[26] Brody, *Responsa of Natronai Gaon* (Heb.), 258.

CHAPTER TWO

※

Sa'adyah Gaon, Revolutionary
Champion of Tradition

RABBI SA'ADYAH GAON ben Joseph was a remarkable figure of the geonic era, aptly styled the 'chief discourser everywhere' by Abraham ibn Ezra. His greatness is reflected not only in what he wrote and said but in his impact on others and in the variety of reactions he elicited. Although the classical Genizah period does not begin until some fifty years after Sa'adyah's death, many documents with a bearing on different aspects of his life and works have come to light since the early days of Genizah research alongside numerous fragments of his writings. This makes Sa'adyah Gaon a more attainable subject for a biography than any other Jewish figure of the first millennium. True, much in his life remains unknown, yet compared to our knowledge of his contemporaries, even the most prominent among them, and considering the fact that no organized archives have survived from his day—if indeed any such existed—the amount of information that has come down to us about his life is truly impressive, almost astounding.

Sa'adyah's Life: A Brief Overview

Sa'adyah, 'the Fayyumite' as he was called, was born in 882 in the Egyptian district of Fayyum to a family originating from the area of Dilas, which is why he is also sometimes referred to as al-Dilasi. About his family background we have scant information aside from the disparaging claims of his adversaries that he was the descendant of local non-Jews who had converted to Judaism, or the scion of church sextons, while he himself traced his ancestry back to Shelah, the son of Judah.

The little we know about Sa'adyah's childhood in Egypt comes largely from his own writings. The precise date of his departure from Egypt cannot be determined, but he was most probably in his late twenties by that time. He left behind a family and a circle of students (his wife and children probably joined him later on, although our sources provide no definite confirmation of this or details about when and where such a reunion might have taken place). What we do know concerning his years in Egypt is that he corresponded with Isaac Israeli, one of the

---

This chapter is closely based on chapter 15 of my *Geonim of Babylonia*, where further details and references may be found.

first Jewish theologians, and that while still in his early twenties he composed a number of works, including the *Egron* and at least one polemical work refuting Jewish sectarians.

There is not much information about the next phase of Sa'adyah's life—prior to 921—either. We know that he sojourned in Palestine, Babylonia, and Syria during that period, but we cannot trace his route or establish how long he spent in each location. Presumably, he stayed in Palestine for some time, as indicated by a letter he wrote to his Egyptian students in 921 or early 922, implying that the reason they had not asked him about the Babylonian stand in the current calendrical dispute was that they had believed he was still in Palestine. As a young man who had grown up in the Jewish community of Egypt, traditionally aligned to Palestine, it is only natural that his first destination on leaving his homeland to seek out the cultural and intellectual hubs of the Jewish world would be Palestine and specifically Tiberias. Sa'adyah's acquaintance with Tiberian Hebrew (and Aramaic) dates from this period and is reflected in a number of his compositions. The only explicit evidence that we have relating to his stay in Palestine comes from a contemporary, the Muslim writer al-Masʿudi who mentions Sa'adyah's studies with one Abu Kathir Yahya al-Katib, a Tiberian Jew with whom al-Masʿudi had conducted a religious disputation. The precise identity of Abu Kathir is uncertain and we do not know which subjects he taught Sa'adyah, but we may reasonably suppose that philosophy and theology were among them.

Sa'adyah stepped into the spotlight of history during the great calendrical dispute of 921–3 CE, although the role he played in this polemic and a variety of other facts clearly indicate that he had risen to prominence in the Jewish world even before that time. The dispute between the Babylonian academies and the Palestinian sages, led by Gaon Aaron(?) ben Me'ir, involved the astronomical calculations according to which the dates of Rosh Hodesh were determined. These calculations replaced the ancient system of declaring the new month on the basis of actual sightings of the new moon—a practice the Karaites continued to follow, like their Muslim neighbours. In brief, without going into the technical details, the average lunar month is a little longer than 29.5 days, and consequently the Jewish month is 29 or 30 days long in most cases. In order to compensate for the slightly greater length of the lunar month and to avoid certain calendrical problems (such as the possibility of the New Year or Yom Kippur falling on a day adjacent to the sabbath), a degree of flexibility in the cycle was retained: the months of Heshvan and Kislev could be calculated either as defective (with 29 days each), alternating (Heshvan 29 days and Kislev 30 days), or complete (30 days each). The sages of Palestine claimed that in the year 921–2 these two months had to be defective and therefore the first day of Passover that year would fall on Sunday, whereas the Babylonian authorities argued that both months should be complete and therefore Passover would fall on a Tuesday.

Beyond the technical aspects of the controversy, the roots of which remain obscure despite the efforts of numerous scholars, a major struggle for hegemony over the Jewish world ensued between the two ancient centres of Babylonia and Palestine. The right to determine the calendar was a long-established Palestinian prerogative, and talmudic sources had ruled that intercalated years (years in which the Hebrew calendar contains a thirteenth month, in order to compensate for the discrepancy between the lengths of the solar and the lunar years) had to be ascertained in Palestine. Moreover, as late as the ninth century the Babylonians had still acknowledged the Palestinian gaon and his academy as their superiors in this sphere, and even sent a delegation of scholars (apparently shortly after 835) to study calendrical matters with them—yet now they were claiming authority in this field too. Although the Babylonians had long considered themselves the supreme arbiters in other matters of halakhah (see pp. 18–19), this audacious claim to pre-eminence in a traditional Palestinian purview was indeed far-reaching. The Babylonians eventually prevailed in the protracted struggle that ensued and their halakhic tradition emerged triumphant.

Sa'adyah was seen as one of the leading figures of the Babylonian camp and he made full use of his rhetorical skills and wide connections to present the Babylonian point of view. Although he, like other Babylonian scholars, failed to convince the sages of Palestine to adopt the proclamations of the Babylonian authorities, it is largely to his credit that the Babylonian position eventually won out. Among other things, he wrote a book called *Sefer hamo'adim* (The Book of Appointed Times), in which he took on the role of official spokesman for the Babylonian position on the calendar debate. The book circulated widely among the Jewish communities before Rosh Hashanah and seems to have contributed a good deal to the Babylonian victory. By the summer of 922 at the latest, Sa'adyah had attained the rank of *aluf* (see pp. 7–8 above), either because of his role in the calendar dispute or in recognition of his earlier achievements. For the next five years we hear only of his literary activities. In 926 he published an important anti-Karaite polemic and a halakhic treatise, apparently his last work in this genre. The halakhic treatise seems to have been composed in Baghdad—by then the home of the exilarch and the geonic academies—where in all likelihood Sa'adyah resided during most, if not all, of this period.

The next great milestone in Sa'adyah's career was his appointment as gaon of the academy of Sura in 928. The academy had dwindled in size by the early years of the tenth century, and prior to Sa'adyah's appointment serious thought had been given to closing it down and absorbing what remained of it in the Pumbedita academy. Sa'adyah's proven abilities and literary accomplishments together with his achievements in the public sphere made him an obvious choice as gaon, but he had several disadvantages as well. Unlike previous geonim, he had not been brought up in the academy or even in the Babylonian community, and his wide-ranging and innovative writings may have been frowned on by the more conventional sages. Moreover, he was highly independent and unafraid of confrontation. The exilarch conferred with one of the leading members of the Babylonian community, Nisi al-Nahrawani, who advised him to appoint a much less impressive candidate named Tsemah ben Shahin in his stead, for 'although he [Sa'adyah] is a great man of prodigious wisdom, he fears no one in the world and looks with favour upon no one in the world'.[1] Nevertheless, the exilarch chose to appoint Sa'adyah.

Around this time Sa'adyah dispatched several letters to the Jews of Egypt, in one of which he wrote: 'Similarly any desire or request you may have of the government, tell us about it, for then we will order the prominent householders of Baghdad, among whom we live, the children of Mar Rav Natira and Mar Rav Aaron . . . and they will respond to you on behalf of the caliph, as God our stronghold enables them; do this without fail.'[2] Such a suggestion, if the exilarch viewed it as usurping his functions, may have strained his relations with the gaon, but it was not until two years later, when Sa'adyah refused to endorse one of the exilarch's rulings, that a fierce dispute broke out between the two. At this point the exilarch deposed Sa'adyah and installed in his stead Joseph ben Jacob, who was 'lacking in years and was much inferior in scholarship to Sa'adyah'.[3] Consequently, Sa'adyah tried to replace the exilarch with his brother Josiah, better known by his Arabic name, Hasan. The Babylonian Jewish elite then split into two factions. The Joseph ben Jacob faction included supporters of the exilarch, among them prominent members of the Pumbedita academy (for example, its head, the gaon Kohen Tsedek, who owed his appointment to the exilarch) and a wealthy merchant named Khalaf (Aaron) Sarjado, who reportedly bribed the Muslim authorities. Sa'adyah's faction included scholars and other prominent members of the community, such as the powerful Natira family of court bankers, mentioned above. Attempts to involve the Muslim authorities failed to resolve the crisis and the stalemate continued for another six or seven years. Each camp published broadsides levelling severe accusations at the other side. Eventually a prominent leader, Bishr ben Aaron (the father-in-law of Sarjado) intervened, and the exilarch and Sa'adyah were reconciled. Sa'adyah was once again universally recognized as gaon and Joseph ben Jacob was pensioned off. Soon after, the exilarch died and Sa'adyah remained gaon until his demise in 942, shortly before his sixtieth birthday. Although he had served as gaon of Sura for nearly fourteen years, his position had been weak and in dispute for half the term.

It is unclear to what extent Sa'adyah succeeded in his post during these years; what is certain is that his writing continued to flourish. We know of at least three

---

[1] Neubauer, *Mediaeval Jewish Chronicles*, ii. 80.

[2] This letter has been published several times, most recently in Gil, *Kingdom of Ishmael* (Heb.), ii. 27–30.   [3] Lewin, *Epistle of Sherira Gaon* (Heb.), 118.

treatises that he composed during this period: in addition to the *Sefer hagalui*, devoted mainly to his conflict with the exilarch and his supporters, he published his two great theological works, a commentary on *Sefer yetsirah* (The Book of Creation, an early work on cosmogony) and *The Book of Beliefs and Opinions*.

Sa'adyah the Revolutionary

Sa'adyah's background worked both for and against his career. On the one hand, he was able to draw on personal contacts in various Jewish communities, particularly in his native land, Egypt; on the other hand, his attempts to enter the ranks of the Babylonian Jewish elite were met with mistrust and jealousy. His unconventional education had an even more striking impact in the cultural and intellectual spheres. Normally the geonim of Babylonia were selected from amongst families of sages with long-standing connections to the central academies, who had been educated within their walls or at affiliated institutions and whose interests lay almost exclusively in the areas of the Babylonian Talmud and halakhah. These sages had only a limited knowledge of Jewish life in other communities (including the Palestinians and Karaites) and were little acquainted with the surrounding Muslim and Christian cultures. The great intellectual changes that took place in the world of the Babylonian geonim were largely due to Sa'adyah Gaon's introduction and legitimization of many new spheres of knowledge.

From his youth Sa'adyah's cultural exposure had been far broader than any Babylonian yeshiva student's. Egyptian Jews of his day were under the sway of the Palestinian tradition, which fostered biblical philology and liturgical poetry among other disciplines. Sa'adyah had also been exposed from an early age to important areas of Muslim culture—as we may learn, for example, from the introduction to his *Egron* (a dictionary that he produced at the age of 20), in which he explains that he composed it because, among other things:

Just as the children of Ishmael recount that one of their notables saw people who did not speak Arabic eloquently and this distressed him, and he composed for them a brief discourse from which they would learn eloquence, I too saw that many of the children of Israel do not know the basic eloquence of our language, let alone its more difficult [parts] ... and so I felt duty-bound to compose a book in which to gather most of the words in two collections.[4]

As mentioned earlier, Sa'adyah had engaged in correspondence with the Jewish philosopher Isaac Israeli even before he left Egypt. Many of his writings on these and other subjects antedated his appointment as gaon of Sura. Although the cultivation of these fields never became obligatory in Babylonian scholarly circles, Sa'adyah's example lent them legitimacy and prestige, and at least one or two of his successors in the geonate followed him in pursuing each of these areas.

[4] Allony, *Egron* (Heb.), 150–3, and cf. 30–1.

Moreover, Sa'adyah led a quiet revolution even in areas of traditional Babylonian expertise. The geonim before him had concerned themselves exclusively with tannaitic literature and the Babylonian Talmud, not with the Palestinian Talmud or Palestinian aggadic midrashim. Sa'adyah was well acquainted with these works and made use of them in many of his writings. He relied on the Palestinian Talmud even in his halakhic works, though to a limited extent, and this had a decisive impact on his successors, who were prepared to recognize its authority so long as it did not contradict the Babylonian Talmud.

Sa'adyah's innovativeness in halakhah extended to the forms of his literary activity: whereas earlier geonim had limited themselves to the writing of responsa, Sa'adyah, even before his appointment to the geonate, wrote a series of halakhic monographs on various topics. This innovation was adopted by several of his successors and led to a fundamental change in the general character of rabbinic literature from that time onward.

In addition to those areas traditionally cultivated in Babylonia or Palestine or both, Sa'adyah engaged in disciplines—such as biblical exegesis—scarcely touched before by other Jews, at least not Rabbanite Jews. Although he was not the first to translate selected biblical books into Arabic, Sa'adyah may well have been the first Rabbanite Jew to write commentaries on books of the Bible. In the spiritual life of the Babylonian sages Bible study was of marginal importance. In Palestine, too, where there was an intense pursuit of Masoretic studies (concerned with the establishment of the precise consonantal text of the Bible, its vocalization and punctuation by means of cantillation signs) and where a command of biblical literature and language was essential for composers of liturgical poetry, we hear nothing about a framework for advanced study of the Bible or the composition of biblical commentaries. Here the influence of the surrounding Muslim and Christian cultures on Judaism was especially significant, both in terms of the centrality of scriptural interpretation and in terms of the specific modes of thought and expression that characterized their exegesis. Growing competition from other religions and rival Jewish groups increased the need for systematic exegesis as a means of grounding Rabbanite Jewish ideas and refuting the arguments of opponents (in Karaite Judaism, too, biblical exegesis began to play a central role at about this time).

In this context, we should emphasize another aspect of Sa'dayah's literary output: in addition to the polemical elements he introduced to his commentaries and other writings, he composed separate works dedicated mainly to contesting freethinkers and Jewish sectarians. In this he apparently stands alone among the geonim, perhaps as a result of his unique rhetorical skills, his forceful and assertive personality, and his exposure to various religious currents both inside and outside the Jewish world in the course of his travels from Egypt to Palestine, Syria, and Babylonia. Though some of his successors incorporated polemical elements in their writings, particularly in their biblical commentaries, none of them wrote special works dedicated to intra-Jewish polemics.

Sa'adyah's view of his role contrasts sharply with that of other geonim, particularly his predecessors, who had been raised within a relatively closed world and focused mainly on their responsibilities within the academies and their *reshuyot* (see Chapter 1). Their relations with more distant Jewish communities were rather passive: they expected and encouraged them to send questions and contributions and made certain efforts to bring the Jews of Palestine and the diaspora under the halakhic hegemony of Babylonia, but in general they were more reactive than proactive. Sa'adyah, on the other hand, had since early youth considered himself responsible for the welfare of the entire Jewish world, in both his own generation and future ones. The most explicit expression of this sense of mission is found in the *Sefer hagalui*, where he declares that 'God does not leave his nation in any generation without a scholar who instructs and enlightens her [the nation], so that he may counsel and instruct her, and her condition be bettered'. He goes on to clarify that he is writing these words because 'I am aware regarding myself of the grace that God has bestowed upon me and her [the nation]'.[5] Hints of this attitude were in evidence long before Sa'adyah attained any official standing. As we have seen, by the age of 20 he had undertaken to bring about a revival of the Hebrew language rather than wait for someone older or of greater authority to do so, and it was to this end that he wrote the *Egron*. He also composed polemics against those whom he considered threatening to Rabbanite Judaism, such as Anan and Hivi of Balkh. Concerning his attack on Hivi, he declared many years later that the heretic's treatise had circulated for six decades without a proper riposte, which he had felt able and duty-bound to provide without delay. Although the new symbiosis that Sa'adyah created between his roles as defender of traditional Judaism and as head of the academy left a definite mark on the remaining century of geonic life, no other gaon, or medieval Jew, for that matter, ever burned with such a sense of mission.

Daring in the Service of Tradition

As we have seen, Sa'adyah was innovative, even revolutionary, in his literary and public activities. On the other hand, we should remember that he enlisted all his originality in the service of a single lofty cause: the preservation of an idealized form of Jewish and Rabbanite tradition. The idea of tradition played a central role in Sa'adyah's thought, most conspicuously perhaps in his epistemological discussions in the *Book of Beliefs and Opinions*. There he argues that in addition to the three sources of knowledge recognized by all humanity—namely, the senses, intuitive intellectual perception, and logical inference—there is a fourth one,

---

[5] Harkavy, *Fugitive Remnants*, 155 (Arab. original), 154 (Heb. trans.).

acknowledged by the 'community of monotheists' (adherents of the monotheistic religions): authentic tradition. Yet there is nothing extraordinary about relying on transmitted knowledge, or tradition, since all human beings must do so, in religious matters as well as in their economic and social dealings. No one can lead a life based solely on individually acquired knowledge, but religious traditions provide a unique safeguard against possible error:

> Were it not for the fact that men felt satisfied in their hearts that there is such a thing in the world as authentic tradition, no person would be able to cherish legitimate expectation on the basis of the reports he receives about the success of a certain commercial transaction or the usefulness of a specified art . . . Nor would he heed the warnings he had received about the harm which would result from following a certain path, or the call to avoid a certain act . . . nor, were there not in this world an authentic tradition, would a person know what the legacy of his father was and the heritage of his grandfather. Nay, he would not even be certain of being the son of his mother, let alone the son of his father. And as a result the affairs of men would always be subject to doubt, to the point where human beings would believe only what they perceived with their senses and only at the time of its perception . . . Now when we ponder these two things [and] how to guard tradition against them, our reason arrives at the conclusion that incorrect thoughts and malice can only affect the individual without being exposed. In the case of a large community of men, however, their [innocently] incorrect thoughts would not be in agreement. On the other hand, had they deliberately conspired to create a fictitious tradition, that fact could not have remained a secret to the masses, and wherever the story [that they fabricated] came out, the story of their agreement would have come out with it; and when the tradition is free of these two there is no third cause which makes it necessary to reject it. Accordingly, if the traditions transmitted to us by our ancestors are examined in the light of these principles, they will be found to be proof against these criticisms, correct and unshakable.[6]

Here Sa'adyah attempts to legitimize reliance on tradition in general, and in what follows he explains his adherence to Jewish tradition in particular, including the belief in the mission of the prophets and in the biblical canon. Elsewhere he defends Rabbanite tradition against the Karaites, who recognized biblical authority but claimed that the rabbinic 'tradition' was in fact a fraudulent later invention. Sa'adyah's central argument in this context, as it appears with certain variations in a number of his writings and those of other Rabbanite authors, runs as follows: the succinct wording of many laws in the Bible would render them impracticable without the amplification provided by the Sages (in fact, he contends, the very language of the Bible would be incomprehensible without their help; see pp. 84–5). A fine example of this line of reasoning appears in the introduction to his commentary on the book of Genesis:

---

[6] *Book of Beliefs and Opinions* (Arab.), ed. Landauer, 126–8. The following translation modifies that of Rosenblatt in *Saadia Gaon*, 156–7.

And we find in the non-rational laws [explained below] seven principles that necessitate our turning to tradition, one more important than the other:

(1) Because there are biblical commandments that entail qualities that are left unexplained, for example, the method used to prepare fringes, or build the booths of Sukkot and so forth.

(2) Because there are commandments that entail quantities that are left unexplained ... for instance, the exact number of possessions, wives, and horses that a king is permitted to have is not explained, only that he is prohibited from having a great number of them, as is written, 'he shall not multiply horses to himself, neither shall he multiply wives, neither shall he multiply to himself silver and gold' [Deut. 17: 16–17], and so on.

(3) Because there are commandments that leave the means of recognizing something unexplained, as, for example, there is no sensory proof which is the day of the sabbath or the day of the new moon, but we are referred for proofs in this matter to the traditions of the emissary [Moses] ...

(4) Because there are commandments in the Bible that are unexplained in their very essence, such as what manner of work is prohibited on the sabbath, except to say 'All manner of work' [Exod. 20: 10, Deut. 5: 14], or which vessels in particular are liable to become defiled, where only 'every vessel' is mentioned [Lev. 11: 32], and so forth ...

(5) Because it is agreed by the nation that God has enjoined on it certain commandments that are not mentioned in the Bible by name, let alone in their qualities and quantities, such as prayer ... and to this we must add some of the [civil] laws not mentioned in the Torah at all, while necessity requires that we must seek out knowledge of them ...

(6) The account of the years and deeds from the cessation of prophecy up to our time, this can only be comprehended through received tradition ... and it is clear that these things are even more important than the former ones ...

(7) What we anticipate that God will renew for us in the end of days ... all this can be attained by the nation in a way which gives hope only by relying on the explanation of the masters of tradition.[7]

What is notable here is the way in which Sa'adyah blends historical and eschatological knowledge with the information needed to perform the non-rational commandments (those which would not be required by reason and are known only through Divine revelation). The point is consistent with Sa'adyah's historical consciousness, which we will examine further on, but for now let us direct our attention to the halakhic aspects. Sa'adyah does not limit himself to the argument that Judaism cannot dismiss Rabbanite halakhah and base itself solely on the Bible but makes a much more far-reaching claim: that virtually all of the halakhah of the Sages conveys an unbroken tradition that was transmitted orally from the days of the prophets. Rather than emphasize the Sages' ability and authority to interpret biblical laws and to modify them in accordance with changing circumstances,

---

[7] *Sa'adyah's Commentary on Genesis*, ed. Zucker, 13–15 (Arab. original), 181–4 (Heb. trans.).

Sa'adyah presents them as steadfast but passive guardians of tradition. Such, for example, is his succinct account of the history of the oral law:

And at the completion of a thousand years . . . [since the Torah was given] from the days of Moses the man of God, at the end of the remaining prophets in the days of Media, when [prophetic] vision was sealed in the fortieth year after the construction of the Second Temple with few people; when our forefathers saw that the multitude had been dispersed throughout the land and feared lest the Speech be forgotten, they gathered all the words thereof which had been transmitted from ancient times . . . and called them Mishnah. And there remained things which they hoped would be preserved with their occupation of the land [of Israel] since they belonged to the branches of the laws.[8] But we continued to go astray and deviate and were exiled again . . . and fearing lest they be forgotten, the Sages gathered them too and called them Talmud, 500 years after the first time.[9]

In another context Sa'adyah argues that it is not proof of the biblical derivation of particular laws that is offered in countless passages of rabbinic literature but rather biblical support for traditional laws long accepted. Likewise, the so-called 'principles by which the Torah is interpreted' are not exegetical methods used by the Sages to derive the laws from Scripture, but rather principles that they discovered *ex post facto* as a result of painstaking examination of accepted traditions in comparison with the biblical sources:

I preface this by saying that concerning *mitsvot*, the Sages of blessed memory did not rely in their teachings on any analogy [*hekesh*] for they did [not] turn to the analogy of their reason and their opinions, but were rather transmitters [of traditions received] from the emissary [Moses] and bearers of his traditions . . . and it is clear from what we have explained that the Sages did not record these thirteen principles because they proved [the laws] using them but rather compiled them because they found that the *halakhot* that they had could be combined according to these thirteen [principles], but they were not established on the basis of the thirteen. And just as we say of the Masoretic notes that they found that there are ten occurrences [in the Bible] of the plene spelling of 'shall be done', nine of 'in the good' and eight of 'in Babylonia',[10] and these did not come about as a result of the Masorah, but rather the Masorah searched and found them to be so, and just as the grammarians and others searched and found things and classified them . . . so too our Sages recorded these thirteen means [i.e. principles] in accordance with what they found through their painstaking analysis of the commandments.[11]

---

[8] 'Branches' refers to the ramifications of the laws rather than their central core. According to Sa'adyah, the sages had believed that when Israel had its own homeland the people would succeed in preserving certain traditions without the need to organize them in a formal collection.

[9] Schechter, *Saadyana*, 5.

[10] Counting the occurrences of particular spellings and word forms in the Bible was one of the characteristic activities of the Masoretes.

[11] Zucker, 'Fragments' (Heb.), 375–6 (Arab. text), 378 (Heb. trans.).

In keeping with this radical approach, Sa'adyah claimed that familiar laws which had seemingly developed as a result of historical circumstances were in fact ancient laws transmitted to the prophets for future use and preserved over the centuries as a part of Jewish heritage, awaiting the day of their implementation. This is what he asserts, for example, with regard to the use of astronomical calculations among Rabbanite Jews in his day to determine the calendar, as opposed to the system described in rabbinic literature; the addition of a second festival day (*yom tov sheni*) to every festival celebrated in the diaspora; and the version of the prayer service current in his day, which undoubtedly differed from what had been customary during the days of Israel's monarchy (see p. 134 below).

Likewise, Sa'adyah offered a radical response to one of the main arguments of the Karaites, which stated that the existence of countless disagreements among the talmudic and mishnaic sages proved that their tradition was false. Sa'adyah countered that such discrepancies were more apparent than real. Whether he actually believed his own claims or chose them for purely polemical purposes, a tendency to wax nostalgic over an idealized past was certainly characteristic of him. This gained expression, for example, in the realm of poetry, where he drew a distinction between the five great 'ancients' and the more recent writers, whom he quoted only in special cases. In other areas he articulated a desire to restore an idealized past, as in the following passage from the preface to the *Egron*:

The book of *Egron* of the holy tongue, which our God has chosen from primeval times and in which his holy angels praise him . . . There was one language . . . throughout the land from the day when God created man on the face of the earth . . . until the days of the stormy herd [the generation of the tower of Babel] . . . The holy tongue remained in the mouths of the children of Ever [i.e. the 'Hebrews'; Ever appears in the genealogy of Noah's descendants and Abraham's progenitors in Gen. 11: 14–17] alone . . . their feet trod throughout the land and the language did not depart their mouths, and when they left Egypt God spoke to us in it, eloquent words by the hand of his servant Moses on Mount Horeb . . . and one hundred and one years after the destruction of God's city we began to forsake the holy tongue and speak in the languages of the foreign peoples of the land . . . and we were exiled afterwards through all the gates of the land and the isles of the sea, and there was no people among whom our people were not dispersed, and in their midst too did we beget children and learn their languages: and their uncouth speech concealed the beauty of our diction . . . Our heart is appalled, and our spirits too, that the sacred speech is removed from our mouths . . . it behoves us and all the people of our God to study and investigate it always, us and our children and wives and servants; let it not depart from our mouths because through it we understand the laws of the Torah of our Rock that are our life and vitality, our light from the Holy One through all eternity . . . and the collector [*oger*, from the same root as the title of the book] wrote this book to serve as wisdom for all the people of God and all those knowledgeable in law and justice. And He prepared it to speak in riddles and to offer parables and all manner of tropes and rhyming verses . . . And the people of our God will speak in it when they go in and out, in all their occupations and in their bedrooms and to their children; it will not depart from the intelligence of their hearts for through it the Torah of God will be known.[12]

Sa'adyah expressed his metahistorical conceptions in various ways. As we have seen, he singled out eschatology and history as areas in which extra-biblical tradition is of crucial importance, even more so than in the field of halakhah. His placing of the individual and the nation in a broad historical and metahistorical continuum was revolutionary. In this context, it should be noted that Sa'adyah also wrote a chronological work in Arabic and though it was not especially original in content, being based primarily on the ancient work *Seder olam*, it is noteworthy that he considered this text important enough to devote his time to producing an updated Arabic version.

There is a possible link between Sa'adyah's conservative leanings and the sense of mission noted above. Sa'adyah saw himself as a vital link in the historical chain of the Jewish people and its covenant with God. He carried on his own two shoulders, as it were, the full burden of Jewish history and the responsibility for the future of his people. It was not enough for him to address an elite readership. He felt duty-bound to reach a broad enlightened public and to take on the many perils and challenges which this public faced. At the same time, he was quick to embrace anything that he regarded as good and useful from the surrounding cultures of his day, and he never hesitated to admit that there are important things to be learned from people outside the covenant. In everything he did, Sa'adyah Gaon acted in the firm conviction that there is one truth only and its source is the Creator of the universe; that there are different and often overlapping means of reaching various elements of this truth; that all these elements are complementary rather than contradictory; and that uncovering them serves the true purpose of man's life on earth, which is the service of God.

General Characteristics of Sa'adyah's Writing

Most of this book is devoted to the manifold writings of Sa'adyah Gaon, but before proceeding to examine each genre in greater detail, I will offer some general observations about the entire corpus of his work.

First, let us note the functions assigned to the different languages in which he wrote. Roughly speaking, these are Arabic and Hebrew (with Aramaic playing a very marginal role, essentially confined to citations). Arabic was, in all likelihood, the main spoken language of world Jewry at the time and Sa'adyah's language of choice for nearly all writings that were not constrained by existing Hebrew models. It was the language that he used for most of his philosophical, exegetical, and linguistic monographs, and in a large number of halakhic and polemical works as well. His choice of Hebrew stands out primarily in the field of poetry, where his

[12] Allony, *Egron* (Heb.), 156–9.

language was largely determined by the long-standing tradition of *piyut*. Even where he stretched the existing limits of poetry in terms of content and technique, he remained faithful to its linguistic tradition.

In addition to poetic language, which is naturally elevated and stylized, we find at least two other genres of Hebrew writing among Sa'adyah's works. On several occasions he wrote a kind of pseudo-biblical Hebrew, complete with imitation of biblical grammatical forms, verse division, and cantillation signs. In addition to their content, he explains, these writings were intended as paradigms of sophisticated Hebrew that he hoped would contribute to the revival of Hebrew as a literary language (though he was well aware of how difficult it was for many readers to understand his writing, as we shall see). He also presumably wished to show that he could express himself in this elevated style, although he normally used a simpler, prosaic Hebrew for his halakhic responsa (alongside those that he wrote in Arabic—since the language of responsa normally followed the language of the questions) and for his letters, where clear communication was of the essence and a polished style counted for less.

In a departure from earlier Jewish literary convention, Sa'adyah wrote prefaces to most, if not all, of his monographs. Following the model of Muslim writers, he opens his remarks with praises for the Creator, suiting them to the purpose of his book, and proceeds from there to a general discussion of its subject matter and a review of the contents. He ends the preface to some of his Arabic works with a table of contents, divided into numbered chapters—an organizing principle that he seems to have invented and contributed to the world of literature. Even in works with a less definite framework Sa'adyah concludes his preface with a summary of the book's structure and the organization of its contents.

Sa'adyah's innovative use of numbered chapters suited his general inclination to employ numbers as a means of structuring his thought. He often lists opinions that he wishes to discuss, questions that require attention, useful lessons to be learned from a particular source, and so forth. Sometimes this love of 'scientific' organization prevails over ease of application, particularly when he writes in a 'modular' manner: in compositions where a certain element is repeated, he introduces it at the outset and from then on merely refers the reader back to the initial discussion—a sometimes cumbersome and inconvenient procedure (see pp. 126, 133–4).

On the other hand, he provides quite a number of cross-references between monographs, noting that he has previously elaborated on a given point in such and such a work, or intends to do so in a projected work. At other times, he goes into some detail about subjects he has already discussed, undoubtedly because of the special significance they hold for him, as in his many discussions on the importance of tradition in general and the Oral Law in particular, although this is not the only example. Subjects of particular interest to him, such as his meta-

historical perspectives, find their way into a variety of often surprising literary settings (see pp. 34, 80, and 157).

Sa'adyah was adept at 'recycling' not just single passages but entire works. He
published several titles in different editions, notably the *Egron* and *Sefer hagalui*,
both of which came out first in Hebrew and later in expanded Arabic editions.
The Arabic version of *Sefer hagalui* included a literal translation of the Hebrew
original accompanied by philological and substantive annotations to the text. A
similar phenomenon was his occasional use of a text both as a separate composition and as part of a larger, more comprehensive work. So, for example, he treats
his magnum opus in the field of linguistics both as a unified work and as twelve
separate essays. He also notes that a certain treatise on halakhah actually forms
one part of a more comprehensive work that he intends to write later on, although
he apparently never did. In the same vein, it would appear that at least some chapters from *The Book of Beliefs and Opinions* circulated as separate essays, whether
they were originally written as such and were later included in the larger framework or whether they were extracted from the comprehensive work and turned
into independent texts. At least one chapter of *The Book of Beliefs and Opinions* has
come down to us in two very different manuscript versions.

Another facet of what might be termed the 'open' style of much of Sa'adyah
Gaon's writing is the diversity of content and genre which characterizes many of
his works. Any composition of his that is confined to a single area of knowledge is
an exception to the rule. His exegetical and philosophical writings, and even his
linguistic and halakhic works, contain a substantial element of polemic; his biblical commentaries include halakhic discussions; several of his writings were
intended inter alia as paradigms of Hebrew belles-lettres; and some of his linguistic or polemical works contain metahistorical discourses. Sa'adyah seems to have
had so much to say in so many different fields that he was unwilling to limit himself to a single subject in any given work; perhaps he also believed that this diversity would challenge his readers and add to their enjoyment. It is also important to
point out that many of the literary paradigms that Sa'adyah used were his own
creations, and in the absence of precedents he felt free to adapt them to his personal tastes and talents.

Finally, a few words ought to be said about the formal aspects of Sa'adyah's use
of sources. It is only to be expected that he relied mainly on the authoritative texts
of the Jewish tradition, first and foremost on the Bible and talmudic literature,
and, occasionally, on other texts—among them some nearly contemporaneous
works. Interestingly enough, he would often draw on such sources without referring to them directly or even indirectly. A case in point is his use of aggadic materials that provide the background to many of his biblical commentaries and
chronological reckonings. In many cases, Sa'adyah indicates that something
derives from an earlier source and merely paraphrases the contents, while at other

times he cites the original in Hebrew or Aramaic. When he does refer to a source, whether through paraphrase or citation, he is extremely vague. He does not normally cite a specific book of the Bible but merely notes that 'Scripture says', 'the prophet says', or 'the pious man says', and so forth. Nor does he specify which tractate of the Talmud he is referring to, let alone the chapter of the given tractate. He often neglects even to name the work he is quoting. His usual form of citation from classical rabbinic—and occasionally from post-talmudic—literature is 'the ancients said', 'the Sages said', or simply 'they said'. Any reader who does not accept the author's word and wishes to locate the references has to be Sa'adyah's equal in the mastery of the entire corpus of classical rabbinic literature.

CHAPTER THREE

❧

Sa'adyah the Philosopher

CLASSICAL RABBINIC JUDAISM is grounded in a comprehensive system of halakhah that determines behavioural norms in every aspect of life and sets community boundaries accordingly (as opposed to Christianity, with its emphasis on correct belief). Differences of opinion abound on virtually every philosophical subject, and it would be difficult to speak of a well-formed rabbinic theology with respect to even the most basic issues. The literature of the Sages does not expound dogma or attempt to deal in a systematic way with broader questions of belief and outlook. On rare occasions, a particular opinion is denounced, but holding such an opinion carries no penalty in this world; at worst, the believer's place 'in the world to come' is said to be forfeited. A few basic principles of faith, such as the belief in a God who revealed himself to the children of Israel and charged them to keep the Torah's commandments, were presumably shared by all the *tana'im* and *amora'im* (and their contemporaries), but they were little inclined on the whole to theological and philosophical speculation.

The Background to Sa'adyah Gaon's Philosophy

The impetus to orderly theological speculation came from without at a time when both Christians and Muslims were making a concerted effort to systematize their religious principles and buttress them with rationally based argumentation.[1] This activity derived in part from the proliferation of cults within Christianity and Islam, from the controversies that raged among adherents about the tenets of their faith, and from exposure to each other's religions; but an even more important factor in this development was the encounter with the ancient Greek philosophical tradition. While Christians writing in Greek and Syriac had grappled with Greek philosophy long before the rise of Islam, Muslims were exposed to it for the first time during the eighth and ninth centuries, when many Greek works were translated into Arabic (often by way of an intermediary translation into Syriac). Much of the Greek influence on Arabic-speaking culture in the early centuries of Islam came less from those thinkers who identified themselves as philosophers, or *falasifa*—followers of the school of Aristotle, and to a lesser extent of Plato—than

---

[1] For a more detailed discussion of the background to Sa'adyah's philosophy, see Brody, *Geonim of Babylonia*, 284–8.

from the *mutakallimun* (literally, speakers)—members of the broad movement known as *kalam*, meaning speech or discourse.

During this period, adherents of the various religions and sects would often engage in theological discussions. Among the most important cultural events of the time were the *majalis* or sessions open not only to monotheists of all persuasions but to dualists, sceptics, and others. The ground rules at these gatherings stated that no one could advance arguments that relied on a particular religious tradition; any argument had to be based on rational principles accepted by all the participants, who strove to validate their own beliefs and invalidate those of others (including the beliefs of competing sects within their own tradition). This, according to the ground rules, was accomplished by means of well-reasoned arguments and skilful rhetoric, without resort to the scriptures or traditions of a particular faith. One possible consequence of this liberal approach was a relativistic or even fundamentally sceptical attitude towards the whole idea of 'religious truth'.

We have fragments of two theological compositions written by Jews, both in Arabic, that pre-date Sa'adyah's speculative works. The author of one of them was David al-Muqammas, the first known Jewish *mutakallim*, who was apparently active in the mid-ninth century. According to a Karaite contemporary of Sa'adyah Gaon, al-Muqammas converted to Christianity but returned to his Jewish roots some time later and attacked Christian beliefs in two books. Nevertheless, the Karaite informant claims, the commentaries that al-Muqammas composed on Genesis and Ecclesiastes were based on Christian sources. Large portions of his theological work, *'Ishrun Maqala* (Twenty Chapters), have survived in the Cairo Genizah, and demonstrate clearly the tremendous influence of *kalam*, particularly of the Christian variety, on his writing. It is reasonable to suppose that Sa'adyah was acquainted with al-Muqammas' composition and influenced by it. According to one source, he even studied with al-Muqammas, but this is highly doubtful.

The other theologian who preceded Sa'adyah was his older contemporary, a noted Rabbanite Jew named Isaac Israeli, who was active in Egypt and North Africa during the second half of the ninth century and the early part of the tenth. Unlike most contemporary thinkers in the Muslim world, Isaac Israeli inclined mainly to the Neoplatonic stream of Greek philosophy, although his system was eclectic and included some Aristotelian and *kalam* elements as well. We know that the young Sa'adyah, while still in Egypt, engaged in correspondence with Isaac Israeli on scientific topics, but we have no information about the exact contents of their exchange. There is also evidence that Sa'adyah studied with a Palestinian named Abu Kathir Yahya, though very little is known about him or his activities.

There were other Jews besides those mentioned above who participated in the emerging theological discourse. Some incorporated discussions of theology in works that were not primarily theological in content. One such prominent figure was the ninth-century biblical exegete Daniel al-Qumisi, a Karaite who wrote in

Hebrew. Theological works of various kinds may well have been lost in the course of time, but many Jewish intellectuals must also have engaged in debates such as those described above or in less formal discussions on philosophical matters without writing about them. Moreover, there were also 'consumers' of these theological discussions who did not actively contribute to them but attended the sessions or read what others had written. By the early tenth century or even earlier, many Jews regarded Jewish tradition as merely one component of their cultural identity, and not necessarily the dominant one at that. Their familiarity with theological and philosophical discourse may not have been profound, but their knowledge of Judaism—and rabbinic thought in particular—was probably just as limited. This must have been the sort of audience Sa'adyah had in mind when he wrote his foremost theological work, *The Book of Beliefs and Opinions*, as evidenced by his preface to the book:

What prompted me to preface [the book] with this discussion is my observation of the state of many people in terms of their beliefs and convictions. There is among them a type of person who has attained the truth and is cognizant of it and rejoices in it, and of him the prophet has said, 'Thy words were found, and I did eat them; And Thy words were unto me a joy and the rejoicing of my heart.' [Jer. 15: 17] And again there is among them the kind of person who has attained the truth but is nevertheless in doubt about it, being neither wholly convinced nor holding it firmly in his grasp . . . There is further among them the kind of person who holds to be true what in reality is false, thinking that it is the truth, and thus he clings to falsehood and abandons what is right . . . There is [lastly] among them the type of person who for a time follows one school of thought and then abandons it on account of some flaw that he has remarked. After that he moves on to another system but withdraws from it owing to some other objectionable point, and then to yet another which he later rejects . . . and thus he vacillates all his days . . .

When I considered this state of things and the evil thereof, my heart grieved for my species, the species of human beings, and my soul was stirred on behalf of our people, the children of Israel. For I saw in this age of mine many believers whose faith was not pure and whose convictions were unsound . . . And I saw men drowning, as it were, in seas of doubt, sinking in the waters of confusion, without a diver to raise them from the depths, without a swimmer to take their hands and lead them ashore.[2]

Sa'adyah and *Kalam*

As I have noted, many philosophers of Sa'adyah's time belonged to the broad framework of *kalam*.[3] The original and narrow sense of the word referred to an

---

[2] *Book of Beliefs and Opinions*, ed. Landauer (Arab.), 3–4; the translation modifies that of Rosenblatt in his edition of *Book of Beliefs and Opinions*, 6–7. (Landauer's edition of the *Book of Beliefs and Opinions* contains the Arabic text (in Arabic script) with a German preface. Rosenblatt translated this edition into English. There are frequent references below citing the two works in parallel.)

[3] For the contents of this section see Stroumsa, *Sa'adyah Gaon*, and the literature cited there.

Islamic theological system made up of various groups and currents. In the broader and more abstract sense of a certain type of religious speculation, it is possible to speak of a Jewish *kalam* and a Christian *kalam* as well. All proponents of the *kalam* shared the view that there is no real contradiction between the truth (or truths) derived from religious tradition and from rational speculation. Nevertheless, it is impossible to embrace all beliefs propounded by conventional religious tradition; these must be carefully scrutinized in order to arrive at a core of beliefs and opinions that are acceptable both to religion and to reason.

The main challenge faced by *kalam* thinkers was the development of a 'purified' concept of God that would stand up to rational criticism without relinquishing the notion of a personal God of revelation concerned with the fate of mankind, imposing commandments and prohibitions, and bestowing rewards and punishments. To this end, each theologian or group of *mutakallimun* strove to produce a coherent blend of ideas that they considered compatible with both religion and philosophy. The boundaries separating the *mutakallimun* of the different faiths were not very rigid: they shared a great deal of common ground and it is possible to trace their mutual influences. Eventually Muslim *kalam* overshadowed its Jewish and Christian counterparts, but the importance of Christian and perhaps even Jewish *kalam*, especially in the early period, should not be underestimated. After all, Christian thinkers had engaged in the systematization of their beliefs already in pre-Islamic times and their theology exerted considerable influence on the development of Muslim *kalam*.

The dominant school of Muslim *kalam* in the ninth and tenth centuries was that of the Muʿtazilites (lit. separatists). Wasil ibn ʿAta, who was active in the first half of the eighth century, is considered to be the founder of this school. From early on the Muʿtazilites incorporated elements of ancient Greek thought, although actual translations of Greek philosophical writings did not become available until early in the ninth century and their impact on the school is questionable. The Muʿtazilites held certain doctrinal positions which were considered heretical by other Muslims. Central to their system was a radical faith in the unity of God and in Divine justice, as a result of which they were known as the 'advocates of justice and unity' (*ashab al-ʿadl wa-al-tawhid*). It should be emphasized that this approach is based on the premise, shared by the Muʿtazilites, that universal criteria of an intuitive moral order are 'implanted' in man's consciousness by the Creator, and that these assumptions apply no less to the ways of the Creator Himself. Muʿtazilite belief in the absolute uniqueness of God led to their radical concept of indivisibility and a rejection of any type of anthropomorphism. But they went even further in denying the reality of Divine attributes, called *sifat*, which had been accepted in earlier Islam, especially the attributes of Life, Knowledge, and Power, holding that these are merely different aspects of the absolute unity of the Divine. Divine justice implied free will, since it was inconceivable to them that a just God would command or prohibit certain ways of behaviour, let alone reward or punish human beings for their good and evil deeds, if man was not free to choose between different courses of action. They found support for their position in certain verses of the Qur'an, but this entailed a reinterpretation of other verses suggesting that God is in fact responsible for everything in the world, including human actions. Most early Jewish theologians, both Karaite and Rabbanite, were powerfully influenced by this school of thought. However, unlike the Muslim *mutakallimun*, the Jewish theologians considered themselves free to choose ideas and opinions from amongst the various schools inside or outside *kalam*. (An important instance of this was the rejection of some central physical tenets of *kalam*, especially atomism and non-causality.)

Would it be correct, then, to assume that Sa'adyah Gaon was a Jewish *mutakallim*? There is no simple and unequivocal answer to this. He never identifies himself as such in his writings but other sages apparently consider him thus. When Abraham ibn Ezra calls him the 'chief discourser everywhere' (though this particular designation appears in the Talmud as well and Ibn Ezra uses it here in the context of Sa'adyah's linguistic writings) he is probably also alluding to Sa'adyah's role as a *mutakallim*.

It is indeed possible to find important principles in Sa'adyah's philosophy that would allow us to identify him as a proponent of *kalam*, but it is equally possible to point out central elements in it that derive from other schools of thought. For example, he refers to Aristotle's *Logic* (albeit in an abridged and adapted form) as a fundamental work, with ideas essentially similar to his own, particularly with regard to the conventional and arbitrary nature of language (see further pp. 88–9). Yet other motifs, such as the important role he assigns to Divine will (especially in his commentary on *Sefer yetsirah*, see below), reflect a Neoplatonist influence. Nevertheless, if we emphasize the methodology of *kalam* rather than its specific contents, Sa'adyah emerges as a *mutakallim* par excellence.

Kalam discourse is no less characterized by structural elements of a particular kind than by its specific contents—and often even more so. For example, the subjects and the order in which they appear are largely the same across various *kalam* monographs, even when the specific positions and arguments differ. The style of discussion is typically dialectical and polemical, and the argument is often approached *via negativa*, that is, all possible opinions (according to the author) are examined and refuted except for the one which is thus shown to be correct.

These elements are likewise conspicuous in Sa'adyah's writings. The structure of *The Book of Beliefs and Opinions* fits in well with the typical model of comprehensive *kalam* works. The introduction deals with epistemology, the first chapter with the creation of the world, the second with the attributes of the Creator, and after that the author discusses revelation, the commandments, and various facets of reward and punishment. The treatment of the latter includes a discussion of eschatology. The final chapter, which is only loosely related to the rest of the book, argues that the ideal life entails the balancing of different goals rather than focusing on a particular goal to the exclusion of others.

At a lower level, too, there are noticeable *kalam* elements in Sa'adyah's writings. Dialectics and polemics figure prominently in his works belonging to various genres. Sa'adyah's predilection for numbered lists, so evident in many of his monographs, is especially suitable to the *kalam* style, described above, of mapping out all possible arguments and selecting the correct one through a process of elimination. Some of the theories that he reviewed there may not have had any actual adherents but were merely representative of the logical possibilities he chose to raise and dismiss. This commonly used system was known in *kalam* as partition (*taqsim* or *qisma*) and was quite often employed—and even developed and improved—by Sa'adyah Gaon. The sophisticated technique that he used in constructing his lists is particularly noteworthy. If, for example, he wished to dispute two different systems, but some of his arguments applied to both systems while others to only one of them, he would first present and critique the system less vulnerable to attack and proceed to the second with arguments that pertained to it alone, while noting that the arguments pertaining to the first system pertained to the second as well. Sa'adyah, it should be noted, always lists the preferred opinion either first or last, never in the middle. This clearly shows that he has mapped out the opinions he wishes to discuss in advance according to his organizational principles, before embarking on a detailed analysis.

Another *kalam* device that plays an important role in Sa'adyah's philosophical works is the technique known as *ilzam* (coercion), whereby one attacks an adversary's position and attempts to force him to concede the truth of the writer's argument. The focus is on proving the opponent wrong, not necessarily on providing a satisfactory resolution of the difficulties that he raises with regard to one's own position. In order to refute another's standpoint one may accept, for the sake of argument, the opponent's axioms but demonstrate that they are not self-consistent or that they lead to absurd conclusions which the adversary himself must reject. Sometimes Sa'adyah attempts to shift the opponent gradually from his initial position, ultimately forcing him to accept his own position. We find an example of this technique in the first essay of his *Book of Beliefs and Opinions*, where he strives to establish the created nature of the world by refuting all possible alternative theories.

Diametrically opposed to Sa'adyah's position of *creatio ex nihilo* was that of the *dahriyya*, which maintained that the universe is eternal and unchanging. Advocates of this view dismissed intellectual theories, claiming to base their arguments solely on the evidence of their senses, and since they experienced the world as it is, they had no reason to suppose it had ever been different. Sa'adyah asserted that, unlike philosophers who gave up on the possibility of engaging in debate with the *dahriyya* because of their refusal on principle to consider rational arguments, he himself would succeed in defeating them. This he would achieve either by posing questions unanswerable on the basis of sensory evidence alone (for example, what is the nature of snow that falls from the sky?) or by citing aspects of their own behaviour (for example, taking bad-tasting medicine) to prove that in practice they did not conduct their lives according to sensory evidence alone. Then 'they renounce the very basis of their argument and admit the knowledge of something that does not derive from sensory experience'.[4]

Sa'adyah's Theological Writings

Sa'adyah Gaon was the author of two works in the category of theological speculation. Unlike most of his other writings, these books are precisely dated: his *Commentary on the* Book of Creation 931, and *The Book of Beliefs and Opinions* 933. They were composed after his appointment as gaon of Sura and his dispute with the exilarch David ben Zakai.

The *Book of Creation* (*Sefer yetsirah*) is an enigmatic work, written in a curious style of Hebrew, that describes God's creation of the world by means of the twenty-two letters of the Hebrew alphabet and the *eser sefirot belimah* (the ten sefirot of nothingness, apparently referring to the numbers from one to ten). This description is vivid and dynamic, if inscrutable, with numerous allusions to the human body and discussions of the letters of the alphabet, their division into groups, their symbolism, and the role they play in Creation. Most aspects of this pithy book remain shrouded in controversy even today. The text is ambiguous enough to allow for a wide range of interpretations. Kabbalists regard it as an essential work of Jewish mysticism but others refute this view as a distortion of the author's intention, which was to provide a 'scientific' explanation for the origins of the universe. The date of authorship is no less uncertain. *Sefer yetsirah* purports, although never explicitly, to have been written by the biblical patriarch Abraham, but the first unambiguous evidence of its existence appears not much earlier than Sa'adyah's own day. Modern scholars, too, are radically divided on this question: some assign *Sefer yetsirah* to the early centuries of the Common Era, while others place it within a few generations of Sa'adyah.[5] In any event, it is clear that Sa'adyah was not the first author of a commentary on the book since he argues with earlier commentators (without identifying them, as was his wont), and it is possible that one of his motives in writing such a commentary was to offer a rationalistic alternative to prevailing mythico-magical interpretations. This rationalist tendency is quite apparent in his commentary, as we shall presently see, though

---

[4] *Book of Beliefs and Opinions*, ed. Landauer (Arab.), 63–5; ed. Rosenblatt, 75–8.

[5] See, most recently, Liebes, *The Theory of Creation* (Heb.), esp. pp. 7–11; Dan, *History of Jewish Mysticism*, ii (Heb.), 545–640.

one could hardly claim that he comes across as an out-and-out rationalist. In one place he expounds on the influence of the stars and constellations according to astrological theory and in two places he refers to the writing of amulets, though he never takes a clear stand as to their efficacy.

Sa'adyah does not accept the simplistic attribution of *Sefer yetsirah* to Abraham, asserting rather that the book was compiled by Palestinian sages in mishnaic times on the basis of an orally transmitted tradition going back to Abraham. Sa'adyah's approach to the contents of the book is complex: he does not feel obliged to accept the author's every view (any more than he accepts every view of the talmudic sages on non-halakhic matters, see pp. 74–5) and he takes issue more or less explicitly with a number of points in the work. At the same time, he tries to interpret the text as rationally as possible, presenting it as a poetic metaphor based on various cosmogonic speculations (although he remains non-committal regarding the truth of these speculations). An interesting example concerns a paragraph apparently describing the heavens and the earth in a way that is incompatible with the scientific views of Sa'adyah's day and milieu. In this case, he presents several alternative explanations:

And if someone should say that the author of this book seems to believe that the earth is square and the heavens are square and that there are no heavens beneath the earth, and that these two things are contradicted by the consensus of the wise, let us say [in response that] first: it is possible that these things were intended metaphorically and not literally . . . and further we may say that even if they were intended literally, there is nothing in them that contradicts the Sages in either of these respects, in that there are some sages who did in fact assert that the earth is square . . . and it is not to be wondered at that he said something similar. And on the matter of the heavens being over the earth but not under it, R. Eli'ezer and R. Yehoshua both say as much . . . and even though it is agreed by most of us that the celestial sphere and the earth are both round and that the earth is like a point within the heavens . . . and even though the early sages also mentioned this, saying (Pes. 94*b*), 'The wise men of the nations of the world say that the sun travels above the earth during the day and below the earth at night,' and they [the sages] said, 'Rabbi said: their words are more plausible than ours', many of them also held the opinion expounded by the author of this book.[6]

In his relatively lengthy introduction Sa'adyah speaks of the many difficulties involved in understanding the genesis of the world. He considers nine cosmogonic theories. He begins with earlier philosophical systems and their hypotheses of an uncreated universe or of the existence of primal matter, and ends with the system that he believes to be the correct one. According to this system, which he identifies as that of the Torah, God created the world by means of letters and numerals after generating the four physical elements (fire, air, water, and earth) simultaneously and *ex nihilo*. The preceding theory that he presents is one

---

[6] Kafih, *Sa'adyah's Commentary on the Book of Creation* (Heb.), 82–3.

ascribed to *Sefer yetsirah*, which—though very similar—speaks of air as the only medium activated by the letters and numbers in the process of Creation. It appears that, as Sa'adyah sees it, *Sefer yetsirah* does not describe the instantaneous *ex nihilo* creation of the universe, but rather the later stages of its genesis, which is evidently why he called the book in its Arabic translation *Kitab al-Mabadi'* (The Book of Beginnings) rather than 'The Book of Creation'. This distinction may underlie Sa'adyah's view that it is meritorious to enquire into these matters:

> For although they described this as inaccessible and profound, one must not neglect its study, as philosophy corresponds to what occurred as a result of the acts of the Creator, may he be magnified and exalted, of whom it is said, 'He reveals deep things from the darkness, and brings death's shadow to light' [Job 12: 22], and it behoves them, too, to enquire into this as far as they are able.[7]

The same distinction between the first act of Creation and its later stages may also be the reason that Sa'adyah rejects the prevailing opposition to scientific or philosophical enquiry:

> And the third system determines that there was a beginning to all that exists, but forbids enquiry into what preceded that beginning, as it is forbidden by most of the sages, who say, 'Those who contemplate these four things, it were better that they had not entered this world: what lies above and what lies below, what lies ahead and what lies behind' [Mishnah *Hag.* 2: 1] ... And this adage is true, but its interpretation is not what it seems to those in error, namely, that they forbade enquiry into which of the created things were created first, but I say they forbade it rather so that they would not go on to [explore] matters of the Creator may his name be blessed and exalted, and concern themselves with his essence ... but after determining that [all] things were created, it is permitted to speak about which of them came into existence before the other.[8]

Sa'adyah states that he will copy the Hebrew version of each section (which he designates a *halakhah* even though it is not a *halakhah* in any normative sense, as we have seen) before translating it into Arabic. The reason for this, he explains, is that since so few people dealt with *Sefer yetsirah*, its text had been poorly preserved (discrepancies between the book's copies are indeed numerous and profound). In one place Sa'adyah asserts that he uses logic and context to establish an accurate text in contrast to the garbled version that he has found in all the available copies, adding that he has used the same methods to edit a book of another genre.[9] Occasionally he rejects a text that he believes to be corrupted in favour of another text, but there is no basis for the conjecture of certain authors that Sa'adyah himself composed a new version of *Sefer yetsirah* in order to bring it more in line with his own ideas.

---

[7] Kafih, *Sa'adyah's Commentary on the Book of Creation* (Heb.), 18.
[8] Ibid. 24–6.   [9] Ibid. 117–18.

The text on which Sa'adyah comments is composed of eight chapters, but in his view the last four chapters are merely elaborations on ideas found in the first four. As a result, he dispenses with a systematic interpretation of the latter chapters, contenting himself with copying the Hebrew text and offering comments on difficult words and problematic points. The full presentation of a particular 'halakhah' includes the Hebrew text, its translation into Arabic, an explanation of the words, and an explanation of the subject matter, although the last two sections are at times combined. The linguistic component of the commentary is also worth noting: following the treatment of the letters of the alphabet and their attributes in *Sefer yetsirah*, Sa'adyah introduces a number of discussions on linguistic matters, some of them rather detailed, referring the reader to his comprehensive work on grammar, and sometimes even expanding on that work (see pp. 85–7).

The main thrust of the commentary, as we have seen, is to bring *Sefer yetsirah* in line with Sa'adyah's speculative theories by neutralizing the potentially mythic elements of the book. For instance, about the passage that speaks of the *eser sefirot belimah*, the ten sefirot of nothingness 'that flash like lightning but have no end to them and they are spoken of as running back and forth . . . and before His throne they prostrate themselves', Sa'adyah comments:

For the beginnings of things burst out in the intelligence and flash like lightning, as it were, and only afterwards are they revealed and clarified so that they appear diffuse, and then they aggregate and multiply till it is no longer possible to follow them to their end . . . and 'they are spoken of as running back and forth' meaning that every time these numbers arrive at ten they return again and are eternally multiplied . . . but 'They prostrate themselves before His throne' alludes to their obedience to Him and to the authority of His decrees over them, and this is the case with every 'prostration' which should not be understood literally.[10]

Sa'adyah's underlying assumption is that the author of *Sefer yetsirah* is expressing abstract ideas and philosophical concepts in non-philosophical terms and it is up to the commentator to reveal the rational intent beneath the metaphorical mask of the text. For instance, the book opens with a list of ten of the names of God. Sa'adyah explains that they refer to the ten Aristotelian categories: substance, quantity, quality, relation, place, time, position, state, action, and affection. This, he believes, is also hinted at by the fact that precisely ten commandments were given at Sinai.[11] An important means of bridging the gap between the concepts of philosophy and Jewish tradition is the 'special ether' created, according to Sa'adyah's theories, to mediate between the Creator and the physical world, which he identifies with what the Bible calls the 'Glory of God' and with the Shekhinah mentioned in talmudic literature. Sa'adyah also uses this concept to explain the

[10] Ibid. 70, 72–3.   [11] Ibid. 43–7.

dynamics of biblical prophecy and of a lesser form of revelation which the Sages call 'spirit of holiness' or *bat kol* (lit. daughter of a voice).[12]

Two years after composing his commentary on *Sefer yetsirah*, Sa'adyah wrote his magnum opus in the area of theology, *The Book of Beliefs and Opinions*. The book includes a long introduction and ten chapters or essays; it is possible that he wrote some of these initially as separate pieces, which he later incorporated in a more comprehensive work.

The Arabic original of the text is preserved in two comprehensive manuscripts (one now in Oxford and the other in St Petersburg) and in a large number of fragments that have survived in the Cairo Genizah. On the basis both of internal evidence and of the fragments found in the Genizah, the St Petersburg copy seems generally more reliable, although most modern editions of *The Book of Beliefs and Opinions* are based on the Oxford recension, which was more accessible to scholars. Overall, however, there are only minor discrepancies between the two recensions, with the exception of the seventh chapter, which is transmitted in quite different versions. It is nearly certain that both versions were penned by Sa'adyah, who, as we have seen, sometimes published revised editions of his own works. A number of renderings and Hebrew adaptations of the book were produced during the Middle Ages, the most influential of these being Judah ibn Tibbon's Hebrew translation based on an Arabic version that closely resembled the St Petersburg manuscript.[13]

I shall review the structural elements and the contents of *The Book of Beliefs and Opinions* in greater detail later on, and limit myself here to a few preliminary remarks about its general characteristics. The main purpose of the book is to demonstrate the absolute consonance between the truths that were divinely revealed to the children of Israel and the ineluctable conclusions of rational enquiry. Sa'adyah introduces each chapter with the succinct presentation of a central belief in Jewish tradition and then attempts to prove that unbiased rational analysis leads to the same conclusion. He does not stop with the integration of reason and tradition at this level, however, but cites numerous scriptural verses to support his arguments, although in most cases his interpretations of these verses are by no means simple or self-evident. He rarely makes explicit reference to post-biblical sources, except in his discussion of eschatology; this may be a result of his desire to reach the broadest possible audience, including readers unfamiliar with talmudic literature or those who might question its importance and authority.

The polemical element, which figures prominently in so many of the works of Sa'adyah Gaon (see Chapter 8), is especially striking in *The Book of Beliefs and*

---

[12] Kafih, *Sa'adyah's Commentary on the Book of Creation* (Heb.), 108–9; cf. *Book of Beliefs and Opinions*, ed. Landauer (Arab.), 99–100, 106–7; ed. Rosenblatt, 120–2, 129–31.

[13] For further details and references to relevant literature see Brody, *Geonim of Babylonia*, 289–90.

Opinions. As noted earlier, this is an important feature of the theological writings of *kalam*. Sa'adyah often includes numbered lists of opinions that have been voiced (or could be voiced) on various issues, and considers arguments that support these as well as counter-arguments that refute all but the position he himself holds. Sometimes he attributes conflicting views to Jews, at other times to non-Jews, but he often cites such opinions in completely anonymous fashion, and over the centuries much scholarly effort has gone into identifying his opponents. Some of the lists of opinions turn out to have been lifted by Sa'adyah from lists made by other theologians and adapted by him to his own requirements and standpoint.[14]

Such philosophical-theoretical motifs are to be found in many of Sa'adyah's other writings as well, for example, in the prefaces that regularly open with praises of the Creator (see p. 37). We should take special note of the essay which he dedicated to proving that tradition, rather than analogy, is to be followed in interpreting the non-rational or 'auditory' precepts (see pp. 149–50). His biblical exegesis is replete with theoretical discussions—and not merely where clearly invited by the text—for example, in his commentary on the book of Job (which Sa'adyah calls 'the book of theodicy'), but in many far less expected places as well. An especially striking example of this is his commentary on Exodus 14: 31 ('And they believed in the Lord and in His servant Moses'). Here he posits the existence of ten fundamental principles of faith that share four common elements: faith in God, faith in his prophets, faith in the messages they transmit, and faith in the world to come. He then refers the reader to a special section that serves as a kind of appendix to his commentary on the first half of the book of Exodus. In this unit, Sa'adyah interprets ten biblical songs, and the discussion of the sixth song, the Song of David (2 Sam. 22), includes an extensive commentary on the principles of faith. He sees intimations of the ten principles in the ten descriptions of God found in the first two verses. The first three principles refer to God's relationship to the world in general: he is eternal, he comprehends everything, and he created everything. The others concern Divine revelation and the imperative of obeying the commandments. A Jew is required to believe that God has commanded him to carry out religious precepts, to accept them as just, and to commit himself to upholding them. He must also believe that God will redeem his people and protect them in the eschatological wars of Gog and Magog, and that he will reward the righteous and punish the wicked in the world to come. These principles are closely linked to the chapter headings of *The Book of Beliefs and Opinions*, but to the best of my knowledge this is the only place in Sa'adyah's writings where he presents a formal list of normative beliefs—and is among the earliest known lists of Jewish principles of faith.[15]

[14] See e.g. Davidson, 'Saadia's List of Theories of the Soul'.
[15] See Ben-Shammai, 'Sa'adyah Gaon's Ten Articles of Faith' (Heb.).

Sa'adyah's Philosophical Principles

Let us briefly examine Sa'adyah's main concepts, mostly following the course of his arguments in *The Book of Beliefs and Opinions*. The lengthy preface to the book deals primarily with epistemology, a subject of great importance to Sa'adyah in other contexts as well (see pp. 31–2 and 67–8). He enumerates three sources of knowledge that pertain to science or human reason in general—sensory perception, intuitive knowledge, and logical deduction—and to these he adds a fourth source accepted by the 'community of monotheists', namely, true or authentic tradition. Here he offers a succinct argument to the effect that tradition validates the first three sources of knowledge, but his polemics against those who deny some or all of these sources and his proofs of the reliability of tradition are deferred to the body of the work proper.

If, Sa'adyah asks, prophetic tradition and rational speculation lead to similar truths, why are there two distinct ways of reaching the selfsame conclusion? To this he replies that God himself commands us to engage in theoretical speculation and not to be content with revelation, as we see in verses such as Isaiah 40: 21: 'Know ye not? Hear ye not? Hath it not been told you from the beginning? Have ye not understood the foundations of the earth?' On the one hand, such speculation is useful in two ways: it deepens our understanding of the truths transmitted by the prophets and 'actively verifies them for us'; at the same time, it enables us to respond to arguments levelled against various religious beliefs. On the other hand, revelation and tradition are also necessary, because not everyone is capable of reaching the right conclusion through a rational thought process. Furthermore, even those who arrive at the truth do so only after lengthy speculation, and God has no desire to leave his creatures in a state of ignorance and uncertainty.

The first two chapters treat the theme of the existence and unity of the Creator. Near the beginning of the book Sa'adyah asserts briefly: 'Our exalted Lord has made it known to us that all things are created and that he created them *ex nihilo*, as it is written, "In the beginning God created the heaven and the earth" [Gen. 1: 1] and so forth, and as it is written, "I am the Lord that maketh all things; That stretched forth the heavens alone" [Isa. 44: 24].' Sa'adyah adds, 'I have studied this matter to see whether it can be verified as much through rational speculation as through prophecy.'[16] He then offers rational proof that all things in the world were created at a certain point in time and thus are not eternal; that they were brought into being by an external agency and could not have created themselves; and that they were created *ex nihilo*. He goes on to review twelve other theories of the origins of the universe and refutes them one by one. Only some of these, it should be noted, correspond to the theories that he refutes in the preface to his commentary on *Sefer yetsirah*.

[16] *Book of Beliefs and Opinions*, ed. Landauer (Arab.), 32; ed. Rosenblatt, 40.

Sa'adyah devotes the second chapter to establishing the absolute unity of the Creator. This entails a refutation of dualistic concepts and a denial of God's corporeality and of the reality of the qualities attributed to him. Sa'adyah focuses this section of the argument on the three attributes—life, knowledge, and power—which were central to Mu'tazilite thought and may have gained relative importance in the context of debates with Christian theologians. These three attributes, he claims, are logically inseparable aspects of the Creator, and it is only the limitations of human language that necessitate the use of three distinct terms to describe them. In this context, he goes on to voice explicit criticism of four versions of the doctrine of the Trinity representing the beliefs of different (unidentifiable) Christian sects.[17]

The next seven chapters deal with various aspects of the relationship between the Creator and his creation, and may be viewed as an extensive treatment of the second theme of Mu'tazilite *kalam*, namely, Divine justice. God created the world for the benefit of his creatures, and to this end, he gave them commandments and prohibitions that would enable them to earn the rewards of observing his law. As Sa'adyah states at the beginning of the third chapter:

Because it is clear that the Creator, may he be exalted and magnified, was alone in primordial existence, the creation of things was an act of goodness and generous kindness on his part . . . and his goodness and beneficence are attested in Scripture as well, as the verse says, 'The Lord is good to all and his tender mercies are over all his works' [Ps. 145: 9]. And the first of these kindnesses to his creatures is that he brought them into being, that is, he created them when they were not in existence, as he said to the chosen ones among them, 'Every one that is called by my name and whom I have created for my glory' [Isa. 43: 7]. And then he gave them the means through which to attain perfect joy and absolute bliss, as it is written, 'Thou makest me to know the path of life; In Thy presence is fullness of joy, In Thy right hand bliss forevermore' [Ps. 16: 11], this being what he commanded and forbade them to do.

Human intelligence reflects upon this and says: he could have given them perfect bliss and eternal happiness without commanding or prohibiting them, and it would even seem that his kindness would have been of greater benefit to them in this way . . . and I would say in clarification of this matter: just the opposite—making their observance of the commandments the means of attaining eternal goodness is the greatest kindness, as it stands to reason that one who receives benefits for a deed which he has performed is rewarded twice as much as one who receives benefits gratuitously.[18]

Here we find the distinction, which Sa'adyah repeats in several places, between rational and non-rational commandments. Rational commandments are those dictated by the moral intuition bestowed on humankind by God, such as the

---

[17] Ibid., ed. Landauer, 90–1; ed. Rosenblatt, 109–10.
[18] Ibid., ed. Landauer, 112; ed. Rosenblatt, 137.

prohibition against murder or theft or the obligation to honour one's parents. With respect to these commandments, too, self-understood though they are in a general way, there is a need for revelation in order to determine their details, but the main need for revelation and tradition concerns the non-rational commandments. These are not necessitated by reason or moral intuition but are added to the rational commandments in the form of specific injunctions in order to provide additional opportunities for reward to those who observe them. At the same time, in most if not all cases, they also confer a direct benefit that is apprehensible by the rational mind. So, for example, the avoidance of work on the sabbath and festivals provides rest for the body and the leisure to engage in intellectual, religious, and social pursuits. This chapter also includes extensive discussions on the nature of prophetic revelation: why it is necessary, how the prophet knows that he has received a revelation from God, how his listeners recognize it as such, and so forth. Sa'adyah makes a special effort to negate the possibility that some or all of the commandments could be revoked through later revelations, as claimed by Christianity and Islam.

The next six chapters concern topics related to reward and punishment, a central theme that expresses a basic faith in Divine justice. The fourth chapter deals mostly with man's freedom of choice to obey or disobey God's commandments. Faith in freedom of choice is the logical consequence of faith in Divine justice, since it would be unreasonable to command or forbid actions to anyone incapable of obedience, and it would certainly be unjust to reward those who fulfil a commandment or punish those who do not if they had no choice in the matter. Sa'adyah refers the reader to various biblical passages which express this principle, such as 'choose life' (Deut. 30: 19), and to the talmudic statement that 'everything is in the hands of heaven except the fear of heaven'. He also devotes a lengthy discussion to verses which seem to imply that God makes people behave in certain ways, and offers alternative explanations for these.

The fifth chapter deals with merits and demerits and includes a division of human beings into ten categories—righteous, wicked, heretical, repentant, and so forth—according to their religious behaviour. Here Sa'adyah discusses the reward or punishment designated for someone who belongs to each of these categories, his guiding principle being that reward and punishment are in the main reserved for the world to come. One should not be surprised therefore to observe a righteous person who is unhappy or a wicked person who is happy in this world since their accounts will be settled in the world to come, which is the more important one. Sa'adyah expands his discussion on the last category, the repentant individual, and gives a list based on talmudic sources of the essential components of repentance (abandonment of sin, remorse, asking forgiveness, and undertaking not to continue sinning in the future), the cases in which it is not accepted or does not provide immunity from punishment, and the various degrees of repentance.

The sixth chapter discusses the nature of the human soul and its fate after death. Sa'adyah examines six different views on the essence of the soul, refutes them, and concludes that God creates each person's soul when creating his or her body. In its essence the soul is 'a substance as pure as the celestial spheres' but it needs a body in order to be able to act and thus earn reward and happiness. The soul and body act in concert and receive their just reward or punishment together. God has set a time limit on the union of the body and soul, and at the end of this time limit he separates them and the individual dies. The body then ceases to exist but the soul continues alone until the time of the resurrection, when it will be reunited with the body. At the end of the chapter Sa'adyah forcefully rejects the belief in the transmigration of souls found among 'some who are called Jews'.

According to Sa'adyah the resurrection of the dead will be a double event, taking place partly in the messianic age—which will bring the world as we know it to an end—and partly in the world to come. The seventh chapter (which, as we have seen, was published in two versions) is devoted to the resurrection of the dead in this world, and leads to an eighth chapter dealing with the messianic age. The resurrection of the dead in the world to come is discussed in the ninth chapter.

Resurrection in this world applies only to the children of Israel—as opposed to resurrection in the next world which applies to all of humanity—and represents one part of the Divine plan for the redemption of Israel in the messianic age. Sa'adyah bases this dogma on a straightforward reading of various biblical passages and argues that it is a belief shared by most Jews and should be accepted, as there is no valid reason to understand these passages in a non-literal way. In his discussion of specific questions relating to the resurrection of the dead, such as the quality and length of life of the resurrected, he relies on talmudic sources and concludes that the resurrected will live an earthly life after which they will pass on to the next world without dying a second time. Life in the world to come will not involve corporeal activity even though people will inhabit the same bodies that they had during their earthly existence. But this need not surprise us since 'we know that our rabbi Moses, who used to drink and eat, stayed for forty days on the mountain without food and drink, while his body remained in its [former] state'.[19]

The eighth chapter is devoted to the redemption promised to Israel in the end of days. This belief is based on a number of prophecies but it is also dictated by reason. Just as Divine justice requires the giving of suitable rewards to individuals, so it requires a suitable reward at the national level:

And this nation has already been visited with great and prolonged sufferings, and there is no doubt that some of these have been punishments and some are set as tests, and for each of these two conditions there is a finite span of time . . . and when they come to an

[19] *Book of Beliefs and Opinions*, ed. Landauer, 224; ed. Rosenblatt, 281–2.

end he will of necessity stop punishing those [who are being punished] and reward those [who are being tested].[20]

Following the Sages, Sa'adyah concludes that redemption will come when the children of Israel return in repentance and become worthy of it, but even if they do not return in repentance, redemption will come at a time predetermined by God. He enters into detailed calculations of the end of days based on hints found in the book of Daniel, and describes the various stages of redemption according to biblical sources and talmudic traditions. At the end of the chapter Sa'adyah argues against the belief, which he ascribes to 'some who are called Jews' and (in a slightly different version) to Christians, that the prophetic promises had already been fulfilled during the era of the Second Temple. According to these people, the promise of an ideal state that would endure until the end of days had been conditional on the behaviour of the children of Israel. However, the children of Israel had sinned and forfeited their kingdom subsequent to the fulfilment of the prophecies, and so could not expect them to be fulfilled in the future. To these arguments Sa'adyah replies that there is nothing in the language of the prophets to indicate that God's promises were conditional, and that many aspects of the prophecies were not fulfilled during the time of the Second Temple, for example, the return of the entire nation of Israel from exile. Therefore, he maintains, we must believe that the promises will be fulfilled in the future (see pp. 143–4).

The ninth chapter, concerning reward and punishment in the world to come, assumes that God acts justly and rewards individuals according to their deeds. However, it is clear that people do not always receive their just reward or punishment in this world, so there must be a future existence, a 'world to come', where we will see justice done. As Sa'adyah puts it:

It has been shown . . . that the heavens and the earth and all that lies between them were created solely for the sake of man, and this is why God placed man at the centre of Creation and gave his soul an exalted degree of intelligence and wisdom, and also gave it commandments and admonitions so that it might attain eternal life—and this life will be attained when the human beings created according to the requirements of Divine wisdom come to an end, for then God will settle them in another world and reward them in it . . . And it is only reasonable that the Creator, may His name be exalted and magnified, should mete out in his wisdom and omnipotence and goodness a measure of happiness for man's soul there which differs from the delights and pleasures of this world, where every delight is joined with sighing and every joy with grief and every pleasure with pain and happiness with sorrow. And I find . . . that these exist in equal measure, or else sorrow prevails over happiness in this world, and since this is so beyond a doubt, it cannot be that God in His exalted wisdom would have intended the soul's state of pleasure to be so fleeting, but must rather have appointed for the soul a place of unmitigated life and sublime happiness . . .

[20] *Book of Beliefs and Opinions*, ed. Landauer, 230–1; ed. Rosenblatt, 291.

And the souls of created beings that I have known are never tranquil or serene in this world, even if they reach ... the highest station, and this is not due to the nature of the soul, but to its knowledge of a greater world than that of earthly delights, for which it longs and aspires ... Moreover, when we see that people exploit each other and that it fares either well or ill for the exploiter and the exploited and then they both die— because the works of the Exalted One are just, He must already have appointed another world for them where justice will reign and the one will be rewarded for what he suffered through exploitation while the other will be punished for the pleasure that he gained through evil and exploitation. Furthermore, when we see heretics enjoying life in this world and the faithful suffering in this world, it must be that both will receive their just deserts in another world.[21]

The book ends with a loosely related chapter on the subject of the ideal life in this world. The basic contention of the chapter is that rather than pursuing a single goal, however lofty, a person should strive to integrate various pursuits and traits in an intelligent fashion and strike a correct balance between all human possibilities. In Sa'adyah's own words:

And when these thirteen elements are combined ... the man of wisdom will obtain from his food and drink and intercourse enough to satisfy the needs of his body and his seed and, when permissible, he will set his desire free to take its portion, but if it is prone to excess or to taking what is not permissible he should rein it in ... and care for the possessions and progeny that God has allowed him by His grace with the power of His love for them, and build on earth according to the measure of his needs ... and love worldly life for the sake of the world to come, as a corridor to it, not for its own sake. And let him never crave power or revenge ... and let him never behave in an indolent manner. And let him devote the time that remains after he has earned his livelihood to [Divine] service and learning. And when he has combined these actions as we have described he will be deserving of praise in both worlds.[22]

[21] Ibid., ed. Landauer, 255–6; ed. Rosenblatt, 323–4.
[22] Ibid., ed. Landauer, 314–15; ed. Rosenblatt, 399–400.

CHAPTER FOUR

⁂

Sa'adyah the Biblical Commentator

THE BIBLE, as we know, was viewed as sacred by Jews of all persuasions, Rabbanite and Karaite. Yet while the Karaites held that the Bible should be interpreted strictly with reference to the text rather than external sources, Rabbanite Jews transmitted alongside the Bible, which they called the Written Law, a no less authoritative tradition referred to as the Oral Law. This tradition was crucial in determining the correct and binding interpretation of the Bible when it appeared to contradict the overt meaning of the text.

The Bible retained its unique status during the geonic era (and after) as manifested first and foremost in the regular order of synagogue readings from the Pentateuch and selected portions of the Prophets and the Writings that formed a vital part of the prayer service. It also played a central role in such forms of creative endeavour as *piyut* and midrash, more prevalent in Palestinian tradition than in that of Babylonia. There is no indication that the Babylonian sages before Sa'adyah's day engaged in systematic biblical exegesis as part of their higher education, although it is reasonable to assume that their primary education—as in traditional Judaism everywhere—consisted largely of learning to read the Torah and other parts of Scripture. All Jewish males were expected to be able to 'go up to the Torah' in the synagogue and read the passages that fell to their lot (at this time the ancient custom according to which the man who went up to the Torah read the passage himself was still observed, as opposed to the later practice of employing an expert reader or *ba'al kore* to read the Torah for everyone). As far as we know, the sages of the Babylonian academies concerned themselves almost exclusively with the Oral Law and halakhah, and the overwhelming majority of questions sent to the geonic academies from Jewish communities in the diaspora were likewise narrowly focused on these areas. It was relatively rare to address questions of biblical exegesis to the geonic academies.

At least two leaders of the Karaite movement that evolved in the ninth century, Benjamin al-Nihawandi and Daniel al-Qumisi, wrote Hebrew commentaries on portions of the Bible. Moreover, according to recent discoveries, certain parts of the Bible had been translated into Judaeo-Arabic before Sa'adyah's day. But in this area as in others Sa'adyah went further and deeper than his predecessors, and may reasonably be considered the first Rabbanite Jew to engage in systematic biblical exegesis, and perhaps, the first Jew of any persuasion to write biblical commentaries in the Arabic language.

The Scope of Sa'adyah's Exegetical Undertakings

In addition to the often remarkable and surprising interpretations of biblical verses scattered among his writings, in particular in *The Book of Beliefs and Opinions*, Sa'adyah devoted many of his works specifically to biblical exegesis. These include a translation of the Pentateuch into Arabic, a commentary on at least half of it (see below), and pieces combining translation and commentary on a number of books from the Prophets and the Writings. He wrote commentaries on a number of books, including Isaiah, Psalms, Proverbs, Job, and Daniel. With respect to other parts of the Bible, particularly the five scrolls, things are less certain. The Yemenite community preserved Sa'adyah's translation of the Pentateuch over the centuries (though not always with complete accuracy) and, to a lesser extent, his commentaries on Psalms, Proverbs, Job, and Daniel; editions of these, including Hebrew translations, were prepared by the late R. Yosef Kafih. Sa'adyah's commentaries on the Pentateuch and Isaiah, however, have to be pieced together from fragments that survived in the Cairo Genizah and citations that were incorporated in the works of later (mainly exegetical) writers. The difficult task of restoring these commentaries, to which many scholars have contributed over the past hundred years, is far from complete, and there are lingering doubts as to the authenticity of some of the completed sections. The identity of the author of an anonymous fragment of biblical commentary is very difficult to establish solely on stylistic grounds. In the absence of external evidence or other corroborating factors (such as the writer's references to his other works) there is no choice but to incorporate sections that cannot be positively identified (although continuing research in the field of Judaeo-Arabic biblical exegesis will be likely to resolve many open questions as time goes on). At present we have editions of Sa'adyah's commentaries on the first half of Genesis, the book of Exodus, and the book of Isaiah, but large sections of these commentaries are missing. No edition of his commentary on Leviticus has yet been published, although he undoubtedly wrote one, and numerous sections that probably belong to this commentary have appeared in scattered publications.

Sa'adyah assigned special titles to his biblical commentaries according to what he perceived as their central themes and the themes of the biblical books themselves. Thus the book of Isaiah bears the title *The Book of Seeking Perfection of Divine Service* (literally, obedience) *as Revealed to the Prophet Isaiah*; Psalms is called *The Book of Praise*, Proverbs *The Book of the Search for Wisdom*, and Job *The Book of Theodicy*. He bestows a surprisingly long and detailed title on the book of Daniel: *The Book of Kingdoms and Prophetic Visions of Events that Will Take Place at the End of 1,386 Years.* His commentary on the Pentateuch and the Pentateuch itself he calls *Kitab al-Azhar*, meaning either *The Book of Blossoms* or *The Book of Splendour* (or radiance). For his biblical commentaries, like his other monographic writings, Sa'adyah wrote rather lengthy introductions with an overview of the books in question and their principal themes. In addition, some of these—his introduction to the Pentateuch is an outstanding example—contain extensive methodological discussions.

Sa'adyah's exegetical works (and those of the exegetes who followed his example) characteristically consist of alternating sections of translation and commentary. He divides the biblical text into thematic units, first translating each unit and then commenting on it. The commentaries often relate to the translation, explaining Sa'adyah's decision to translate in a particular way. Such works are generally known by the Arabic term *tafsir*, which may indicate either translation or commentary.

Two questions about Sa'adyah's commentary on the Pentateuch that have vexed scholars over the years have yet to be resolved. The first concerns the relationship between his translation of the Pentateuch, which was copied and transmitted as a separate work, and his commentary, which, as we have seen, includes a translation. We have in our possession two (incomplete) prefaces by Sa'adyah to his translation of the Pentateuch. In one of them, he writes the following:

I composed this book only because a petitioner asked me to isolate the simple meaning of the Torah text in a separate work without discussion of language ... [or] any of the questions of the heretics or their refutation; or any of the 'branches' [i.e. details] of the rational commandments or the proper mode of performing the non-rational commandments, but only the translation of the substance of the Torah text itself. And I realized that what he asked [of me] in this regard would be advantageous, so that listeners might hear the substance of the Torah, meaning the stories and the commandments and their rewards, in an orderly and concise manner, and a person seeking [to understand] a particular section would not have to go through tiresome and lengthy proofs touching on every aspect. And if anyone should wish to investigate the ramifications of the rational commandments and the modes of performing the non-rational [commandments] and the means to refute those who dispute the Bible, let him seek it in the other book [i.e. the commentary] ... And seeing [fit to do so] I included in this book only the explanation of the simple meaning of the Torah text, painstakingly arranged [in keeping with] knowledge and tradition; and when I was able to add to the verse a word or a letter to make the desired intention clear ... I did so.[1]

The question is whether Sa'adyah simply extracted the portions of translation from the framework of his commentary and published them independently, or whether he produced a revised translation which could be read as a separate monograph without the accompanying commentary. Undoubtedly, there are dif-

---

[1] Derenbourg, *Œuvres complètes*, i. 4 (Arab. with Heb. trans.).

ferences between the free-standing translation of certain verses and the corresponding translation embedded in the commentary, but these could be due to scribal errors or to the deliberate emendations of copyists and adapters over the centuries. However, it seems more likely that Sa'adyah produced two separate, albeit quite similar, translations, intending the first—which adhered more closely to the biblical text—to be read on its own and the second in the broader context of the commentary, which allowed him to explain unusual translations. (Much of the commentary could actually be described as an annotated translation with numerous passages beginning, 'I translate X because the word Y has Z meanings in Hebrew' and providing additional examples from the Bible to prove the existence of said meanings, almost like an exhaustive dictionary entry). One instance of this phenomenon concerns the term *ets ḥayim* (Tree of Life, Gen. 2–3), which Sa'adyah translates literally in the separate translation but in his commentary renders as 'the Tree of Health' (or well-being), supplying philological arguments in support of this departure from the literal translation.

Another interesting example is Sa'adyah's translation of the biblical expression *ruaḥ kadim*, which is normally rendered as 'an east wind' but which Sa'adyah contended could not be interpreted in this way in every case. In the description of the plague of locusts that struck Egypt (Exod. 10: 13) he understands, perhaps through his personal knowledge of geographical conditions in Egypt, that the wind that brought the locusts was actually a south wind. The translation in his commentary renders it explicitly as 'south wind', and he notes: 'I have translated *ruaḥ kadim* as "south wind", which is also called *reah kavul* on account of its destructive effects'.[2] Nevertheless, in the separate translation, presumably realizing that he could not simply supply a translation which the average reader would find very surprising without providing an explanation, he chose the same term mentioned in the commentary, *reah kavul*, which, according to him, has no definite geographical connotations but refers to the destructive qualities of this wind.

The second disputed question, which has certain implications for the previous one, concerns the scope of Sa'adyah's pentateuchal commentaries. A twelfth-century author, Joseph ben Jacob Rosh Haseder, states that he was inspired to write a commentary on the *haftarot* after studying 'The threefold commentary on the Torah: from "Bereshit" to "Vayetse" [Gen. 1: 1–28: 9] and from Exodus to [the beginning of] Numbers by R. Sa'adyah Gaon; from "Vayetse" to [the beginning of] Exodus and from Numbers until "Shofetim" [Deut. 16: 18] by Rabbi Samuel ben Hofni; and from "Shofetim" until the end of the Torah by Rabbi Aaron ben Sarjado.'[3]

This reflects the custom, widespread in the geonic period, of dividing each of the pentateuchal books in half. A simple reading of the above statement seems to

[2] Ben-Shammai, 'An "East Wind" from the South' (Heb.).

[3] See Mann, 'Fihrist', 426–7 and n. 10.

indicate that Sa'adyah wrote commentaries on the first half of Genesis and the books of Exodus and Leviticus in their entirety; his contemporary, Rabbi Aaron, wrote a commentary only on the second half of Deuteronomy, while Samuel ben Hofni wrote his on the portions not treated by his predecessors, namely, the second half of Genesis, the entire book of Numbers, and the first half of Deuteronomy. Such a reconstruction is supported by various early booklists found in the Cairo Genizah, first and foremost the catalogue of works by Sa'adyah Gaon compiled by his two sons, She'erit and Dosa, only a few years after his death.[4] It is also supported by the vast majority of citations by later writers from Sa'adyah's commentaries, which relate to parts of the Pentateuch on which he wrote commentaries according to this theory.

On the other hand, it is possible that Sa'adyah's original commentary covered all five books of the Pentateuch and an anonymous scholar later on decided to piece together a commentary made up of selected portions of Sa'adyah's work together with the commentaries of two other geonim on the remaining portions of the Torah. There is some prima facie support for this theory in the fact that both Sa'adyah and Samuel ben Hofni are occasionally cited with respect to certain Torah portions on which, according to the former theory, they wrote no commentaries. It is, however, possible that these geonim authored commentaries on selected pericopes in addition to commentaries on whole or half-books, either because they considered them particularly significant or in response to special requests from readers (it appears, for example, that both Sa'adyah and Samuel ben Hofni wrote commentaries on the portion of 'Ha'azinu', Deut. 32). It is also possible that some of the citations derive from commentaries on other Bible portions in which these verses were referred to in the course of the discussion. I tend to believe that each of the three geonim wrote commentaries only on selected portions of the Pentateuch as described above, but the final solution to this knotty problem must be suspended until the exegetical treasures of the Cairo Genizah, many of them as yet unexamined, have been thoroughly perused and identified.

Before we proceed to explore Sa'adyah's biblical commentaries, let us look briefly at the nature of his translations.[5] First, we should note that Sa'adyah allowed himself a great deal of leeway in his biblical renderings, even where he provides no explanation in the accompanying translation, and was often surprisingly bold in this respect. His aim was not to stick to the literal meaning and structure of the source, and even less to reflect the obscurity or ambiguity of many verses. He chose rather to communicate the contents as he understood them based on various considerations, in lucid, unambiguous Arabic to the best of his ability. In order to achieve this aim he was not averse to dropping 'superfluous'

---

[4] This unique source was published in Mann, 'Fihrist'.

[5] See Blau, 'Sa'adyah's Translation of the Pentateuch' (Heb.); id., 'Sa'adyah's Translation of Genesis ɪɪ–ɪ2' (Heb.).

words from the translation or to adding words with no equivalent in the biblical verse in order to facilitate a clear and accurate understanding of the text. As we have seen, Sa'adyah himself declared explicitly, 'When I was able to add to the verse a word or a letter to make the desired intention clear ... I did so.' For example, he renders the words of God to Adam in Genesis 2: 17, proclaiming that on the day that he ate from the tree of knowledge of good and evil he would 'surely die', as 'thou shalt deserve to die', since the death sentence was never carried out.

Nor does Sa'adyah remain faithful to the syntax of the biblical text, often altering it in the interest of greater clarity, especially by replacing co-ordinated clauses with subordinate clauses. We find a striking example of this in the translation of Genesis 1, where each day of creation ends with the repeated words, 'And there was evening and there was morning of day X', which Sa'adyah translates consistently in a way that links it to the following day: 'And after day X of the nights and days had passed'. The tendency to supply connecting phrases between adjacent sentences is common in his translations, but in this case, it should be noted, he ignores the paragraph division of the biblical text. Similarly he does not preserve the rhythms of the original and renders most poetic or quasi-poetic passages as prose. He does not feel bound even by the sequence of the Hebrew text and in many places changes the word order. He even moves whole sections around in the commentaries. For example, in the commentary to Proverbs 9 he skips verses 10–12 in order to discuss verses 1–9 together with verses 13–18, highlighting the parallelism between the first unit, which according to him deals with those who hold right opinions, and the second, which deals with those who hold wrong ones. Only then does he return to the three omitted verses.

In many of his commentaries—and occasionally in other writings as well—Sa'adyah follows and sometimes quotes the Aramaic translations of the Bible. (Since we are in possession of these Aramaic texts, it is relatively easy to determine the extent of their influence on Sa'adyah's translations into Judaeo-Arabic.) His work was also influenced by previous translations into Judaeo-Arabic, some apparently written and others oral, but these, except for a few surviving fragments, vanished almost entirely after the overwhelming success of his translations.[6]

Sa'adyah's highly elevated style became less and less comprehensible to Arabic-speaking Jews over the centuries and his translations were therefore adapted and revised many times. Remarkably, he was not averse to using Qur'anic locutions, as, for example, in his rendering of *benei reshef* in Job 5: 7 with the Arabic phrase *ahl al-nar*, that is, 'people of the fire [of Hell]'. In one extreme case he uses the Qur'anic phrase *baqara safra* (yellow cow) to translate the 'red heifer' of Numbers 19: 2. This phenomenon may be connected to Abraham ibn Ezra's claim that Sa'adyah rendered the Pentateuch 'in the language and writing of Ishmael' in order to make it accessible to adherents of other religions, and above all to

---

[6] See Blau and Hopkins, *Corpus of Judaeo-Arabic Texts* (Heb., forthcoming).

Muslims. If we accept his testimony, we may hypothesize that the background to this was the forum of theological debate between adherents of various faiths, and the desire of Jewish participants to provide their interlocutors with an authorized translation of Hebrew Scriptures to which they could refer in the course of discussion. Such debates were documented at a slightly later period, but there is no reason to suppose that they did not take place in Sa'adyah's own day. If this assumption is correct, it is likely that Sa'adyah published his translations in Arabic script for the convenience of non-Jewish readers as well as in Hebrew letters for his Jewish audience.[7]

Sa'adyah's biblical commentaries vary considerably in scope from one book to another. At one extreme are the commentaries on the Torah, which, as he stresses, include broad expositions of linguistic and halakhic topics as well as refutations of heretical doctrines. At the other extreme, in his commentary on the book of Psalms, he presents certain psalms without any interpretation at all beyond the Arabic rendering, or with only a few interpretative remarks. Midway between these extremes is Sa'adyah's commentary on the book of Daniel. Here we sense his desire to accentuate elements that will offer comfort and encouragement in the anguish of exile, going so far as to calculate dates for the coming of the messiah. Yet he is sometimes terse in dealing with other aspects of the book, and even states that 'Having cut short my explanation of these six chapters [chapters 1–6], I will elucidate the remaining four chapters more fully because of the great importance of understanding the ends [i.e. apocalyptic predictions] and linguistic usages.'[8]

The case of the book of Psalms is complex and raises additional questions. Sa'adyah wrote two separate prefaces to it, one relatively short and the other quite lengthy, and possibly a very brief third preface as well. The short preface concentrates on the startling claim—variations of which we find in some of Sa'adyah's other works (see pp. 134–5)—that the psalms were not composed by King David or others as prayers addressed to God but are actually prophecies representing the words of God to man, even though such an understanding would seem to contradict their formulation. The polemical motive behind this daring proposition is obvious: Sa'adyah was attempting to prove that the early Karaites were wrong to use the book of Psalms as their liturgical text since one cannot pray to God with words that he addressed to man. Prayers must be 'human' in function and purpose,

---

[7] See, most recently, Ben Shammai, 'Old and New' (Heb.). In this context it is perhaps worth mentioning that over a millennium later, when former president Yitzhak Navon met Anwar Sadat, he gave him a copy of Sa'adyah's translation as a gift.

[8] Kafih, *Sa'adyah's Commentary on Daniel* (Heb.), 120. In his preface to the commentary, Sa'adyah enters into a lengthy discussion of the difference between prophecy—through which we obtain well-founded information regarding the future—and astrology, which is a superstitious belief lacking any predictive capacity (see Ben-Shammai, 'Sa'adyah's Introduction to Daniel' (Heb.)).

like the prayers of the Rabbanite tradition. Sa'adyah presents this argument as follows:

Because human guidance is achieved by all manners of speech, the Wise and Exalted One had to make his books aimed at their [i.e. humans'] guidance adapt to these and their divisions. Now among the many devices used by human beings in guiding one another we find injunctions concerning virtue, prohibitions against sin, exhortations, warnings, exemplary tales of righteous men to be emulated, cautionary tales to deter us from following the example of the wicked, in the words of a servant addressing his master and of a master addressing his servant . . . parables and narratives. For man uses the ten devices and their like, finding that they inspire him to accept what is inherently desirable. And there is no need here to adduce examples for each and every one of these . . . since they are perfectly clear, nor is it necessary to cite examples from other books of the Bible, since the examples from the book that we are about to interpret provide sufficient proof . . .

And we found it necessary to preface our remarks with these words so that the reader will not contemplate dividing the book's substance and taking the words expressed in the language of a servant addressed to his master as the words of the servant instead of the master, thinking that 'grant me grace', 'save me', 'hasten unto me', and their like derive not from the visions that God showed His prophets but are only the words of the servant, or that 'they will thank' and 'they will sing' describe the third person and not the second person, or anything else that one might imagine contrary to God's intention, for we must know that all of these [words] come from God, who formulated them in all the manners of speech used by His creatures.[9]

The long preface is largely devoted to the same motif—the claim that all of Psalms was composed by God and revealed prophetically even though much of the wording suggests otherwise—but Sa'adyah develops the argument for his claim in greater detail here. Towards the end of the preface he deals with the order of the psalms, and offers possible explanations for their arrangement. The text ends with an extensive discussion of Psalms 1–4 which includes their translation (not the same translation found in the body of the book itself) and a full commentary, with emphasis on the thematic continuity of these psalms and on the transition from one to the next. In conclusion Sa'adyah writes:

This commentary, may God have mercy on you, completes the four psalms in which I have established the principles for explicating the order of the psalms in this book . . . Doing the same for each psalm would result in too long a book, so I have provided a kind of key, which every reader may study in order to understand the structure of the rest of the book, in a manner that is plausible although not definitive.[10]

Judging by the diversity of material covered by the exegesis of the first four psalms—particularly Psalms 1 and 2, the commentaries on each of which are

---

[9] Kafih, *Sa'adyah's Commentary on Psalms* (Heb.), 51, 53.   [10] Ibid. 50.

divided into a section on philology followed by a section concerning the ideas in the psalm—the preface was intended not only to illustrate how to explain the order of the psalms but also to show how the psalms themselves should be interpreted. Presumably, the various prefaces represent different stages of Sa'adyah's work; it is possible, for example, that the shorter preface accompanied the original publication of the commentary, and that some time later (due perhaps to the response of readers) Sa'adyah decided that he had made it too brief. However, instead of rewriting the work he merely added a preface to it with a sample of the more expansive commentary that he would have written had he not feared that 'it would result in too long a book', together with a recommendation that the reader apply the same principles and approaches to the remaining psalms. But this is only conjecture.

Another case in point is the commentary on the book of Job which has come down to us in two separate editions, both probably authored by Sa'adyah Gaon. The first published version was more concise, and the writer expanded on it in a second edition. Although it is true that the briefer version may have been the work of copyists who were simply too lazy to transcribe the entire book, there is a conspicuous structural difference between the two versions: the shorter one provides a summary of each speech in the book of Job followed by its detailed interpretation, while the longer one presents a summary at the end of each speech. Since Sa'adyah's remarks in the preface agree with the structure of the shorter version, it is more likely that this preface was written for the first, shorter edition and that even when he published the second, expanded version and changed the order of the exposition, he left the preface as it was.[11]

Exegetical Principles

Sa'adyah was keenly aware of the methodological issues confronting biblical exegetes and addressed them at length, particularly in his prefaces to the commentaries. Of special importance are the programmatic discussions in the introduction to his commentary on Genesis. One of these deals with basic questions of human knowledge and their implications. As we have seen (pp. 31–2, 52), Sa'adyah maintains that knowledge is based on sense perception, reason, or tradition, and in his view—as spokesman for Rabbanite Judaism—authoritative tradition encompasses both the Bible, or Written Law, and the talmudic tradition, or Oral Law. Moreover, since there is only one truth, there can be no real inconsistency between the versions of truth arrived at through different channels. Any 'contradiction', then, is merely apparent, for when the issue is studied in depth, one of the conflicting conclusions will prove to have been derived incorrectly.

In the exegetical context Sa'adyah applies this basic principle by means of non-

[11] See Kafih, *Sa'adyah's Commentary on Job* (Heb.), 5, 21, and n. 10.

literal interpretation. Although he maintains that the exegete's first inclination should be to interpret every phrase in accordance with its common and accepted meaning, he adds that one may draw on a variety of alternatives when necessary. The Arabic expression for such interpretation is *majaz*, which can be translated literally as 'transferred'; its range includes metaphor (which has a similar etymology in Greek) but is considerably broader. As Sa'adyah writes:

Now that I have finished explaining the three types of knowledge [i.e. rational, scriptural, and traditional] which are necessary for the commentator on the Torah, I see fit to preface [a description of] the [proper] method of expounding the Torah and the other books of the Prophets. I say: since these three types of knowledge are the very foundations of Scripture, and since every speech includes perforce both unambiguous and ambiguous [expressions, Arabic *muhkam* and *mutashabih*] . . . the exegete should consider all words that accord with the prior dictates of reason and the later dictates of tradition as unambiguous, and words that are inconsistent with one or the other as ambiguous.

To explain further: a reasonable person should always understand the Torah according to the external meaning of its words, that is, the meaning generally recognized among speakers of the language—because the purpose of any book is to convey its meaning perfectly to the reader's heart—except where perception or reason contradict the usual meaning of a particular expression or where the usual meaning of an expression contradicts an unequivocal verse found elsewhere in Scripture or a tradition. However, if retaining the simple meaning of an expression leads the exegete to profess one of these four things [discussed below] he must know that this expression is not to be understood according to its simple meaning, but that it carries one or more non-literal meanings [*majaz*]; and once he knows the type of *majaz* involved . . . in order to bring [the expression under consideration into agreement with] its unambiguous equivalent [Arabic *muhkam*], the verse will be reconciled with the senses, with reason, with other scriptures and with tradition.[12]

Sa'adyah follows this with four examples of contradiction, one for each of the four types mentioned. The description of Eve in Genesis 3: 20 as 'the mother of all living things' cannot be interpreted literally, since to do so would contradict the perception that animals such as lions are not born of human mothers. We must assume therefore that the verse is elliptical and translate it as 'the mother of all living things who speak', that is, human beings. Similarly the statement in Deuteronomy 4: 24 that God is a 'consuming fire' should not be interpreted literally, because reason tells us that fire is mutable while God is not. Since the commandment in Deuteronomy 6: 16, 'Ye shall not try the Lord your God as ye tried Him in Massah', is understood as an unequivocal prohibition against the testing of God, the expression about 'trying God' in Malachi 3: 10—'Bring ye the whole tithe into the store-house, that there be food in My house, and try Me now herewith saith

---

[12] Zucker, *Sa'adyah's Commentary on Genesis*, 17–18 (Arab. text), 191 (Heb. trans.), with thanks to Haggai Ben-Shammai for corrections to Zucker's Arabic text based on a new collation of manuscripts.

the Lord of hosts, if I will not open you the windows of heaven and pour you out a blessing that shall be more than sufficiency'—must be interpreted according to a rarer and lesser-known meaning. Sa'adyah does not explain what this meaning may be, but promises to explain it 'in its place', that is, at a later time, when he comments on the book of Malachi. As far as we know, the Gaon did not live to write a commentary on Malachi, but he solved the apparent contradiction in *The Book of Beliefs and Opinions* by interpreting the prophet's words to the children of Israel not as an exhortation to try the powers of the Lord, but as a call to test their own virtue and their worthiness to receive the blessings that God pours out through the windows of heaven.[13]

Last but not least, the thrice-repeated prohibition in the Torah[14] against seething 'a kid in its mother's milk' is interpreted more broadly as a prohibition against eating milk with meat. This accords with rabbinic tradition, which is to be accepted because the Sages based it on 'sense perceptions and manifest things which they saw with their own eyes'—apparently meaning that the children of Israel learned the parameters of the prohibition from the example and instructions given by Moses, who was the authorized mediator and interpreter of Divine revelation.

Sa'adyah then proceeds to a more detailed discussion that includes a long list, only part of which has survived, of linguistic and stylistic phenomena with which an exegete must be familiar. For example, a word may sometimes appear only once in a verse but must be understood as if it appeared twice, as in Psalms 137: 3: 'For there they that led us captive asked of us a song, and they that tormented us [asked of us] mirth'. The exegete must also pay attention to syntax and consider alternative ways of grouping the words of a verse in line with their content. For example, for theological reasons—to avoid anthropomorphism—Sa'adyah cannot read Isaiah's description 'above Him stand the seraphim' (Isa. 6: 2) literally and therefore analyses the structure of the verse as follows: 'the seraphim who stand above [are] His'; that is, God has seraphim who stand on high.

At the end of this discussion Sa'adyah deals with a question that seems obvious according to his approach:[15] why was the Bible written in a way that is so difficult to understand and demands so much effort from the interpreter? He answers that God wishes to benefit his creatures and to reward them for the great effort that it takes to understand his words (this fits in with a central tenet of his philosophy, namely, that God's reason for giving many of the commandments was to enable humans to earn reward for observing them) and, moreover, since they have the Oral Tradition to guide them and alleviate their doubts, they are assured of staying on course.

[13] *Book of Beliefs and Opinions*, ed. Landauer (Arab.), 102; ed. Rosenblatt, 415–16 (and cf. Landauer, 212–13, Rosenblatt, 266).   [14] Exod. 23: 19 and 34: 26; Deut. 14: 21.

[15] Zucker, *Sa'adyah's Commentary on Genesis*, 20 (Arab. text), 195–6 (Heb. trans.).

Theological and Polemical Dimensions

It is not surprising that Sa'adyah's general education should occasionally find expression in his biblical commentaries. A striking instance of this is the concept of the four elements (earth, air, fire, and water), rooted in the ancient world and still prevalent in the scientific thought of the Middle Ages. Sa'adyah applies this concept several times in his writings; for example, in the classification of the ten plagues inflicted by God on the Egyptians according to these four elements.[16]

We find an especially interesting application of the theory of the four elements in Sa'adyah's commentary on the story of Creation in the book of Genesis.[17] Here he claims that the first verse of Genesis ('In the beginning God created the heaven and the earth') describes the creation of the heavenly spheres (a theory likewise derived from the physical sciences of ancient Greece) and the element of earth. The second verse ('and the earth was unformed and void and darkness was upon the face of the deep and the spirit of God hovered over the face of the waters') includes the elements of air and water in the scheme of Creation.

And should a person ask why [Scripture] omits any mention of the creation of fire, we answer: if by this he means the fire of the heavenly spheres, it is mentioned in the verse on the creation of the spheres. And if his question alludes to the fire that is latent in the earth, like that which is in water and stone and dust and trees and so forth, Scripture has already mentioned the creation of its bearers, so there is no need to mention its creation.

Sa'adyah's words about the nature of Creation in the preface to his commentary on the second half of the book of Exodus are also of interest:

The beginning of its [the earth's] perfection is that he created it round and spherical as established by geometers and confirmed by mathematical demonstrations; and as stated in Scripture [Job 26: 7] that the earth is suspended, as it were, in the middle: '[He] hangeth the earth over nothing'. This is because the sphere is the most perfect and unchanging of geometric shapes, unlike the square with its angles and the triangle with its sides and other shapes . . . And it is also the most balanced among them because the point called the centre is equidistant from all points on its circumference—hence the earth is equidistant from all points on the [celestial] sphere.[18]

Many of Sa'adyah's translations and commentaries are intended to resolve theological difficulties. As we have seen, he considers the biblical verse 'for the Lord your God is a consuming fire' to be an exceptional instance when a verse cannot be understood literally, because doing so would contradict the theological certainty

[16] Ratzaby, *Sa'adyah's Commentary on Exodus* (Heb.), 25.

[17] Zucker, *Sa'adyah's Commentary on Genesis*, 27–30 (Arab. text), 210–17 (Heb. trans.); the quotation is from p. 29 (p. 215).

[18] Ratzaby, *Sa'adyah's Commentary on Exodus*, 214 (Arab. text), 103 (Heb. trans.).

that God is unchanging, since fire is mutable. As we know, attempts to avoid anthropomorphism in speaking of God are already present in the Aramaic translations of the Bible, and this tendency was intensified in Judaeo-Arabic exegesis, first and foremost in the exegesis of Sa'adyah Gaon, owing to the heightened philosophical awareness which had developed in the Arabic-speaking milieu. Sa'adyah went further and attempted to avoid the attribution of human qualities or feelings to the Creator. The following text from his commentary on the verses leading up to the flood in Genesis 6: 5–8 exemplifies a number of characteristic elements. These verses are usually translated, 'And the Lord saw that the wickedness was great in the earth ... And it repented the Lord that He had made man on the earth and it grieved Him at His heart.' Sa'adyah is particularly troubled by the attribution of regret to God and offers two possible solutions, one lexicographical and the other stylistic and theological. In the first approach Sa'adyah distinguishes, as he often does elsewhere, between various significations of a single biblical lexeme (according to his linguistic theories), while the second approach relies on a more general technique of reading verses which appear to relate to God as though they actually related to human beings. The main points of his interpretation are as follows:

I have translated *vayinaḥem* [usually understood as 'repented'] as 'He warned them' because this word involves six different meanings: repentance, in its most familiar sense— 'And the people repented them for Benjamin' [Judg. 21: 15]; threat and warning, as in 'Behold, thy brother Esau threatens to kill you' etc. [Gen. 27: 42]; comfort—'And Isaac was comforted after his mother [died]' [Gen. 24: 67]; atonement—'And He atoned for them according to His great mercies' [Ps. 106: 45]; heat—'Ye that inflame yourselves among the terebinths' [Isa. 57: 5]; observation—'Then I will look on the good' [Jer. 18: 10] ... and according to this interpretation, we should understand 'and it grieved him at his heart' as referring to man, for the entire verse is written from beginning to end in the singular. And he added 'that He had made man' and 'for I warned them in creating them', as we have established [in the translation, namely: for I warned them by having created them], for He who created them out of nothing has the power to destroy them, because their destruction is no more difficult than their creation, indeed it is easier ...

And it may be that the verb *vayinaḥem* is used here with the meaning of regret according to the usual sense of the word, whereas the word 'grieved' refers to the creature. Nor does this imply a shortcoming in His power, as I shall elucidate further. For we say that God fears evil [befalling] those who love Him, inasmuch as He says, 'Were it not that I dreaded the enemy's provocation' [Deut. 32: 27]—this does not mean that fear [actually] overcomes Him but that He is warning them. Likewise, we say that He desires something on behalf of His creatures, as it is written: 'Oh that they had such a heart [always to fear me, and keep all my commandments]' [Deut. 5: 25], but the desire is not in Him but applies to them. And in the same way He rejoices [as it were] in the deeds of the righteous, though [in fact] He possesses no joy; yet it is written, 'Let the Lord rejoice in His works' [Ps. 104: 31], the proper meaning of which is that He praises them for their deeds. And it is possible to say the same in relation to 'And it grieved Him at heart', that the grief and worry do not pertain to Him but to the unbelievers who have sinned and transgressed His commandments. And thus 'God repenteth' [should be understood as] 'God made them regretful', involuntarily, so much so that it were better had they not been on earth and had God not created them. And this is the interpretation of the end of the verse 'that He created man on the face of the earth'.[19]

There are also instances of theologically motivated exegesis not directly related to the Divine nature, as, for example, in Sa'adyah's interpretation of Genesis 2: 15, 'And the Lord took the man and put him in the Garden to dress it and to keep it'. Sa'adyah finds it necessary here to explain the verse in a way that is fully consonant with his radical views on free will: 'One should not conclude from this that God forces his will on man, for God does not directly impel man to act. Rather, the "putting" [mentioned here] was by means of a commandment, and what is most likely is that he sent man an angel and commanded him to cross into the garden.'[20] Worthy of attention in this regard is Sa'adyah's astounding interpretation of the frame story of the book of Job, which is intended to refute the existence of a supernatural evil power, even if ultimately subordinate to the word of God, in the guise of Satan. According to Sa'adyah, both the 'sons of God' and Satan himself are only human beings.[21] In keeping with this interpretation, of course, only God himself and not Satan could bring down the calamities described in the book. For example, Job 2: 7, 'So Satan went forth from the presence of the Lord and smote Job with boils', is to be understood as follows: 'Satan was not the performer of this deed but God himself, who is mentioned before when it is said [that he went forth] from the presence of the Lord, to which he added by saying that the Lord smote Job, and therefore I have added [God's] name in order to make it explicit.'[22]

A characteristic tendency that derives from Sa'adyah's theology and is frequently evident in his commentaries expresses itself in his search for a manifestation of Divine wisdom (*Wujuh al-Hikma*; literally, the faces of wisdom) underlying every act of God and everything related in the Bible. Sa'adyah formulates this as a basic premise, 'For it is impossible that the Torah should contain anything which is not beneficial.'[23] This principle applies at both the general and the particular levels. In the preface to his Pentateuch commentary Sa'adyah explains that the entire Torah, with its diverse contents, is meant to prepare man to worship the Creator, and he writes:

And we have seen that the best preparation for human acceptance of the commandments is threefold: commandments, notification of reward, and moral lessons. Commandments: 'do' and 'do not'. Notification of reward: exposition of the consequences of

---

[19] Zucker, *Sa'adyah's Commentary on Genesis*, 100–1 (Arab. text), 333–4 (Heb. trans.).
[20] Ibid. 62 (Arab.), 272 (Heb.).   [21] Kafih, *Sa'adyah's Commentary on Job* (Heb.), 26–7.
[22] Ibid. 38.   [23] Zucker, *Sa'adyah's Commentary on Genesis*, 9 (Arab. text), 175 (Heb. trans.).

actions which have been mandated or prohibited. Moral lessons: accounts of people who kept the commandments and flourished, and of those who transgressed them and perished... And because the All-Wise knew that we should derive the greatest benefit from the conjunction of the three types, he made these three pillars the foundations of the Torah.[24]

We find an example of how Sa'adyah applies this principle at the particular level in his fourfold explanation of the Torah's account of the creation of various components of the universe, which he repeats several times in the course of his commentary on Creation.[25] The purpose of these descriptions is: (1) to move us to worship the Creator; (2) to prevent us from worshipping his creations; (3) to engender belief in the biblical accounts of miracles involving these creations, and (4) to foster obedience to those commandments which are connected to these creations.

As I observed at the beginning of this chapter, Sa'adyah himself mentions polemics as a central component of his commentaries, alongside linguistic and halakhic discussions. We may reasonably assume that the need he felt to dispute biblical critics from outside the Jewish tradition, and his possibly even stronger drive to argue with critics of Rabbanite Judaism from within the tradition, were among the leading motives for his entire exegetical program. Several leading Karaites had dealt extensively with biblical exegesis, and heretics such as Hivi of Balkh had attacked not only the Rabbanite tradition but also the Bible itself. Sa'adyah felt obliged to take on these adversaries (see pp. 144–7). Moreover, it seems that certain constituents of the Jewish community had been exposed to the arguments of adherents of other religions, particularly Islam and Christianity, and Sa'adyah felt it necessary to refute some of these arguments in his commentaries.

As in his other writings, Sa'adyah directs the polemics in his commentaries against a variety of groups—and perhaps even individuals—but it is not always possible to identify his addressees. A particularly interesting and complex example of this phenomenon occurs in his commentary on Genesis 1: 14–19, which relates the story of the creation of the sun and moon and describes their function in the calendrical system as 'signs for seasons and days and years'.[26] Here Sa'adyah cites a variety of calendrical systems and brings arguments in favour of the Rabbanite system, which combines a lunar calendar and a year of the same average length as the solar year by means of a fixed cycle of normal twelve-month years and intercalated thirteen-month years. He attributes only some of the systems that he critiques to specific sects or individuals. Among these we find groups known from ancient times, including the Samaritans, Zadokites, and Boethusians, mentioned alongside relatively recent groups such as the followers of Anan

---

[24] Zucker, *Sa'adyah's Commentary on Genesis*, 7–8 (Arab.), 171–2 (Heb.).

[25] Ibid. 32–3, 35, 40–1, 46, 50 (Arab.); 221–2, 222–3, 225–6, 236–7, 246, 251 (Heb.).

[26] Ibid. 41–2 (Arab.), 237–8 (Heb.).

and Benjamin al-Nihawandi, while other groups appear anonymously. There are conspicuously anti-Karaite polemics in Sa'adyah's commentary on verses such as Exodus 35: 3, 'Ye shall kindle no fire throughout your habitations upon the Sabbath day', which the Karaites interpreted as a prohibition against kindling a fire even before sunset on the sabbath eve that would continue to burn on the sabbath; this was one of the more prominent controversies between Rabbanite and Karaite Jews.[27]

A rare instance of anti-Christian polemics may be found in Sa'adyah's commentary on Genesis 1: 26, 'And God said, "Let us make man in our image and after our likeness"'. The plural form, he notes, is used by Christians as an argument for the Trinitarian doctrine whereas he interprets it as an instance of the 'royal we'. He points out that Christians do not take other expressions in the passage literally but believe that God created man in his image only in a figurative sense. Nor do they believe that God has male and female characteristics, as might be understood from the passage: 'In the image of God He created them, male and female He created them' (Gen. 1: 27). The attempt to base the Trinitarian argument on a literal reading of 'Let us make man' is therefore arbitrary and tendentious.[28] In other cases—for example, when Sa'adyah tries to prove that there is no essential inconsistency between two laws in the Torah and that neither revokes the other—we cannot be certain whether his argument is directed against Christianity or Islam, or both.

Attitude to Talmudic Literature[29]

As in most of his writings, Sa'adyah rarely cites talmudic sources verbatim in his biblical commentaries. Normally he paraphrases their contents in Judaeo-Arabic, often without any indication that he is summarizing the words of his predecessors. In other cases, also quite numerous, he attributes citations to the Sages of old by means of an epithet such as 'the early ones' or 'our fathers'; only on the rarest occasions does he note a specific source such as the Mishnah. This habit of paraphrasing the words of the talmudic sages in Judaeo-Arabic made it easier for Sa'adyah to adapt them, and he often reworks the sources that he cites—at least the aggadic ones—sometimes introducing extensive changes.

[27] Ratzaby, *Sa'adyah's Commentary on Exodus*, 407–10 (Arab. text), 242–6 (Heb. trans.).

[28] Zucker, *Sa'adyah's Commentary on Genesis*, 50–1 (Arab. text), 252 (Heb. trans.). Ben Shammai, in his review of the Hebrew edition of this book ('An Important Monograph' (Heb.), 181–3), pointed out that Sa'adyah's treatment of the 'suffering servant' of Isaiah 52–3 (Ratzaby, *Sa'adyah's Commentary on Isaiah*, 118–20 (Arab.), 332–7 (Heb.)), although not explicitly marked as such, is a thinly veiled anti-Christian polemic.

[29] See Ben Shammai, 'Midrashic-Rabbinic Literature' (Heb.); Brody, *The Geonim of Babylonia*, 312–14.

With regard to halakhah, Sa'adyah was of course committed to the talmudic tradition. As we have seen, he considered the study of the particulars of the commandments, which he omits from his separately published translation, to be one of the major components of his commentary on the Pentateuch. It was also his habit to introduce peripheral halakhic elements into biblical stories, apparently in an effort to strengthen the link between the Bible and the Oral Law in the framework of his polemics with the Karaites and others. Thus, for example, he interprets Abraham's words to his servant Eli'ezer, '[Thou shalt go unto my country, and to my kindred,] and take a wife for my son' (Gen. 24: 4) as describing Eli'ezer's appointment as an agent to conduct the rites of betrothal (*kidushin*), stating further that Eli'ezer's attendants were to act as witnesses for the betrothal. Elsewhere he uses the opportunity afforded by one or another biblical verse to enter into halakhic discussions which are quite tangential to their interpretation. For example, he inserts a discourse on the different stages of maturation and their legal implications into his commentary on the verses: 'And the child grew, and she brought him unto the Pharaoh's daughter . . . And it came to pass in those days, when Moses was grown up, that he went out unto his brethren' (Exod. 2: 10–11).[30]

Sa'adyah's attitude to the aggadic literature of the Sages is far more complex. On the one hand, he often follows their statements even in non-halakhic matters, sometimes implicitly and sometimes explicitly. Nevertheless, he appears to consider himself less strictly bound by aggadic sayings than by halakhic ones. This is suggested even in places where he accepts certain aggadic interpretations, but the style in which he does so hints at his exegetical autonomy and freedom to adopt or reject interpretations according to his judgement. So, for example, he cites talmudic sages on the separation of men and women in Noah's ark with the phrase 'some say', noting that this saying is reasonable.[31] In other cases, his language suggests reservations, for example, when he notes that 'one of the ancients' (apparently referring to the Targum of Jonathan) interprets the light promised to the righteous in the verse 'But they that love Him be as the sun when it goeth forth in its might' (Judg. 5: 31) as a light 343 times brighter than sunlight. He adds:

At the root of this interpretation are the words of Isaiah: 'Moreover the light of the moon shall be as the light of the sun and the light of the sun shall be sevenfold, as the light of the seven days' [Isa. 30: 21], on the premise that 'sevenfold' here means seven times seven . . . And since he adds 'as the light of the seven days' . . . forty-nine should be multiplied by seven . . . which is a correct interpretation if we accept the premise.[32]

There are instances where Sa'adyah goes even further; for example, he asserts that neither the biblical account nor the tradition enables us to determine how

[30] Ratzaby, *Sa'adyah's Commentary on Exodus*, 263–4 (Arab. text), 6–8 (Heb. trans.).

[31] Zucker, *Sa'adyah's Commentary on Genesis*, 103–4 (Arab. text), 339 (Heb. trans.).

[32] Ben Shammai, 'Midrashic-Rabbinic Literature' (Heb.), 55–7.

long Adam lived in the Garden of Eden, although reason suggests that it was several days, despite the well-known aggadah that God banished him from Eden on the very day of his creation.[33] Even more radical is the way in which he refers to an aggadic claim that the Land of Israel was not inundated during the Flood, remarking: 'Someone of our nation imagined that the Land of Israel was not inundated during the days of the flood, and he only entertained this idea because he thought . . . and we must explain his error in this matter'.[34]

Sa'adyah thus draws a distinction between ideas which he believes to be based on tradition and those that he believes reflect the personal opinion of one or another of the Sages. So, for example, in his commentary on the last chapters of Exodus he supplies, in the name of a tradition of the Sages, detailed descriptions of the vessels of the sanctuary. Similarly he decides, at the beginning of his commentary on the book of Job, that the Land of Uz where Job lived was the land of Abraham's nephew Uz, on the grounds that 'many of those who came before us transmitted this'.[35] Conversely, he presents anything that is unacceptable to him as the saying of 'one of our nation' or as not being part of (authoritative) tradition. It is not clear, however, whether Sa'adyah had any objective criteria for distinguishing between 'tradition' and 'personal opinion'. He seems to have reserved the right to dismiss any aggadic saying that struck him as unreasonable (or perhaps even one intended humorously) as a personal opinion that he did not feel himself obliged to accept, notwithstanding his commitment in principle to the authority of the Sages.

In spite of his reserved attitude towards the aggadah, Sa'adyah seems to have been deeply influenced by its characteristic modes of thought, even when he was not following a particular aggadic interpretation. Not a few of his comments sound homiletical although they have no direct rabbinic source as far as we know. For example, he explains the seemingly redundant words 'of the sea' in Genesis 1: 26, where God says that Adam will have dominion over the 'fish of the sea', as indicating that Adam will also have dominion over water, using pumps to draw it, or damming rivers, and the like.[36]

In some cases, Sa'adyah attributes exegetical significance to the orthography (with or without *matres lectionis*) of a particular biblical word. For example, he observes that in three places the word *ḥalilah* (forfend) is written without a *yod* (iota) and offers the suggestion—though this, he notes, is only speculation—that the spelling is meant to signify that not even an iota of evil can be imputed to God, 'not even like a *yod*, which is the smallest of the letters'. Elsewhere he interprets

---

[33] Zucker, *Sa'adyah's Commentary on Genesis*, 81 (Arab. text), 300 (Heb. trans.; cf. n. 505 ad loc.).

[34] Ibid. 109 (Arab.), 349–50 (Heb.; cf. n. 77 ad loc.).

[35] Kafih, *Sa'adyah's Commentary on Job* (Heb.), 23.

[36] Zucker, *Sa'adyah's Commentary on Genesis*, 53–4 (Arab. text), 258 (Heb. trans.).

the three different spellings of the word *meḥato* (from sinning) as signifying three different degrees of sin: light, medium, and heavy.[37]

At times Sa'adyah produces long, well-structured homilies, many—if not all—of which are a kind of personal contribution to the midrashic genre. For example, the following passage is based on the idea that the words of Simon the Righteous as they appear in the Mishnah (*Avot* 1: 2) are also hinted at in Scriptures. We find this idea in separate rabbinic sources with regard to two verses, one from the Torah and one from the Prophets. Sa'adyah joins these two sources and adds a parallel homily, probably of his own invention, based on a verse from the Hagiographa. In this way he arrives at a threefold interpretation in accordance with the classical midrashic model of 'as written in the Torah and repeated a second time in the Prophets and a third time in the Writings'. He explains:

Of the verse 'Thou in Thy love hast led' [Exod. 15: 13] the ancients said, 'On three things the world is sustained: on the Torah, on the [Temple] service, and on deeds of loving kindness.' When they said 'on service' they referred to [the service of] the Temple. These three [things] are grouped together in three verses: the first one in the Torah, and this is the words of the fathers [in Exodus], 'Thou in Thy love hast led'. The words 'in Thy love' hint at deeds of loving-kindness . . . 'by Thy strength' hints at the Torah, as it is written 'The Lord will give strength unto His people' [Ps. 29: 11]. 'To Your Holy Dwelling' [Exod. 15: 13] is clearly the Holy Temple, as it is written, 'Look upon Zion, the city of our solemn gatherings; Thine eyes shall see Jerusalem a peaceful habitation, A tent that shall not be removed, the stakes whereof shall never be plucked up' [Isa. 33: 20].

The second verse is from the Prophets and it says, 'And I have put My words in thy mouth' [Isa. 51: 16], meaning the Torah, for that is the word of the Lord, and it continues, 'and have covered thee in the shadow of My hand', by which he means love and deeds of loving-kindness, because there are places where 'hand' refers to this, as is said 'and I told them of the hand of God which was good upon me' [Neh. 2: 8]. And further on he said, 'To say unto Zion thou art My people', and this is clearly the Temple, for it says, 'And the Lord dwelleth in Zion' [Joel 4: 21].

And the third verse is from the Writings and it says, 'Loving-kindness and truth preserve the king; and his throne is upheld by loving-kindness' [Prov. 20: 28]. Now 'loving-kindness' is explicitly loving-kindness; 'truth' is the Torah, as it says, 'a Torah of truth was in his mouth' [Mal. 2: 6] etc.; and 'throne' is the Temple, as it is written, 'And at that time they shall call Jerusalem the throne of the Lord and all the nations shall be gathered unto it, to the name of the Lord, to Jerusalem' [Jer. 3: 17].[38]

Another indication of Sa'adyah's 'midrashic mentality' is his parallel presentation of multiple interpretations of a single passage, not because he is uncertain about which of them is correct, but because he considers them to be simultaneously legitimate at different levels. He explains the name Kiryat Arba (literally

---

[37] Zucker, *Sa'adyah's Commentary on Genesis*, 127, 134–5 (Arab.), 381–2, 393 (Heb.).

[38] Ratzaby, *Sa'adyah's Commentary on Exodus*, 288–9 (Arab. text), 61 (Heb. trans.).

'the town of four', another name for Hebron) in four ways, one of which he considers the *peshat* or simple explanation, and the other three based on opinions in rabbinic literature:

(1) And this is the simple explanation: it is the name of a place or the name of a person. (2) Because four heroes inhabited it, a giant and his three sons . . . (3) Because it is fated to be divided in four, that is, to the tribe of Judah in general and to the Levites in cities surrounded by pasture land [see Num. 35: 1–5] and to the priests in the cities of refuge, and its fields for Kalev ben Yefuneh. (4) Because exactly four pairs of righteous ones would be buried there: Abraham and Sarah, Isaac and Rebecca, Jacob and Leah, according to Scripture, and Adam and Eve according to tradition.[39]

Elsewhere he offers an interpretation according to the simple meaning and three homiletic interpretations of a single verse, only this time the homiletic interpretations appear to be his own as well:

And in the saying 'And thou shalt be the father of a multitude [*hamon*]' [Gen. 17: 4] four matters are included: (1) this is closest to the language of the text—an allusion to three nations: Israel, Edom, and Ishmael, and Abraham is the father of them all; (2) an allusion to the spirit of prophecy which will fill his sons, and this is called 'multitude' as it is written, 'And the voice of his words like the spirit of the multitude' [Dan. 10: 6]; (3) prayer to the Creator, may he be exalted, and response to it, as it is written, 'The *hamon* of Thy heart and Thy compassion, now restrained toward me' [Isa. 63: 15]; (4) [an allusion to] the Torah that was given to his children, as it is written concerning this, 'Then I was by Him as a nursling [*amon*]' [Prov. 8: 30].[40]

We find a striking instance of Sa'adyah's layering of meanings in his interpretation of the verse 'Prepare thy work without, and make it fit for thyself in the field; and afterwards build thy house' [Prov. 24: 27].[41] The simple explanation that Sa'adyah offers is a metaphorical interpretation, well known in rabbinic literature, in lieu of a literal one; and beyond this he presents two additional layers of meaning. In the following, he also expresses important views about the values and roles of the various types of commandments:

In its overt aspect this verse advises a man who is preparing to wed a wife not to begin until he finds a profession and knows that what he will earn from it will suffice to support her and the child or two he may have . . . and 'the house' according to this explanation is the wife . . . And its inner [meaning is] that a man meets the inescapable needs of this world before he [engages in] matters of the world to come, for one cannot reach the things of the world to come except by [first meeting] natural needs, food and clothing and a dwelling place . . . and 'the house' here, according to this explanation, is the world to come. And one of its secrets is that wisdom has beginnings which are like the corridor

---

[39] Zucker, *Sa'adyah's Commentary on Genesis*, 144 (Arab. text), 403–4 (Heb. trans.).
[40] Ibid. 118 (Arab.), 366 (Heb.).   [41] Kafih, *Sa'adyah's Commentary on Proverbs* (Heb.), 191–2.

of a house; do not approach that science [i.e. wisdom] before having them as preliminaries because they open it up, and the Greeks call the introduction to any science—logic and astronomy and geometry and medicine—*isagoge*, and the student who begins to read the book before the preface will not understand it. And in the same way the worship of God has introductions which are the key to it and one part will be of no use to a person without the second part. And the explanation of the matter is this: that the non-rational commandments, such as fasting and the sabbath and the Feast of Unleavened Bread, will be of no value to a person who holds to them unless he proceeds from the rational commandments such as truth and justice and [civil] law ... And the matter [of the verse] will be: perfect your behaviour towards human beings and only then between yourself and God; and do not steal and then give alms thereof, nor fornicate and fast to make up for it.

CHAPTER FIVE

※

Sa'adyah the Linguist

FROM HIS EARLIEST YOUTH, Sa'adyah Gaon was drawn to the study of Hebrew. Hebrew linguistics did not develop as an independent field but as an ancillary discipline to biblical exegesis, on the one hand, and to poetry on the other. Biblical exegetes sought to plumb the linguistic depths of a particular sacred corpus, and their relationship to the Holy Tongue remained essentially passive, whereas the writing of poetry required an active knowledge of the appropriate language (which was not quite the same as biblical Hebrew). Both areas of study and creative effort played an important role in the Palestine-centred Jewish culture of Sa'adyah's upbringing, and before Sa'adyah's time Masoretes and liturgical poets alike had devoted considerable energies to linguistic study, each in their own way. But Sa'adyah was the first to respond to these needs within Jewish culture and to the development of Arabic linguistics in the surrounding Muslim culture by studying the Hebrew language in a comprehensive and systematic way.

First Breakthrough: The *Egron*

While still in Egypt, at the precocious age of 20 Sa'adyah published the first edition of the *Egron*, which may have been his earliest work.[1] In his preface to the book, written in a lofty style and pseudo-biblical language, he presents a historical survey of the Hebrew language and a statement of his reasons for composing such a work, referring to himself as 'the collector' or 'compiler'. Hebrew, he explains, is the Holy Tongue, the language of God and the angels, and man's primordial speech from Creation, until the sin of the Tower of Babel led to the dispersal of the various nations and languages, as recounted in Genesis 11. Thereafter the Hebrew language became the unique heritage of the sons of Ever, apparently identified with the original 'Hebrews', in consequence of their faithfulness to God. The nation of Israel evolved out of this group and retained its language in the course of many wanderings 'throughout the earth' until at last they returned to the Land of Israel. But after the destruction of the First Temple, when most of the Jews were exiled from their land, the status of the Hebrew language declined. Later, during the period of the return to Zion, Nehemiah discovered that the Jews who had

---

[1] See Allony, *Egron*, 23.

stayed behind in the Land of Israel had taken wives from among the other nations, and 'Their children spoke half in the speech of Ashdod and could not speak in the language of the Jews' (Neh. 13: 24), not to mention the Jews who remained in exile. The young Sa'adyah viewed this as a tragedy but also a challenge, and he wrote the *Egron* in the hope of reviving the Hebrew language so that the Jewish people would use it in their daily lives. As Sa'adyah himself explains:

The *Egron* of the Holy Tongue, which God chose from all eternity, in which His holy angels ever sanctify Him in their song, and therewith all beings worship Him on High. The whole earth was of one language and of one speech from the day when God created Adam and conferred wisdom upon him . . . until the band of the tempest [the generation of the Tower of Babel] . . . and the land was divided into languages according to the number of its peoples, but the Holy Tongue remained in the mouths of the descendants of Ever alone. Because they were truthful in the sight of God, and from their stock issued our forebears, our father Abraham, His beloved, Isaac, His chosen one, Jacob, His cherished one, and all the tribes of God. Their feet trod the land, through the kingdom of Canaan and Patros beyond, and the Holy Tongue never departed from their mouths, and when they left Egypt, God spoke in it eloquently to us through His servant Moses, the man of God, on Mount Horeb, [instructing us in] the laws and commandments. Generation after generation it has been our heritage, from the time we dwelled in the land of our inheritance, given to us through the tender mercies of our Holy One, [it was the language used] for the occupations of our kings, the hymning of our Levites, the music of our priests, the visions of our prophets, the right reason of our governors, until [the people of] Jerusalem were exiled to Babylonia in the days of Zedekiah . . . when we began to abandon the Holy Tongue and speak in alien tongues . . . In the days of Nehemiah the governor and all his men he saw us speaking the language of Ashdod and was angered and rebuked the people and contended with them. And afterwards we were exiled through all the gates of the land and the islands of the sea; there was no nation our outcasts did not reach, and in their midst we raised our children and learned their languages. Their halting speech enshrouded the fairness of our words and this was not right: the eastern diaspora spoke Greek and the language of Persia, and in Egypt they spoke in Coptic. And the children of Kenaz and Sepharad spoke foreign tongues,[2] those who sojourned in Yatet likewise, and so [forth] in the language of every nation. Our hearts and spirits are aghast at this for we are bereft of the stronghold of our holy speech, and all the visions of its prophecies and its speeches are like a sealed book to us, and in waking from a vision we stumble in our language in the lands of our captivity. So it behoves us and all the nation of our Lord, us and our children and our wives and servants, to enquire and understand and investigate it always, so that it may never depart from us again, for through the Holy Tongue we understand the laws of the Torah of our Rock, which are our very life . . . for all eternity.

---

[2] Sa'adyah is probably using *no'az* as equivalent to the biblical *lo'ez*, substituting one 'liquid' consonant for another (in accordance with the belief that certain phonetically similar consonants may be substituted at will); see p. 87.

And in the year 1214 [of the Seleucid era, i.e. 902 CE[3]], from the day that vision and prophecy were sealed, the collector [i.e. Sa'adyah] wrote this book to serve as [a source of] wisdom for all the people of God and for all those who know the law and the tradition. And he prepared it [to teach them] to riddle riddles and to speak in parables and to write works of all kinds, and rhyme every rhyme … The people of our God will converse in it, in their going out and coming in, in all their occupations, and in their bedrooms, and with their children. Never more will the Holy Tongue leave their minds or depart from their hearts, for through it they will know the Torah of God.[4]

At a later, undetermined, date Sa'adyah reissued this work in a Judaeo-Arabic edition, disclosing more about the background of the book and his motives for writing it in his preface:

And just as the children of Ishmael recount that one of their notables saw that the people did not speak Arabic eloquently and this distressed him, and he composed for them a brief discourse from which they might learn eloquence, so too did I see that many of the children of Israel are ignorant of the most essential articulacy in our language, let alone its more difficult [aspects], and when they speak, much of what they say is ungrammatical; and when they compose poetry, few are the ancient elements they adopt and many those they forget … till even Scripture is like unintelligible and incomprehensible speech to them. And so I was compelled to write a book wherein I collected most of the words in two lists: the first grouping together all words beginning with *alef*, and then all those beginning with *bet*, and similarly *gimel* and *dalet* and all the other letters; and the second list grouping together all words that rhyme with *alef* in one place, and similarly all words ending with *bet* and then with *gimel* and *dalet* and *heh* and so forth to the end of the alphabet, so that it will be easy to grasp everything and retain it [in memory], and so that the [words of the] language, both simple and difficult, will be preserved … and I hoped that this would satisfy the needs of the seeker, who would take from the first element what is most appropriate to his desires and build on it according to his intentions and conclude the rhyme with what is suitable to his intention.[5]

From the above it is clear that Sa'adyah drew inspiration from a Muslim writer who felt impassioned about the Arabic language and distressed at the low level of spoken Arabic in his day. Like him, the young Sa'adyah was deeply troubled by the state of the Hebrew language, which had probably degenerated even further than Arabic. The Jews in Muslim lands used Arabic for most of their needs, and many of them probably aspired to no more than a passive knowledge of Hebrew at a fairly basic level, mainly for use in prayer and participation in the synagogue service, by reading from the Torah and selected portions from other parts of Scripture. Most of the congregants did not necessarily understand the language of the prayers and the biblical selections. The majority were even less able to express themselves in Hebrew, and their writing was impoverished and full of

---

[3] See p. 3 above.   [4] Allony, *Egron*, 156–9.   [5] Ibid. 150–3.

grammatical errors, at least in Sa'adyah's opinion. He became so distressed at this state of affairs that he set out, at the age of 20, on a mission to improve the state of his nation and its Holy Tongue.

The first edition of the book included a preface in elevated Hebrew and two wordlists.[6] A large portion—perhaps most—of the preface has come down to us, as well as a significant portion of the first list, but only a few words from the second list. As we have seen, the first and perhaps most important part of the preface consists of an overview of the history of the Hebrew language and of Sa'adyah's motives in writing the book. This is followed by a concise treatment of linguistics, fragmentary and rather opaque, but apparently intended to facilitate the use of the book. The contents of this section are further elucidated in other works by Sa'adyah, as we shall presently see. The final portion of the preface apparently included a discussion of poetics and rhetoric, but only the ending of this section survives. The preface, as noted, was written in a pseudo-biblical style, meant to serve as a paradigm of 'eloquent' Hebrew prose. This style is apparent not only in Sa'adyah's use of syntactical features, such as the conversive *vav*, and certain lexical items—for example, the word *ya'an* (because)—which were no longer current in the later strata of the language, but also in his division of the text into verses, vocalized and marked with cantillation signs like the biblical text itself. This procedure, which he followed in at least two other works as well, laid him open to the accusation that he was claiming the stature of a prophet—despite his assertion in the above-quoted passage that he had composed the *Egron* 1,214 years after 'the day that vision and prophecy were sealed'.

The two wordlists, as Sa'adyah explains further, are meant as aids to the composition of poetry. The first list offers the poet a choice of words arranged in alphabetical order to suit the requirements of acrostic structures (spelling out the alphabet, the poet's name, etc.); the words in the second list are arranged alphabetically according to their terminal letters to facilitate rhyming. The alphabetical arrangement applies to the first two letters of each word in the list, but entries beginning with the same two letters are not always listed alphabetically; this system was utilized in Arabic dictionaries of the period as well.

The *Egron* is commonly described as the first dictionary of the Hebrew language, but, although it represents a great advance in Hebrew lexicography, it is not strictly speaking a dictionary, for a variety of reasons. First, as we have seen, the author's stated intention was not to incorporate all the words of the language but only a majority of them (although it is possible that he declared this simply to forestall critics who might otherwise attack him by pointing out words which had escaped his notice). In effect, the book contained at most 4,000–5,000 lexical items—far fewer than in modern Hebrew dictionaries, but an admirable begin-

---

[6] The surviving sections of the preface: Allony, *Egron* (Heb.), 156–63; the first list: 164–380, the second list: 381–5.

ning all the same. Secondly, here and there the author labels certain letter combinations as 'non-existent'—sometimes incorrectly, as his critics pointed out. As for the selection of entries, let us clarify two principles: (1) Most words are derived from biblical Hebrew; even where the exact form of an entry does not appear in the Bible, it may be constructed by analogy on the basis of biblical data according to Sa'adyah's linguistic theories, which we shall discuss later on. At the same time, there are a substantial number of entries drawn from rabbinic Hebrew and the Aramaic of the Bible and the Babylonian Talmud. (2) The headings of the entries are nominal forms according to Sa'adyah's conceptions (a category that includes verbal nouns, infinitive/imperative forms and participles) rather than roots or unambiguous verbal forms (see below).

A more fundamental reason that disqualifies this work as a dictionary per se is its lack of any systematic attempt to provide definitions. Not a few entries present nothing but the word itself. Sometimes Sa'adyah adds a biblical or rabbinic quotation to contextualize a word (or one of its derivatives) or cites a more familiar form of the word listed as an entry (for example: *evev* from *aviv*). Entries providing actual definitions are a minority, albeit a substantial one, of all entries. Most of these definitions are quite general, for example: '*abuv*: a musical instrument' or '*ayah*: a bird'. The entries of the *Egron* include many proper nouns, often rare biblical names (such as '*gazaz*: a man's name' or '*horan*: a city'), although here, too, the author clearly did not aim at comprehensiveness.

Sa'adyah frequently includes in his entries pairs of homonyms which could be used to produce stylistic effects in poetic composition, distinguishing between two (or three) homonyms by means of various techniques. For instance, the book's first pair of entries provides differential definitions for the word *av*, one of which is supported by a biblical citation: 'progenitor [i.e. father], as in "your father and mother" [Ruth 2: 11]; Av: [the name of] a month', while the following pair of definitions is supported by a context and a definition: '*gez* [shearing]: of your sheep [Deut. 18: 4], *gaz*: pass away'.[7]

Apparently the first edition of the *Egron* did not employ Arabic, as exemplified by the aforementioned entries, but succeeding copyists sometimes inserted concise Arabic definitions (generally in Hebrew letters) in the manuscripts of this edition. In the second edition Sa'adyah introduced changes, most conspicuously the addition of Arabic translations for many of the entries, though some were left untranslated or with only their Hebrew definitions, while others had only Arabic definitions and still others both Hebrew and Arabic.[8] Aside from this difference in the wordlists that comprise the bulk of the original work, Sa'adyah added a new introduction in Judaeo-Arabic to the original Hebrew preface. Much of this introduction is extant, and it is fascinating to compare it with the Hebrew

[7] Ibid. 164, 206.   [8] See ibid. 19–22.

preface.[9] The decision to add material to the second edition in Judaeo-Arabic was not merely technical but involved a change of perspective, if not an essentially new aim: instead of the particularist mood of the Hebrew preface, with its emphasis on the unique sanctity of the Hebrew language and the special relationship between the people of Israel, the God of Israel, the Hebrew language, and the Land of Israel, Sa'adyah now speaks in general terms about forgetfulness and the decline of knowledge, and the sage's responsibility to preserve and spread knowledge (although we should note that since both prefaces have reached us in fragmentary form, any comparison between them is unavoidably incomplete).

At the end of the new introduction Sa'adyah describes another important addition: a systematic discussion of poetics, with sections on the different types of sentence (indicative, interrogative, imperative, and so forth) as well as on the modes of description and similes. He writes here that when he issued the first edition of the *Egron* he believed that it was sufficient to aid poets with the composition of acrostics and rhymes, and only later did he realize that poets also needed help with 'those middle parts which are the poem itself, whereas the two extremities are only the sentinels.'[10] His discussion of this subject must have been rather thorough for he states that he will bring proof-texts from early poets, as well as from some more contemporary poets whose writing he finds praiseworthy. Since none of the fragments from this section have been identified with any certainty, we cannot discuss its contents.[11]

Sa'adyah's Other Linguistic Works

Sa'adyah devoted two other works specifically to Hebrew linguistics, while many that belong to different genres in principle also contribute in some measure to the field of linguistics. The two linguistic works were written in Judaeo-Arabic and are known as *Explanation of the Seventy Isolated Biblical Words* and *The Book of the Eloquence of the Language of the Hebrews*.

The *Explanation of the Seventy Isolated Biblical Words*, which has been preserved more or less intact, contains explanations of rare biblical words (not all of them strictly speaking hapax legomena) on the basis of their usage in rabbinic Hebrew, where they appear with greater frequency and their meanings are well understood. In fact, the book contains close to a hundred entries; it would appear that Sa'adyah later decided to add several entries to the original complement of seventy but left the title unchanged.[12] On the face of it, this is a simple

---

[9] For the Arabic introduction and Hebrew translation see Allony, *Egron* (Heb.), 148–55; for the Hebrew introduction, ibid. 156–63. Cf. Allony's summaries of the contents of the two introductions in parallel columns, ibid. 20.

[10] Ibid. 152–5; the quotation is from 154–5.   [11] See ibid. 127–9, 386–9.

[12] See Klar, *Researches* (Heb.), 265 and n. 56; Allony, *Collected Papers* (Heb.), i. 76, gives the total number of entries as 96.

lexicographical work, but the author makes no attempt to conceal his broader motives—to refute the Karaite position that Scripture is a self-contained and self-explanatory corpus, fully explicable without reference to rabbinic tradition. This argument figures prominently in Sa'adyah Gaon's anti-Karaite polemics, but in this case he tries to prove its truth from a purely linguistic point of view. As he writes in the preface:

And I saw that there are some among the Hebrews who reject whatever is transmitted from the prophets by way of the unwritten precepts and laws, and similarly those who reject whatever they have heard by way of language in the speech of the nation and have not found in Scripture. And I have found many words in Scripture which cannot be understood except through the language that the nation used in teaching, and when it was intended to establish the Oral Law, they introduced whatever [extra-biblical language] was necessary and this speech came naturally . . . And I found that whoever does not acknowledge the truth of the halakhah is greatly perplexed by these words and cannot uncover their true meaning, so I needed to collect them from Scriptures and explain them, word by word, and I brought evidence from the prosaic speech of the Mishnah, which was as well known to those people as [their] common speech. And I knew that this would be useful in various ways, for the meanings of these words would be revealed to the nation and they would be relieved of any perplexity concerning them, and they would see that the transmitters of the Mishnah and the Talmud were the most proficient in the language, especially so because they were closest [in time] to the prophets . . . and perhaps this book will bring back some of those who have deviated from their [the Sages'] interpretation, when it becomes clear [to them] that one cannot fathom the truth of what is in Scripture without recourse to their [the Sages'] speech and their words.[13]

In contrast to this slim volume, an abridged version of which survived outside the Cairo Genizah and was printed several times beginning in the mid-nineteenth century, and most of which is now available in its original form,[14] Sa'adyah's pioneering work on grammar, *The Book of the Eloquence of the Language of the Hebrews*, did not fare well. It disappeared from the horizon shortly after its composition, possibly because the field of Hebrew grammar developed in very different directions after Sa'adyah's day. Important parts of the book survived in the Cairo Genizah, and a large fragment was identified at the end of the nineteenth century, during the early days of Genizah research, but almost a hundred years passed before this manuscript was published in full, along with additional Genizah fragments of the work.[15] Whole sections are still missing, and in some cases even the subjects they treat remain obscure, as we shall presently see.

[13] Allony, *Collected Papers* (Heb.), i. 83–4 (Arab. text), 86–7 (Heb. trans.).
[14] See ibid. 29–39 (introd.), 40–66 and 83–5 (Arab. text).
[15] The comprehensive edition is Dotan, *First Light* (Heb.); for the history of scholarly treatments of this work beginning with Harkavy's identification of the Leningrad fragment, see ibid. 23–9.

Sa'adyah's was the first systematic work on grammar in the history of Hebrew linguistics. It derived to a considerable extent from lists and pamphlets produced by the Masoretes that were based on their intimate acquaintance with the biblical text, but it far surpassed them in methodology and linguistic approach. Sa'adyah had learned much from the Arab grammarians active before and during his time and he applied many of their principles to the Hebrew language, although he also had to deal with some issues specific to it. Yet he did not follow the Arab grammarians blindly, either in terms of analysis or of nomenclature, and in some ways even went beyond their achievements, as we shall see.

The Book of the Eloquence of the Language of the Hebrews is divided into twelve sections, which Sa'adyah calls variously 'twelve books', 'twelve discourses', and 'twelve parts'. Sometimes he refers to the text in the plural as 'the books of grammar', which raises the question: should we view the book as a comprehensive work or as twelve discrete monographs devoted to specific topics of Hebrew grammar? Indeed, certain sections of the larger work seem to have circulated individually as self-contained essays. Moreover, Sa'adyah himself appears to have decided at a certain stage to facilitate the study of certain parts of the text independently of the others, and he therefore added the following note to the second edition of the fourth chapter: 'I have seen fit to preface the beginning of this discourse with a brief summary of certain matters already described in the preceding three [chapters] for the sake of those readers who may begin with this section before studying the other three.'[16]

It seems that Sa'adyah originally intended for the different sections to form a single complete work, and in the course of writing began to view the chapters as discrete essays that could be studied separately. Such a change of perspective is indicated by his use of the Arabic term *juz'*, meaning 'section', to refer to the first six chapters, and the term 'discourse', or *maqala* in Arabic, beginning with the heading of the seventh chapter.[17] The fourth chapter, as mentioned, has come down to us in two versions, both authored by Sa'adyah—a phenomenon that we know from another of his works (see p. 50).

Apart from the revision of the fourth chapter, which was meant as an aid for those who read the sections separately or out of order, we know of another revision that Sa'adyah undertook at the request of a reader. He added a whole section at the beginning of the third chapter and wrote:

And one who wished to learn the language of the Hebrews requested that I supplement the book of conjugation that I composed with a chapter that would include the full range of verbal inflection, in past, present, and future tenses. And so I have obliged him, knowing that it would be of assistance to those who study this book.[18]

---

[16] Dotan, *First Light* (Heb.), 414–15.   [17] See ibid. 53–9.   [18] Ibid. 332–3.

Here, too, we discern the later view of the third chapter as a 'book' to which a 'chapter' (*fasl* in Arabic) may be added, but this addendum was incorporated in the comprehensive work as well.[19]

Sa'adyah describes the first four chapters as dealing with consonants and the next five as dealing with vowels. Fragments of the first eight chapters in our possession allow us to flesh out this description. The first chapter treats the consonants of the Hebrew alphabet and the possible and impossible consonantal combinations (although most of the chapter has been lost and its full extent cannot be surmised); the second treats the augmentation and elision of words (see below); the third discusses verbal and nominal inflection and contains the first conjugation table in the history of Semitic grammar; the fourth looks at the rules governing *dagesh* and *rafeh*; the fifth treats the vowels; the sixth the *sheva*; the seventh the effect of laryngeal consonants upon vocalization; and the eighth discusses the vocalization of the laryngeal consonants themselves. According to Sa'adyah, as we have seen, the ninth chapter deals with certain topics relating to vowels, but we have no way of knowing what these topics were. All we know about the last three chapters is that one of them had to do with 'substitutions', most probably referring to possible substitutions of one consonant for another with the same place of articulation (in the example cited by one of Sa'adyah's critics from this chapter, the substitution of *nun* (*n*) for *lamed* (*l*)), and, accordingly, the interchangeability of words comprising similar consonants. It is quite feasible that after his treatment of consonants and vowels, Sa'adyah devoted the final three chapters to words and possibly to syntax, but we can only speculate on this until more fragments belonging to this part of the composition are identified.[20]

Let us conclude this section with a brief survey of some other writings by Sa'adyah that are not linguistic works as such but nevertheless contribute to an understanding of his linguistic ideas. First and foremost among these is his commentary on the Mishnah, which mainly concerns the explication of 'difficult words' in Arabic and could almost be considered a lexicon of mishnaic Hebrew, were it not arranged in the order of the mishnaic text. The linguistic element also figures prominently in Sa'adyah's biblical commentaries, although it occupies a smaller proportion of these. Particularly noteworthy are the many dictionary-like passages analysing the multiple meanings of certain words (see pp. 61, 70). His commentary on *Sefer yetsirah* includes elaborate linguistic discussions with an emphasis on the letters of the alphabet, their divisions into groups, and their combinations. In this commentary he refers to his grammatical work and goes beyond it in comparing the Palestinian and Babylonian traditions of Hebrew with respect to the influence of laryngeal consonants on vocalization. Finally, let us mention the *Sefer hamo'adim* and *Sefer hagalui*, where, as in the preface to the *Egron*,

---

[19] Ibid. 442–3.   [20] Ibid. 41–4.

Sa'adyah sets out to provide models of eloquent Hebrew prose. I shall discuss this attempt in the following section.

General Conceptions

Like other Jewish scholars in the Muslim world during the Middle Ages, Sa'adyah was fluent in three Semitic languages: Hebrew, Aramaic, and Arabic. Hebrew and Aramaic were inseparable elements of rabbinic learning and sacred Jewish tradition, while Arabic was the language of the surrounding culture, used by members of all religions and at every level of society to implement most of their needs. Presumably, it is to these languages that he refers several times as 'every language that we know'. On occasion he points to a phonetic phenomenon in Greek or Persian, but these scattered bits of information seem to have reached him indirectly—presumably by way of Arabic—because some of his generalizations are applicable only to Semitic languages and not to Indo-European ones.[21]

Within the scope of the Semitic languages that he knew, Sa'adyah laid the groundwork for a comparative Semitic linguistics that was elaborated and developed in the later Middle Ages by Arabic-speaking Jews.

Sa'adyah's interest in language led him to reflect on various problems of general linguistics as well. Already in his preface to the *Egron* he states that 'When the idea of writing this book first entered my heart ... I gave my heart over to imagining all the words of mankind and all the expressions of the lips and all the utterances of the mouths that exist in every nation's language.' Likewise, in the prefaces to several chapters of his work on grammar he deals with fundamental issues, such as different types of syllable, in a conscious attempt to establish universal principles.[22]

Of particular interest is Sa'adyah's approach to the question of the origins of language, which greatly occupied Muslim thinkers and went back to the ancient Greeks: is language 'natural'—or, to put it in medieval terms, God-given—or is it the 'artificial' creation of human beings? Sa'adyah's ideas on this question are complex and subtle, but on the whole he views language as a human creation and the choice of particular words to convey certain ideas in a specific language as arbitrary and based on convention.[23]

In one of two discussions where he develops this idea, he deals with the question why certain verbs with weak first consonants are vocalized in the future tense with an *i* vowel, while other verbs of the same class take an *e* vowel:

It is inappropriate to enquire into such matters. Why should this be so? ... Because we have investigated the primary principle, namely the assignment of basic nouns, and

---

[21] Dotan, *First Light* (Heb.), 108–9, 338–9, 500–1; cf. Brody, *The Geonim of Babylonia*, 138–40 and nn. 8–9.   [22] Allony, *Egron* (Heb.), 160–1; Dotan, *First Light* (Heb.), 108–9.
[23] Dotan, *First Light* (Heb.), 96–104.

found no proof [in these matters], and the proof for people is consensus, that they have agreed and assigned a name to every object in existence so that knowledge of existent things [may] be conveyed to us . . . not because something dictates that we bestow a certain name on each thing which distinguishes it from other things, for if this were so, the entire world would necessarily speak a single language, and true speech could not be achieved in any other language; and what is called *even* [i.e. a stone] in Hebrew would not be called *hajar* in Arabic . . . but the case being otherwise proves that names are a matter of convention. And similarly, if people agreed to change them, it would be possible to call *nahar* [Arabic: day] *duhn* [oil] and, conversely, to call *duhn nahar*.[24]

Elsewhere Sa'adyah explains that particular words, chosen arbitrarily by the 'founder of the language', are nevertheless binding on its current speakers because language 'is preceded by a consensus and this requires us not to deviate from its bounds'.[25] He uses the expression 'the founder of the language' not in the way certain Arab writers do, to refer to God, but to indicate human agency (at least in the case of languages other than Hebrew), namely, the first speaker of a given language or, perhaps more precisely, its first group of speakers. To God he applies the expression 'the Author of speech' because he endowed human beings with the faculty of speech, an ability that they utilize to create their respective languages. Where Hebrew is concerned, it is Adam to whom Sa'adyah refers as the 'founder of the language' in accordance with Genesis 2–3. But it is not altogether clear how this fits in with the belief set forth in the *Egron* that 'the Holy Tongue, which our Lord chose from eternity', is the language 'in which all the holy angels and supernal beings sing his praises and adore him on high'. Perhaps Sa'adyah changed his mind on this point sometime between his earlier writing and the composition of the work on grammar, or perhaps he deliberately chose a phrase open to more than one interpretation.[26]

Yet another remarkable aspect of Sa'adyah's unique approach to the Hebrew language is the hope—which he expresses in the preface to the *Egron*—that his fellow Jews will use Hebrew not just in their literary pursuits but also in their everyday affairs. Whether helping them to 'riddle riddles' and 'offer parables and to write works of all kinds and to rhyme every rhyme' or in the writing of prose, Sa'adyah hoped that Hebrew would be studied and understood by 'all the nation of our Lord, us and our children and our wives and servants, that we enquire and understand and investigate it always, so that it may never depart from us . . . The people of our God will converse in it, in their going out and coming in, in all their occupations, and in their bedrooms, and with their children'.[27]

Familiarity with the Holy Tongue, according to Sa'adyah's view, was essential for more than synagogue use. It was necessary for Jews to have an active know-

[24] Ibid. 508–11.   [25] Ibid. 398–9.
[26] Ibid. 98–9, 103; Allony, *Egron* (Heb.), 156.   [27] Allony, *Egron* (Heb.), 159.

ledge of Hebrew—to speak it eloquently in every sphere of life, in every situation. This applied to all ranks of the Jewish people, not merely those who 'pluck instruments and sing songs'. Here Sa'adyah draws on the Arabic concept of eloquence, *fasaha*, the finest exemplar of which he finds in the Holy Tongue of the Bible, just as the Muslims find it in the language of the Qur'an. But unlike Muslim thinkers, who regarded the language of the Qur'an as miraculous, supernaturally beautiful, and thus inimitable, Sa'adyah believed that it was possible and even desirable to imitate the language of Scriptures. He himself attempted to do so in three different places: in his preface to the *Egron*, in *Sefer hamo'adim*, and in *Sefer hagalui*. In the Arabic preface to the expanded edition of *Sefer hagalui* he explains the ten different aims of the book, seven of which relate to specific sections and the remaining three to more general aims:

The first is to teach the nation eloquence in Hebrew, for I have seen that [the influence of] Arabic and Aramaic have overpowered it . . . and the people have forgotten their eloquent and elevated language; and the second is to teach the nation the composition of speech . . . and the third to teach combination, for the knowledge of any [type of] speech is perfected only by means of the combinations which bind it together.[28]

It appears that this explanation applies in principle to the *Egron* and *Sefer hamo'adim* as well. In these three places Sa'adyah uses pseudo-biblical language and style and gives his texts the external form of the Bible, divided into verses and provided with Tiberian vocalization and cantillation marks.

At the same time, it is worth noting that Sa'adyah does not limit the eloquent form of Hebrew to the vocabulary of the Bible. Those who wish to use this elevated language are free to augment it in two essential ways: by grammatical analogy and from extra-biblical, primarily rabbinic, sources. As we shall see in the following section, Sa'adyah devotes a major portion of his work on grammar to clarifying the rules of conjugation by means of which speakers of the language may form verb constructs that are not found in the Bible but are contained *in potentia* in biblical Hebrew. Sa'adyah himself introduces many such neologisms when he writes in elevated Hebrew, particularly in his poetry. He bases the theoretical licence to use words which have no source in Scripture, even in other forms, on the correct perception expressed at the end of his *Explanation of the Seventy Isolated Biblical Words*. In the passage below, taken from the latter work, he discusses the indispensability of rabbinic language for biblical interpretation:

The Bible was not written as a means of teaching the language, but only so that we might learn from it the story of people from the past who acted well and gave thanks [for the reward they were given] or acted badly and regretted [their punishment], and in order for us to know what our Lord has commanded us to do and what he has forbidden

---

[28] Harkavy, *Fugitive Remnants* (Heb.), 152–7 (Arab. text and Heb. trans.); for the correct interpretation of this passage see Tobi, 'A New Page', 56–8.

us to do, and that we might look forward to what he promised us by way of reward and fear that of which he has warned us by way of punishment—and whatever [portion of the] language found its way into these matters entered it [the Bible], but whatever happened not to enter it nevertheless remains a part of the language ... for the language is more extensive than the Bible and the Bible forms only part of it, and this is clear from reason and from testimony.[29]

Sa'adyah's basic conception of the Hebrew language (and perhaps of languages in general) is one of timelessness. He is concerned neither with diachronic linguistics nor with historical explanations of linguistic phenomena, but offers his own unique explanations for what modern Hebrew linguists view as obvious examples of different historical strata, as we shall see. He must have been aware, for example, of the differences between biblical and rabbinic Hebrew (already in the Talmud it is stated that 'biblical language and rabbinic language differ'), but there is no easily discernible statement to that effect in any of his writings. He may well have deliberately stressed linguistic continuity, as he did with other elements of Jewish tradition, as part of his struggle against the Karaites and others who wished to sever the connection between the Bible and rabbinic Judaism.

Grammatical Theories

Like most medieval grammarians, Sa'adyah does not distinguish systematically between 'letters' and 'consonants', that is, the phonetic essence represented by the letter in its written form. The term that Sa'adyah most commonly uses in this context is *harf*, which embraces both meanings, though what he typically has in mind are the sounds symbolized by the letters, that is, the consonants. Nevertheless, he sometimes uses other words when he wishes to emphasize that he is referring not to the written representation but to the sound of the consonant itself.

The consonants are divided into five groups according to their places of articulation: *alef–heh–ḥet–ayin*, *beit–vav–mem–peh*, *gimel–yod–kaf–kuf*, *dalet–tet–lamed–nun–tav*, and *zayin–samekh–tsadi–resh–shin*. In this system of division (as well as in his presentation of the letters of each group in alphabetical order) Sa'adyah follows *Sefer yetsirah*, which he regards as an ancient text of great authority and on which he wrote a comprehensive commentary. In addition to this phonetic division, he separates the letters into various functional groupings as well.[30]

Following the Masoretes, Sa'adyah recognizes seven vowels, divided into three phonetic groups in descending order: high vowels—*ḥolem* (o) and *shuruk* (u); middle vowels—*kamats* (ā), *pataḥ* (a), and *segol* (e); and low vowels—*tsere* (e) and *ḥirik* (i). Nevertheless, in order to describe vowel shifts as part of the process of inflection (see below), he moves the *shuruk* from its natural position in the

---

[29] Allony, *Collected Papers* (Heb.), i. 66.   [30] Dotan, *First Light* (Heb.), 111–12.

phonetic scale to the bottom of the scale. The *sheva* is not counted as a vowel at all, and is placed outside the phonetic scale, although the mobile *sheva* (*sheva na*) is always pronounced as one of the vowels, not as a special phonetic element, as it is in contemporary Hebrew. Here, too, Sa'adyah follows the Tiberian Masoretic tradition, which had already established many of the rules that distinguish the quiescent *sheva* (*sheva naḥ*) from the mobile *sheva* (*sheva na*) and determine the pronunciation of the latter, but Sa'adyah rose to new heights of theoretical abstraction and systematization, presenting a compact scheme of rules covering the majority of possible categories.[31]

The foundation of the linguistic analysis of Hebrew which has prevailed over the last millennium is the root system, in which verbal and nominal forms are derived from a root composed of three (or, in a few cases, four or five) consonants, representing a certain basic meaning. Sa'adyah takes a different approach: he views the primary form of a word not as an abstract root but as an actual linguistic 'basis' (Hebrew *yesod*, Arabic *asl*), meaning a legitimate form from which all other forms may be derived through one or more stages of inflection and ramification. (It should be noted, however, that in some of his grammatical discussions Sa'adyah comes close to the idea of roots in the distinction that he draws between two-letter words and words composed of three or more letters, where by letters he means 'true' consonants, excluding *alef, vav,* and *yod,* which are generally, though not always, used as *matres lectionis.*[32])

According to Sa'adyah's conception, the basic form is always nominal, though it need not take the form of a noun as such but can appear as a verbal noun (e.g. 'saying' (*omer*) or 'desire' (*ḥefets*)) or as an infinitive such as 'walk', or *halokh* (according to Arabic grammarians, the infinitive is the basic form from which all other verb forms are derived). In many cases, letters are deleted from the basic form in the process of deriving other forms. For instance, the word *maḥaneh* (camp) is the basic form, not the root *ḥ-n-ḥ* (to encamp); and because of this the elision of the *mem* should be considered an early stage in the ramification of the basic form leading to all forms of the verb. In the same way the *heh* drops from the verb *halakh* (he went) in its future forms; for example, in *elekh* (I shall go).[33] This is one type of elision discussed in the second chapter of the grammar book; but there are also various types of augmentation or elaboration (*pe'ur* in Hebrew, *tafkhim* in Arabic), such as reduplicating the final consonant or the last two consonants of the basic form. An example of the first type is *veyitpotsetsu,* 'And the everlasting mountains are *dashed in pieces*' (Hab. 3: 6), as opposed to *mapets,* 'And with thee I will *shatter* the nations' (Jer. 51: 20). An example of the second type is *salseleha,* '*Exalt her* and she doth lift thee up' (Prov. 4: 8), as opposed to *mesilah,* 'Clear ye *the way* of the people' (Isa. 62: 10).[34] Even forms that we consider archaic

---

[31] Dotan, *First Light* (Heb.), 113–24.   [32] Ibid. 127–32.

[33] Ibid. 127, 133, 324–5.   [34] Ibid. 186–7, 318–23.

reflections of an earlier period in linguistic development, preceding the elision of final vowel sounds—such as the form *beno be'or* rather than the usual *ben be'or* for 'the son of Be'or' in Numbers 24: 3—were considered by Sa'adyah to be examples of *pe'ur* or augmentation.[35]

The system of ramification, in Sa'adyah's view, includes structural changes of the type we call conjugation or declension, as well as additions such as the prefixes *b-*, *h-*, *v-*, *k-*, *l-*, *m-*, *sh-*. As noted earlier, the process of ramification can be highly complex, taking place in several stages, and in such cases any form that is a point of departure for another stage may be termed a 'basic form', even if it is derived from a previous development and is not a basic form in an absolute sense. In other words, the term 'basic form' is relative. It is worth pointing out here that Sa'adyah's grammatical terminology in general is not entirely precise and consistent. A number of overlapping terms may serve a single purpose, or a single term may have a number of meanings. These shortcomings of his system may be explained partly by his being a pioneer in the field of Hebrew linguistics, seeking the most suitable and appropriate terms to express his ideas, and partly by his emphasis on practical applications rather than abstract theories, as well as by changes that may have occurred in his thinking over time.[36]

As we have seen, underlying Sa'adyah's system of ramification is the nominal form, although sometimes it is 'nominal' in a broader sense that includes verbal nouns or infinitive forms. With respect to nouns there are three principal means of ramification: assignment (transformation to the *status constructus* or the addition of one of the ten possessive pronominal suffixes), formation of the plural, and the addition of prefixes. These processes may take place singly or cumulatively—a basic noun may take a prepositional affix (as in *bedavar*, 'by a word'), a construct form (*devar*, 'the word of'), or a plural form (*devarim*, 'words'). The construct form can also take a prepositional affix (as in *bidvar*, 'by the word of'); the plural can take a prepositional affix (as in *bidvarim* 'by words') or a pronominal suffix (as in *devarekha*, 'your words'). Furthermore, the plural form with a pronominal suffix can also take a prepositional affix (as in *bidvarekha*, 'by your words').[37]

The basic nominal form can be changed into a verb by adding a time element, thus generating a secondary system of conjugation. The basic form of this system is the third person singular past form (for example, *katav*—he wrote). Sa'adyah distinguishes three tenses: past, 'constant', and future. The 'constant' is not the same as what we call the participle (for example, *kotev*), which is considered a noun (and indeed behaves as one in biblical syntax), but is rather an infinitive form which indicates an action that is simultaneous with another action, as in *midei dabri bo* (whenever I speak of him), or a continuous action. The future tense is

[35] Ibid. 144–5, 244. A further example of *pe'ur* is *shekamti devorah* rather than the expected *shekamt devorah* (you arose, Deborah) in Judg. 5: 12.

[36] See Dotan, *First Light* (Heb.), 131–2, 134, 155–6, and *passim*.   [37] Ibid. 137–8, 338–47.

divided into two categories, the indicative and the imperative. The past, the future indicative, and the future imperative have two subdivisions each: 'acting on itself' and 'acting on others'. (We have no way of knowing whether or not Sa'adyah further divided the 'constant' due to lacunae in the manuscript of his grammatical work.) This division is reminiscent of the distinctions made in modern Hebrew grammar between transitive and intransitive verbs, or between the simple (*kal*) and causative (*hifil*) conjugations.[38] However, we must bear in mind that Sa'adyah does not classify verbs according to conjugations, and his system of verb division is functional in nature. He distinguishes between actions that take place within the agent, even if they are described by what we would call transitive verbs (for example, *shama*—he heard, or *akhal*—he ate) and actions that take place outside the agent, whether described by a transitive verb in the *kal* (for example, *harag*—he killed) or by a verb in *hifil* (for example, *hishmia*—he caused (someone) to hear). In each such sub-system there is a further division by person: ten in the past tense and the future indicative, and four in the imperative. Prefixes, pronominal object suffixes, or both, may be added to these forms. In contrast to this, the 'constant' forms are not divided according to person, although they too may take prefixes or pronominal object suffixes. It is unclear why Sa'adyah treats only what we call the *kal* and *hifil* forms in his comprehensive discussions and conjugation tables, although he seems to have also taken into account additional conjugations (in our terminology) when he states that a single basic form can give rise to as many as 19,169 different forms![39]

Although there is no place in Sa'adyah's linguistic scheme for a theoretical discussion of the various *binyanim*, and the concept itself is extraneous to his analysis, he relates in his own fashion to the phenomena that we call conjugations, and distinguishes between active verb forms (belonging to the *kal* and *hifil* conjugations according to our terminology) and passive verb forms (*pual*, *hufal*, *nifal*, and *hitpa'el*). He uses the term 'compulsion' (*qahr* in Arabic) to indicate the intensive constructs, *pi'el* and *pual*. Following Arab grammarians he treats the geminated forms (those with a *dagesh*) as pluralized, as opposed to ungeminated forms; this pluralization can refer to the agents of the action, to its objects, or to the number of actions. What we call the *hitpa'el* conjugation is described as a 'compulsion [of the agent] acting on himself', that is, as a form that incorporates both active and passive elements. Sa'adyah mentions passive geminated forms, or forms with a *pual* vocalization, but provides no examples of the more common use of *pual* as the passive equivalent of the *pi'el*, but only as a form whose active equivalent is the *kal*;

[38] Translator's note: For lack of a better word I use this to translate *binyanim*, i.e. the various forms of the verbal stem in Hebrew (and similarly in other Semitic languages), where the first *binyan* (*kal*) is the basic form of the verb and the others are derived stems.

[39] See Dotan, *First Light* (Heb.), 134–40, 146–51, 342–3, 348–95.

for example, *shafakh* (he poured) as opposed to *shupakh* (was poured), or *avad* (he worked) as opposed to *ubad* (was worked).[40]

Sa'adyah presents a systematic account of vowel shifts through inflection both in nouns (in the transition from singular to plural, or from the basic to the assigned form, that is, to the *status constructus* or to forms that include a possessive suffix) and in verbs (changes in vocalization that depend on tense and person). He classifies the possible variants in two groups, ascending and descending in the phonetic scale, and then according to the different vowels and the circumstances in which each one shifts to a higher or lower position on the scale.[41]

The last factor that Sa'adyah identifies with respect to vowel alternation is that of the pausal (*hefsek*) and context (*heksher*) forms of both nouns and verbs. This, it should be stressed, is one area where he was utterly innovative, since he could not learn this from either the Arab grammarians (the phenomenon does not exist in Arabic) or the Masoretes (who did not deal with this sort of theoretical question). In contrast to the explanation offered by modern diachronic linguistics, Sa'adyah believed that the *heksher* forms are the basic forms—perhaps because they occur much more frequently—and that the pausal forms are derived from them. He considers the pausal form to be a factor in vowel alternation, and gives the example of *arim aser* (ten cities; Josh. 21: 5) as opposed to the context form *eser yadot* (ten parts; 2 Sam. 19: 44). In Sa'adyah's terms, the *segol* sound /e/ rises two steps in the vowel scale, to the *kamats*, when the word *eser* comes at the end of a sentence (it is interesting that here as elsewhere he shows his preference for unusual examples, taken from relatively obscure places in the Bible, instead of frequently occurring examples such as *erets–arets*).[42]

Sa'adyah approves in principle of the creation of unattested forms through linguistic analogy—for example, the noun *petsah* (roughly speech) from the verb *patsah*, or the masculine form *la'an* from the extant feminine form *la'anah* (wormwood). These may be viewed as back-formations, that is, reconstructions of a hypothetical basic form whose absence from the biblical vocabulary is merely accidental in Sa'adyah's view. He seems to have believed that in principle it is possible to generate all the derived forms in the tables of conjugation and declension not only from every basic form attested in biblical Hebrew, but from reconstructed forms as well.[43] He goes even further in his approval of another type of formation by analogy: he sanctions the creation of augmented forms by doubling the final consonant or the two final consonants of an existing element, on condition that this is done according to the rule that he sees as governing such augmentation. In this case he addresses the reader and explains:

[40] Ibid. 146–9. [41] Ibid. 120–4.
[42] See ibid. 151–4, 452–3, 460–1. [43] Cf. ibid. 135–46.

The reduplication of two letters after [the same] two letters, making them four, is the second way in which nominal augmentation [literally embellishment] takes place, as you say *solu solu hamesilah* ['Cast up, cast up the highway', Isa. 62: 10], and as you say *salseleha uteromemeka* ['Exalt her and she doth lift thee up', Prov. 4: 8] ... and in relation to this we must set up a rule so that no one will be able to claim that any noun may be augmented with two adjacent letters, such as ... saying *shemama* as the augmentation of the basic form *shama* or something like that, and will err in thinking that it is like *gilgel* [rolled] ... of which the basic form is *vayagel* ['and he rolled the stone', Gen. 29: 10] ... and [so] we will say: the difference between these two is that when you say *shama* ... the action is in the agent, and when you say *galgal* ... the action is in another, and this is the rule. We say: any word that may be augmented by means of reduplicating two letters is one in which the action takes place in another, whereas if the action takes place in the agent himself it may not be augmented by duplicating two letters.[44]

Construction by analogy was very common in the language of liturgical poetry, and Sa'adyah used it both in his poems and in his works of elevated prose. In keeping with his aspirations, he was not content merely to describe the documented idiom of Scriptures, but aimed at providing the reader with tools to enrich and enhance the Hebrew tongue, as he himself had done.

It was Sa'adyah's innovativeness and his creation of new words and linguistic forms in poetic language that left their mark on his successors, while his treatise on grammar quickly disappeared, as we have seen, and had little impact on Hebrew linguistics, which developed in different directions. Today, with the publication of a significant part of this pioneering work (though much of it is still missing) it is possible to appreciate the scope of Sa'adyah's undertaking and the maturity of his thought in this as in other realms.

[44] Dotan, *First Light* (Heb.), 320–3.

CHAPTER SIX

※

Sa'adyah the Poet

O F ALL THE DISCIPLINES in which Sa'adyah excelled, it was in poetry that he worked within the most highly structured frameworks, though here too he brought great originality to his praxis, as we shall see later in the chapter. Medieval Hebrew poetry—and, to some extent, the poetry of late antiquity—is typically classified in contemporary research as either liturgical or secular according to its formal function: poetry intended for use in religious ceremonies (essentially in the obligatory prayers) is classified as *piyut* or liturgical poetry, while poetry that is not so intended is classified as secular. I will also make use of these categories in describing Sa'adyah's poetic oeuvre, with the reservation that before the end of the first millennium no truly 'secular' Hebrew poetry existed in the Orient in terms of atmosphere and content, and the so-called 'secular' poetry that Sa'adyah wrote served religious ends, as we shall presently see.

The Foundations of Hebrew Liturgical Poetry

Liturgical poetry as I have defined it was known by various names in earlier sources.[1] Already in rabbinic times, composers of *piyut* were referred to as *paitanim*, and in the Middle Ages their poetry was called *ḥazanut* or *ḥazana* (in the Judaeo-Arabic form). We cannot date the earliest stages of this type of poetry with any precision, or identify its earliest surviving fragments. Its flowering may date back to the Second Temple period, in contexts such as that of the *hoshanot* that accompanied the ceremonial circling of the altar of the Temple in Jerusalem during the festival of Sukkot (and in later times the circling of the *bimah* or platform of the synagogue). In any case, there is evidence of a tradition of *piyut* in Palestine during the amoraic era (3rd–4th c. CE) but this early period is quite obscure. The first *paitan* that we know of by name is Yosi ben Yosi, generally presumed to have been active during the fifth or sixth century CE.

Piyut was originally intended to replace central portions of the standard synagogue prayers. The early prayers were composed in a spiritually elevated but stylistically simple prose, and although the liturgical formulations were not absolutely fixed in rabbinic times—halakhah concerns itself mostly with fixing

---

[1] The best introduction to this field, and the basis of most of the following pages, is Fleischer, *Hebrew Liturgical Poetry* (Heb.), supplemented by many more detailed studies, especially by Fleischer and his student Shulamit Elizur.

the concluding eulogies of the benedictions—they varied only slightly and were probably generally standardized in the prayer services of particular congregations. Moreover, halakhah decreed that whenever people worshipped together in public, the central part of the service, the Amidah, was first recited silently by the congregation and then out loud by the precentor (called a *ḥazan* in later periods and down to our day). The congregation would participate in the repetition to a limited extent, for example, by pronouncing *amen* after each of the benedictions and reciting the Kedushah prayer, which was inserted into the Amidah on certain occasions (and about which I shall have more to say later). This frequent repetition of fixed formulations—both by individuals in the course of their daily or sabbath prayers and in the immediate repetition by the precentor—eventually led to dissatisfaction and produced a strong desire to introduce some freshness and variety into the service as a way of avoiding boredom. The *paitanim*, most of whom apparently served as cantors on a regular basis, took up the challenge, composing new prayers that corresponded to the fixed prayers in terms of content but were different in form. This allowed the cantor to express his religious feelings and display his artistry, while the congregants took pleasure in new and varied creations, more suitable to their aesthetic tastes than the fixed prosaic prayers of the service.

As mentioned above, the liturgical poems were originally intended to replace most sections of the standard prayers, not to supplement them, although in later periods many congregations had it both ways, retaining the full text of the standard prayers alongside passages of *piyut*.[2] Nevertheless, fragments found in the Cairo Genizah clearly indicate the ancient role of liturgical poems in the service. In these manuscripts the texts of the *piyutim* are separated by abbreviated references to certain short passages from the standard liturgy, in a way which shows that the actual performance consisted of reciting the *piyutim* together with only a few words of the liturgy—not, as in the later usage of many congregations, treating the *piyutim* as additions to the full text of the standard prayers. These passages consist mostly of the concluding eulogies of the benedictions (of central importance in rabbinic tradition, as stated earlier), a small number of scriptural verses which had become firmly established within the set prayers, and brief introductory or transitional passages such as the opening words of the Amidah.

Presumably the aim of the *paitanim* was to provide a new poetic liturgy for each occasion of public prayer—that is, to use each poetic composition only once; indeed, we know of certain *paitanim* who wrote a number of different liturgical cycles to fill the same niche in the service. But although this may have been their original intention, the practice did not persist for long. Even the most talented poets found it difficult to compose full sequences of new *piyutim* for each occurrence of a particular sabbath or festival, let alone those precentors who were incapable of producing liturgical poetry of any merit themselves, yet did not wish

---

[2] This practice continues today in most synagogues on the Jewish festivals.

to forgo the new fashion and limit themselves to the standard prayers. Thus it became usual for precentors—some of whom were highly gifted *paitanim*—to reuse the most successful *piyutim*. In time, certain liturgical poems achieved canonical status and became permanent features of the prayer service, indispensable and irreplaceable, contrary to the revolutionary spirit of the early *paitanim*. Even when a particular poem was not selected to fill a particular liturgical slot, rigid and almost binding templates were established for various categories of *piyut*, and poets often emulated specific works by outstanding predecessors. In some categories this resulted in a sense of surfeit, so that the *paitanim* of a given period stopped producing in those categories and began composing in less well-developed modes.

The main types of early *piyut* derive from the central portions of the prayer service, where they were meant to offer variety. The two pillars of the Rabbanite prayer service are the recitation of the Shema and its blessings and the Amidah. The Shema is made up of three biblical passages, Deuteronomy 6: 4–9, Deuteronomy 11: 13–21, and Numbers 15: 37–41, which, according to rabbinic law, must be recited every morning and evening. In the opinion of some this is prescribed in Deuteronomy 6: 7, 'and thou shalt talk of them . . . when thou liest down, and when thou risest up'. These verses comprise words that God addressed to the Jewish people and are thus not classified as prayers but rather as a declaration of principles, or, in rabbinic language, 'an acceptance of the yoke of the kingdom of Heaven'. In the liturgy, however, the passages do not stand on their own but are encompassed by benedictions and eulogies addressed by the Jewish people to God. In the morning the recitation of the Shema is preceded by two blessings and followed by one, and in the evening it is preceded by two, corresponding to the morning blessings in content but differing in their formulations, and followed by two.

The other central portion of the service, the Amidah or standing prayer, is the quintessential prayer in talmudic literature and throughout Jewish tradition. In contrast to the Shema, however, the number of daily recitations of the Amidah is not uniform. On weekdays it is recited three times: in the morning, afternoon, and evening services, though its status in the evening service is somewhat shaky and it is considered—officially, at least—to be optional. On special days—sabbaths, the new moon, festivals, and the high holidays, Rosh Hashanah and Yom Kippur—a fourth prayer (*musaf*) is added, and on Yom Kippur a fifth prayer too, known as *ne'ilah* or *ne'ilat she'arim* (the locking of the gates) because it is recited towards evening, at the end of the fast. The Amidah is made up of between seven and eighteen—or, according to the Babylonian tradition followed nowadays by all Jewish communities, nineteen—extra-biblical blessings. The first three blessings are usually categorized as eulogies, and the last three as benedictions of thanksgiving, and these vary only slightly from one Amidah to another. The main differences concern the central portion of the prayer: on weekdays this includes twelve (or in the Babylonian tradition thirteen) blessings petitioning for the fulfilment of needs, whereas on the sabbath, festivals, and Yom Kippur it includes only one blessing, known as 'the holiness of the day'. The *musaf* or additional prayer service for Rosh Hashanah is exceptional in that its middle section consists of a sequence of three blessings devoted to the subjects of God's kingship, remembrance, and the blowing of the ram's horn.

The recitation of the Shema and the Amidah is obligatory for every Jew, whether praying alone or with a congregation (according to halakhah, women are also obligated to pray but they are exempt from the recitation of the Shema). Another element of the Amidah recitation, the Kedushah, is specific to public prayer and is inserted during the precentor's repetition of some of the Amidah prayers. There is a variant of this prayer among the blessings that precede the morning recitation of the Shema, and here opinion is divided as to whether or not a person praying on his own may recite it. All Kedushah prayers depict the angels praising God, with an emphasis on two verses that describe this scene: Isaiah 6: 3 ('And one called unto another and said, "Holy, holy, holy is the Lord of Hosts"') and Ezekiel 3: 12 ('Blessed be the Glory of the Lord from His place'). These two verses are common to all versions of the Kedushah, but the extra-biblical passages around them change from prayer to prayer and from one tradition to another (and additional biblical passages are included in the Kedushah in some prayers). In the Kedushah before the morning recitation of the Shema there is only a description of the angels' praise, while the Kedushah of the Amidah depicts the congregants as participating in the angels' song. The number of times the Kedushah was recited differed in the two centres of Jewish tradition. In Babylonia it was recited at every service except in the evening (when prayers were not repeated by the precentor, since, as I have noted, its obligatory nature was questionable); in the Palestinian tradition it was recited on special occasions only: during the morning prayers of sabbaths, festivals, new moons, intermediate days of the festivals, and Hanukah; in the *musaf* prayers for Rosh Hashanah and Yom Kippur; and in the afternoon and closing prayers for Yom Kippur.

The native soil of *piyut* was Palestine, where it had been cultivated exclusively for hundreds of years. For this reason, there is an essential distinction between the Amidah prayers that included the Kedushah and those that did not. As we have noted, the main types of early *piyut* attempted to add variety to the two central portions of the standard prayer service: the recitation of Shema and the blessings of the Amidah. In each case this was accomplished by means of entire series of liturgical poems rather than isolated ones. The series that was originally meant to replace the benedictions surrounding the recitation of the Shema in the morning prayers is called *yotser* (maker), after the opening words of the first benediction in the standard prayer service ('maker of light and creator of darkness'), while the series replacing the benedictions of the Shema for evening prayers is called *ma'ariv* (creator of evening). The generic name for the series of poems intended for the Amidah is *kerovah* (offering), and the *kerovot* (plural) are divided into those that include the Kedushah and are thus called *kedushtot*, and those intended for prayers without Kedushah, known as *shivata* (seven) if the prayer is said on the sabbath or a festival—when only seven blessings are recited—or as a '*kerovah* of eighteen' if said on a weekday.

These series, with the exception of the *kedushta*, incorporate one poem corresponding to each benediction and to each of the fixed verses in the parallel sequence of the standard prayer service: five in the weekday *yotser*, seven or eight in the sabbath and festival *yotser*, six in the *ma'ariv*, seven in the *shivata*, and eighteen in the Amidah. The *kedushta* has more liturgical poems (at least nine) than the number of benedictions in the standard service but the series of poems ends where the Kedushah is inserted in the prayer—either before or after it—while the final four benedictions are recited in the standard fashion. It is possible that the *kedushtot* too, like the *shivatot* and '*kerovot* of eighteen', originally poetized all the benedictions of the Amidah prayer, but over time they ceased to versify the concluding benedictions as a result of the protracted recitation of the Kedushah. The 'abridged' version prevailed quite early on, and we know of only a few examples of *kedushtot* that include poems for the benedictions after the Kedushah.

The early liturgical poems shared a number of linguistic and stylistic features beyond structural aspects such as metre, rhyme, and template. Most striking in terms of style is their quality of allusiveness. Like the poets of other cultures, *paitanim* preferred allusion to direct statement. There was an inherent tension between their desire to be understood by their audiences and their wish to avoid the overly transparent and prosaic. They were sparing in their use of metaphor and imagery, preferring a different poetic technique known as *kinui*, or denomination, to create a special atmosphere. A *kinui* is a word or combination of words used metonymically to allude to a central concept in the world of *piyut*, such as God, the people of Israel, the patriarchs, the Temple, and so forth, without referring to them overtly. Such expressions are often derived from a verse of scripture and sometimes—as in the second example below—specifically from the rabbinic interpretation of a verse. For instance, the sky is called 'curtain' (Isa. 40: 22) or the community of Israel 'awesome' (S. of S. 6: 4), while other *kinuyim* refer to a particular trait or an event in the life of the figure that they represent. Some of these *kinuyim* eventually grew stale and banal, but there were *paitanim* of talent who would then create fresh ones to suit a certain context. The variety of *kinuyim* lent the poems much of their aesthetic appeal while providing the audience with the enjoyable challenge of deciphering their allusions.[3]

---

[3] See Fleischer, *Hebrew Liturgical Poetry* (Heb.), 104–7.

The *piyutim* had several prominent linguistic features as well.[4] Clearly evident in their vocabulary is a desire to preserve the purity of Hebrew. Words which contemporaries might have identified as foreign in origin, particularly Greek words, rarely appear and are replaced, wherever possible, by 'native' Hebrew words. Only foreign words which had become fully naturalized in Hebrew and whose alien origins were no longer discernible—for example, *zug* (pair) from the Greek, or *ganaz* (hid) from the Persian—could gain entry to the sphere of poetic language. Some exceptions were, however, made for Greek words that sound Hebrew which could be 'sneaked' into the poems in a Hebrew guise. The most prominent example of this is the Hebrew word *gai* (valley), which takes on the added meaning of 'land', borrowed from the Greek *gaia*, in the language of the *paitanim*.

Where nouns are concerned, there was a common tendency to alter their formations. The *paitanim* showed a predilection for certain nominal patterns, particularly the segolate, and created many new forms—such as *eneḥ* for *anaḥah* (groan) and *da'ag* for *de'agah* (worry). Quite a few of these new creations fall in the category of masculinized feminine nouns, that is, masculine nouns formed from feminine nouns; for example, the masculine noun *shoshan* from *shoshanah*, the grammatically feminine word for 'rose'. There were also many new nouns derived from verbs, such as *la'at* (eating) from the verb meaning 'to swallow', and *eter*, in the sense of prayer, from *atar* (he prayed). A similar process occurred on a wide scale in the opposite direction as well, deriving verbs from nouns; for instance, *hidrir* (he freed) from *deror* (freedom), and *hilin* (he made bitter) from *la'anah* (wormwood).

As for Hebrew conjugations, or *binyanim*, the frequent use of *pual* and *hofal* forms should be mentioned, although quite often these do not convey the passive sense that historically characterized their usage. Thus, for instance, we find the passive forms *suredu* and *husredu* in the sense of *saredu* (survived). In contrast to this, there was a tendency to attribute to the *hifil* construction the prevalent causative sense even in verbs whose *hifil* form had carried a different sense in earlier Hebrew. As a result, many new forms were created in the common *kal* construction—for example, *kashav* (he listened)—while the old forms took on a new, causative, sense—thus, *hikshiv* no longer meant 'he listened' but 'he caused someone else to listen'.

With respect to conjugation, one outstanding feature of the language of the *paitanim* was a certain blurring of lines between different categories of weak verbs in which one of the root letters is lacking or silent in certain forms. To put it more precisely, in their usage weak verbs may behave like 'hollow' verbs—those with medial *vav* or *yod*—in the past tense and in a few other instances. We find a large number of forms such as *ats* for *ya'ats* (he advised), *as* for *asah* (he made), or *sa* for

---

[4] The most extensive study of paitanic Hebrew to date is Yahalom, *The Language of Early Palestinian Liturgical Poetry* (Heb.).

nasa (he travelled). We may also note the widespread use by *paitanim* of the prepositions *b-*, *k-*, *l-*, and *m-*, which in classical Hebrew only appear before nouns, with verbs in the past tense—for example, *kehalekhu* (when they went), *kedibart* (as you (feminine) spoke)—and the substitution of the first person singular possessive pronominal ending *-i* for the objective pronominal *-ni* in forms such as *limdi* instead of *limdani* (taught me).

The Evolution of Liturgical Poetry before Sa'adyah's Time

Liturgical poetry evolved in the Orient, first in Palestine and later in Babylonia and North Africa, until approximately the end of the tenth century.[5] After that, two major centres of *piyut* developed in Europe, one in Spain and the other in Italy and Ashkenaz, and the Spanish influence began to move eastwards as well. The long period when poetic activity was confined to the East may be divided into three further periods, conventionally classified as the pre-classical, the classical, and the late Oriental periods. In order to understand Sa'adyah's place in the history of *piyut*, let us consider briefly the main characteristics of each of these three subdivisions.

The most striking fact about the *piyut* of the pre-classical period is that rhyming was not yet a fixed element of the genre, though here and there we find pararhyming. In the absence of rhyme, the main structural feature defining the poem was metre, and here we should bear in mind that throughout the ages of Oriental *piyut* we do not find the kind of precise metre, based on vowels or syllables, familiar from the later Hebrew poetry of Spain and adopted from Arabic models. In the pre-classical period there were several standard metres or rhythms, based on the number of stress units in each poetic line. The most prestigious of these appears to have been the so-called 'quadruple' metre in which long poetic lines were divided into four units with an equal number of stressed syllables, generally two in each.

Another poetic device was the acrostic, in which the initial letters of the first words of each line create a significant sequence. During the period in question the acrostics were alphabetical, as we find already in certain biblical chapters (in a number of psalms and most of the chapters of the book of Lamentations). The poets of this period did not yet provide acrostic signatures and they are all anonymous with the exception of Yosi ben Yosi, apparently the greatest and perhaps the last of them. Even in his case, it is thanks to the testimony of copyists or later authors (among them Sa'adyah) that we are able to identify some of his poems. Yosi ben Yosi's years of activity appear to have coincided more or less with the transition from the pre-classical to the classical period, and though we have no

[5] For a comprehensive overview of this topic see Fleischer, *Hebrew Liturgical Poetry* (Heb.), 47–275.

precise dates, his works are generally assumed to have been written some time in the fifth or early sixth century CE.[6]

The classical period lasted several hundred years, ending approximately in 800 CE. Many gifted *paitanim* were active during this time, most of them in Palestine. Of these, only a handful were known before the discovery of the Cairo Genizah, chief among them the foremost *paitan* of all times, R. Elazar berabi Kalir, known as Hakaliri. However, over the past century many other *paitanim* of the classical period have been discovered, in addition to previously unknown works by *paitanim* some of whose works survived outside the Genizah. Today we know of thousands of poems composed during the classical period by scores of *paitanim*, and the work of identifying and publishing them will undoubtedly continue for a very long time.

The most prominent structural innovation of the classical period was the systematic use of rhyme, which became a near-essential element for all *piyut*. In most types of long poem the normal division was into strophes, each adhering to its own monorhyme scheme. For example: a *piyut* of twenty lines might be divided into five strophes, each made up of four rhyming lines, with the rhyme scheme changing from strophe to strophe. Only rarely do we find a fixed rhyme sustained throughout a *piyut* of any length.

Another novelty worth noting was an acrostic form used not only as an organizing principle (alphabetical or reverse alphabetical order and so forth) but as a means of spelling out the poet's name with the first letter of each line of the *piyut*. This makes it easier to identify the composer of a *piyut*, although it is still no simple matter, since poets wove their name into only some of their works (usually one or two poems in a series, such as a *yotser* or a *kedushta*), and, more often than not, only fragments of the series survived in the Genizah. At best, we can reconstruct such series by comparing overlapping fragmentary copies. What is more, a *paitan* would sometimes insert the name of another person into his own work, for reasons that are not entirely clear. For example, the acrostic might name the cantor for whom the *paitan* had composed a certain piece. In other words, the acrostic signature of a given *piyut* is not necessarily the name of the actual poet, although it usually is.

During the classical period regular templates crystallized for the main types of *piyut*. Each type comprised a certain number of *piyutim* of more or less fixed length, and certain less pronounced structural elements (for example, the different kinds of acrostics and rhyme patterns used, and embellishments such as the repetition of key words or the use of biblical endings) also became fixed.

The subjects addressed by the various *piyutim* in the series were likewise firmly established. It is worth noting here that although the *piyutim* were intended to replace major portions of the regular prayer service, their contents did not always

---

[6] For an edition of his surviving poems see Mirsky, *The Poems of Yosi ben Yosi* (Heb.).

conform to this liturgical purpose (which was one of the main criticisms levelled at *paitanim* over the centuries). Already in pre-classical times, it was customary to devote considerable space in certain *piyutim* to themes only vaguely related to the essence of the prayers—as, for instance, in the lengthy *piyutim* called *sidrei avodah* (orders of service) inserted in the Yom Kippur prayers, which recount the history of the world in brief and then describe the Temple rituals performed by the High Priest on Yom Kippur. In the classical period it was the *kerovot* and especially the *kedushtot* that were most intensively developed. Their crystallization as literary genres was related to the Torah portions and the selections from the Prophets, or *haftarot*, read during the synagogue service on the sabbath and on festival days. That is, the *kerovah* for a given sabbath in the cycle of Torah readings referred to that particular weekly Torah portion and *haftarah* and even quoted the first few verses of the two readings. Similarly, a *kerovah* that corresponded to a festival would incorporate contents drawn from the day's special readings from the Pentateuch and the Prophets (this custom allows researchers to study the different customs concerning the division of the Torah into weekly portions and their associated readings in the prophets.)

The treatment of sabbath and festival portions read in the synagogue usually involved a poetic elaboration, sometimes quite lengthy and detailed, of halakhic and aggadic elements connected with the biblical portion and drawn from the rabbinic literature of Palestine—the writings of the sages of the Mishnah, the Palestinian Talmud, and aggadic midrashim (some of which have not survived). These sources were adapted to the paradigms of liturgical poetry. As noted, the poets normally preferred subtle allusion to explicit statement, so that even these halakhic and aggadic contents were obliquely alluded to in a way that demanded considerable erudition on the part of the audience and intense effort to fathom the poet's intentions. As to the density of rabbinic contents and their level of opacity, there is great disparity among the various *paitanim* and even among different compositions by the same *paitan*.

In the late Oriental age of liturgical poetry (approximately the ninth and tenth centuries) several important changes occurred. In this period we find, for the first time, considerable poetic activity outside the borders of Palestine, particularly in Babylonia. The poets of this era rarely wrote *kerovot*, putting most of their efforts into the composition of *yotserot*, possibly out of a sense that the potential of the *kerovot* had been exhausted during the classical period or because certain compositions in this genre had already become too 'canonical' to compete with. The most outstanding structural innovation was the addition of alternating refrains in some types of *piyutim* (in contrast to the repetition of certain lines at fixed intervals, found already in the classical period). These refrains were probably sung by the choir, which began to play an important role in the synagogue service at about this time. Another noteworthy phenomenon was the waning of the classical convention of writing whole sequences of poems. In the later period many *paitanim* took to reworking the poems of their predecessors, adding a few original compositions of their own (some of which were choral arrangements of existing works) to the older series. Existing series were also taken apart and reassembled to form new ones. A series of *piyutim* recited or copied during this period might therefore include segments composed by various poets, and perhaps even serve different liturgical functions than the ones they had originally served. Such practices often make it difficult to identify the authors and the original context of the poems.

Towards the beginning of the late Oriental period, the ninth century CE, we see a general decline in the creative level of poetic production. This is reflected in the linguistic superficiality of many *paitanim*, their use of timeworn *kinuyim*, and the explicitness of their writing as opposed to the allusive, riddling style prevalent in classical *piyut*. This situation was lamentable in Sa'adyah's view and he tried his best to overcome it in a variety of ways, as we shall see.

The Place of Liturgical Poetry in Sa'adyah's World

Liturgical poetry grew out of the soil of Palestine. Centuries passed before it spread to other lands. A central feature of Palestinian Jewish culture, *piyut* was cultivated by poets of considerable erudition in all classical fields of Jewish learning, biblical, halakhic, and aggadic. Creativity in the realm of *piyut* was truly enormous and it was undoubtedly one of the more important means of expressing the ideas and the national and religious sentiments of the Palestinian rabbinic elite (by the tenth and eleventh centuries we encounter accomplished poets among the high-ranking sages of the central rabbinic academy in Palestine). The attitude towards *piyut* in the competing centre of Babylonia was far less favourable, although its sages differed in their views. Some vehemently opposed it (chief among them Pirkoi ben Baboi, the zealot who contested all forms of Palestinian culture) while others accepted its use in the synagogue service so long as it conformed to halakhic criteria. However, no Babylonian sage that we know of before Sa'adyah's day spoke in praise of *piyut*, though works in the genre had been composed in Babylonia and had been used in the prayer service there at least as early as the ninth century.[7]

The great importance of liturgical poetry for Sa'adyah from his early youth reflects his upbringing in Egypt under the cultural hegemony of Palestine. We find a clear expression of the young Sa'adyah's high regard for the genre in the first edition of the *Egron*. The *Egron*, as we have seen, was intended to help poets find words that would meet the main requirements of classical *piyut*, namely, acrostics and rhyme. It was to this end that Sa'adyah provided his alphabetical wordlists,

---

[7] See Beeri, 'The Beginning of Poetic Creativity'.

one arranged according to initial letters, and the other according to word endings. He also composed many *piyutim* himself, though most of them cannot be dated with any certainty. Nevertheless, the contrast between the unrestricted style of some of his poetry (and private prayers) and the strict halakhic requirements set forth in his prayer book would suggest that he composed the *piyutim* at a much earlier date, when he was more heavily influenced by the poetics of earlier *paitanim*. In his prayer book Sa'adyah limited himself to a few examples of especially prestigious types of *piyut* which had already become part of the standard liturgy—*azharot* (warnings) for Shavuot (see below), *teki'atot* for Rosh Hashanah, *hoshanot* for Sukkot, *sidrei avodah* for Yom Kippur, and *selihot* for fast days.

The limited number of these poems does not, however, reflect a negative attitude towards *piyut*. The avowed aim of his prayer book was to present the basic canon of prayer in its pristine form (see p. 134) and, as he declares several times, it was not intended to include 'cantorial' material, that is, liturgical poems, although he records a few of these notwithstanding. In one place he even apologizes for the irrepressible urge that he feels to include his own poem, one of several *sidrei avodah* that he composed for Yom Kippur: 'As I have already explained, it was not my intention to include liturgical poems [in this prayer book] and I would have refrained from including this one were its composition not so extraordinary.'[8]

Sa'adyah's taste in poetry derived from his preference for the classical forms of *piyut*. He did not think much of contemporary *paitanim* and reverted to models from the classical period (at the latest), as evidenced by his words in the preface to the Judaeo-Arabic version of the *Egron*:

And where I saw fit to bring support for this from the early poets, Yosi ben Yosi and Yannai and Elazar and Joshua and Pinhas, I have done so, but as to those poets closer to us [in time], you will not find me mentioning them except to praise those whose words are desirable, and [therefore] I will say 'as so and so expresses well' and refrain from saying the opposite, 'as so and so expresses poorly'.[9]

This preference is also reflected in Sa'adyah's prayer book: the *piyutim* that he chooses to include in it are either from the pre-classical period (he ascribes some of them to Yosi ben Yosi) or his own compositions.[10]

As far as we know, Sa'adyah did not write many *kerovot*, and the few he did compose were intended for the festivals and Yom Kippur.[11] Four *shivatot* for sabbaths are attributed to him in one manuscript, but this attribution is uncertain. Most prominent among his *kerovot* for the festivals are two *shivatot*, poems for the

---

[8] Assaf et al., *Sa'adyah Gaon's Siddur* (Heb.), 289.

[9] Allony, *Egron*, 154 (Arab. text), 155 (Heb. trans.).

[10] See Assaf et al., *Sa'adyah Gaon's Siddur* (Heb.), introd., 21.

[11] The following survey of Sa'adyah's poetic oeuvre is based primarily on Tobi, *Sa'adyah Gaon's Liturgical Poems* (Heb.).

musaf service of Shemini Atseret, on which date a reference to rain begins to be added to the Amidah: 'Who causes the winds to blow and brings down the rain'. One of the *shivatot* was intended for recitation only when the festival fell on the sabbath, and the other when it fell on a weekday. It should be noted that the attribution of these two *shivatot* to Sa'adyah is well established, even though he signed them with the names of two other men, David and Elazar, probably the cantors who were to perform them.[12]

Sa'adyah's most extensive poetic work is the *shivata* for the festival of Shavuot which is found in his prayer book, though it seems to have been added by a copyist and may not have been included in the original edition.[13] The core of this composition is a remarkable section devoted to *azharot*, that is, an enumeration of the 613 precepts contained in the Torah according to the well-known rabbinic tradition. The custom of including poems of this type in the prayer service for Shavuot, the festival of the giving of the law, was widespread and accepted well before Sa'adyah's day. The innovative element in Sa'adyah's *azharot* is his grouping of the precepts as branches of the Ten Commandments—an idea that figures elsewhere in his writings as well. This *shivata* is one of Sa'adyah's more abstruse *piyutim*, filled with allusions to every precept in the Bible (by his count). In the section below, for example, he deals with the third Commandment (Exod. 20: 6): 'Thou shalt not take the name of the Lord thy God in vain'.

> You shall not take in vain the greatness of the Name, mightier and more
>   hallowed than any god
> Lest you defile and pronounce it, yea, defile it in dismay
> In saying what you will and will not do, fail not to execute [your] speech . . .
> I counsel you: keep the king's command, and that regard in the oath of God
>   [Eccles. 8: 2] . . .
> Make speech virtuous, pursue justice, from bribery desist
> Lest you commit iniquity and pervert the Law, for I will search you out
>   from hair to fingertips,
> My seers have found me and said, Be not respecters of persons,
>   commands our exalted Lord
> That respects not the persons of princes, nor regards the rich man more
>   than the poor [Job 34: 19].[14]

Another *piyut* of the *azharot* type which Sa'adyah includes in his prayer book may be part of a second *shivata* that he composed for Shavuot, which we only have in fragmentary form.[15]

---

[12] Tobi, *Sa'adyah Gaon's Liturgical Poems* (Heb.), i. 62.

[13] Assaf et al., *Sa'adyah Gaon's Siddur* (Heb.), 184–216 (cf. the variant reading at the beginning of p. 184); discussed in Tobi, *Sa'adyah Gaon's Liturgical Poems* (Heb.), 81–8.

[14] Assaf et al., *Sa'adyah Gaon's Siddur* (Heb.), 199.

[15] Ibid. 157–83, discussed in Tobi, *Sa'adyah Gaon's Liturgical Poems* (Heb.), 93–103.

It is not clear whether Sa'adyah composed complete *kedushtot* but there is no doubt that he wrote whole sequences of *piyutim* intended as expansions of the *kedushtot* for Yom Kippur and Shavuot. The elaborations that he composed for the Yom Kippur prayer are many and varied, among them *sidrei avodah* and confessions. Let us now look more closely at two Yom Kippur *piyutim* of other types. One of these, a monumental poem entitled 'Bless the Lord, O My Soul', is in the genre known as *rehitim* ('running' poems) that poeticize biblical verses. It is based on the first four verses of Psalm 104 and is intended for use in the prayer service for Yom Kippur as a kind of philosophical hymn. Based on the words 'Bless the Lord, O My Soul', the opening lines illustrate the style of the poem as a whole:

> Bless you, great and strong one, and render glory and praise forever
> To the Great and Strong One exalted on high forever.
> Bless you, created being with an end to your allotted days and by time encumbered,
> The Creator of all Creation, without end and years without number
> Bless you, O Lady who rules the body but whom none may rule or restrict
> The Almighty who rules alone . . . to gather and sift.
> Bless you, who rise above all works of men while they study you
> He who rises above the earth and the sphere of heavens that with His word came to be.
> Bless you, who fills the body and by whom its greed is stilled
> He who fills heaven and earth and cannot be contained even by many such as they.[16]

Another type of liturgical poem for Yom Kippur in which Sa'adyah made his mark was the *tokhaḥah*, a very early type of *piyut* on the theme of man's negligibility and his absolute dependence on the mercy of his Creator, as befitting the atmosphere of Yom Kippur. Sa'adyah's poem in this genre is one of the most impressive of its kind ever written and in it he introduces a major structural innovation: he dispenses with rhyme, which had for hundreds of years been a necessary element in *piyut* of this kind. Sa'adyah's *tokhaḥah* is composed of twenty-two strophes of eight lines each, and the only formal structuring that he employed—other than a metre of three accents to each half-line—was a simple alphabetical acrostic at the beginnings of the strophes.

To appreciate the spirit of the *tokhaḥah*, let us look at selections from the opening and closing strophes.

> If You have chosen, our Rock   This paltry being man . . .
> As for his form or lineaments   Like pottery taken from clay
> Fountains of blood and spittle   The abode of worm and maggot
> My spirit is grieved   When I speak of his acts
> My soul bows low   When I recall his deeds
> Woe unto him for his [evil] craving   Woe unto him from his Creator
> His hand is turned against all creatures to destroy them   And the hand of all is
>   against him to destroy him

[16] Zulay, *Sa'adyah Gaon's Poetical School* (Heb.), 111–12.

In his world he seems   To tread among thorns
And all the days of his vain life   To walk on a lattice
Icy hail and storm   Searing heat and scald . . .
Flailing out when full   Furious in his hunger
Even at night his heart is bestirred   For all his days are pain and rage
House by house he arrives   Four cubits for a burial suffice
Let him heed this and stand ashamed   And yield before his Maker . . .

We are sojourners before You   Our days on earth are few
We besought Your forgiveness and have been foolish   Perhaps we may find
        favour with You
Deal with us for Your name's sake   For we know our deeds are naught
Amend our latter days by Your will   That our hope be not dashed
Be slow to anger with us   And may Your glory restrain [anger] for us
Act according to the quality of Your mercy   Renowned of yore
May fasting atone on our behalf   And the suffering of our soul achieve
        forgiveness for it
Accept our penitent return to grant us life   And set us among those of the
        world to come.[17]

In addition to the genres that I have reviewed here, Sa'adyah's poetic oeuvre includes two series of *piyutim* of the type known as *ma'arivim*, meant to replace the standard blessings before and after the evening recitation of the Shema, as well as a number of *seliḥot* and *hoshanot*. His greatest work of liturgical poetry, however, was the series of *yotserot* that he wrote for each sabbath in the year, according to the annual reading cycle of the Pentateuch customary in Babylonia. Here, too, he did not sign his own name but rather the name 'Solomon', and sometimes even 'Solomon Suleiman'. The motives for this action are unclear, and at one time it raised doubts as to the true authorship of the poems in question, though they are evidently Sa'adyah's work. Each series is composed of seven *piyutim* (eight if we count the section beginning with the words 'And how long' as a *piyut* in its own right). The first *piyutim* in the series relate closely to the weekly Torah portion, and are generally more difficult to understand.[18] I have chosen as an illustration the last two (or three) poems of Sa'adyah's *yotser* for the portion of 'Tazria', Leviticus 12 and 13. This portion first deals with purification after childbirth (Lev. 12), and Sa'adyah includes the birth motif in the various *piyutim* of the *yotser*. The fixed words, characteristic of this type of *piyut*, are printed here in bold. The acrostic (which unfortunately cannot be reproduced in translation) disregards them, however, and, building on the first letter in the line following the fixed words, spells out the signatures 'Solomon' in 'Who Is Like Unto Thee' and 'Solomon Suleiman' in 'God Is Our King—And How Long'. At the end of the

[17] Zulay, *Sa'adyah Gaon's Poetical School* (Heb.), 65, 76–7.
[18] Tobi, *Sa'adyah Gaon's Liturgical Poems* (Heb.), i. 160–90.

first *piyut* a reference is made to a passage from the standard prayer which begins 'He is the Rock of our Redemption', and at the end of the last *piyut* there is another reference to a longer passage that concludes the standard benediction after the recitation of the Shema. Here, then, are the *piyutim* in full:

Who is like unto You, curing our three matriarchs of barrenness
To conceive and bear progeny of righteousness that is measureless
And who is Your equal, making the barren woman dwell in her home,
    joyful in dearness
Singing to extol You at the sea of the first light of clearness:
This is the Rock of our Redemption

God our King who judges us till the time of birthing, my sanctuary having fled
For travail and giving birth to wickedness within me are spread
They ruled us and weakened and sapped the strength of the four species by
    rank oppression[19]
Like a woman in travail, her heart distrait with each contraction
We have been beset, impregnated, delivered as though birthing wind

And till when did every hair stand on end and the eyes grow dark
Awaiting that day when the cloud [of glory] will cover the Temple and assemblies
Alvim and Yetetim[20] out, to draw all barbarians away from them
Retain the native-born, created with the finery of her youth
The sons of Zion will be born at once and all will be alarmed to hear and see
As it is written 'Who has heard such things' and so on[21]
And as is said 'Our redeemer' and so on
Blessed be the Redeemer of Israel.[22]

Distinctive Features of Sa'adyah's Poetry

There are a number of characteristics of marked interest in Sa'adyah's poetic oeuvre that distinguish him from most of the earlier *paitanim*. In terms of content, I have already noted the prominence of philosophical themes in some of his works. A further remarkable feature is the personal tone that he often lends these themes, so different from the collective perspective of early *piyut*. The allusions to rabbinic writings in Sa'adyah's poetry vary from one *piyut* to another and from

[19] The interpretation of this line is unclear; I have taken it to be a reference to the midrashic motif according to which the four species used on Sukkot represent a fourfold division of the Jewish people, see e.g. *Leviticus Rabbah* (ed. M. Margaliot), 709–10, and the additional sources cited in the editor's note ad loc.
[20] Two nations, mentioned in Gen. 36: 23, 40, whom Sa'adyah has chosen to represent the oppressors of Israel.   [21] Isa. 66: 8: 'Who has heard such things? Who has seen such things?'
[22] Tobi, *Sa'adyah Gaon's Liturgical Poems* (Heb.), ii. 38–9.

genre to genre, but there are generally fewer than we find in the works of the leading *paitanim* before his day.

In terms of structure, Sa'adyah had a predilection for longer than average lines: in addition to the *piyutim* with three or four accents to a line, in some of his more elaborate works we find lines of five or six stressed syllables, often divided in two by a regular pause or caesura in the middle. He also introduced striking innovations in rhyme, experimenting with new schemes such as the a/b/a/b/ form that broke the classical *piyut* tradition of monorhyme strophes. No less important is the scheme known as 'quasi-girdle rhyming', in which all lines but the last rhyme with each other in a strophe, and the rhyme changes from strophe to strophe, while the last lines of all the strophes rhyme with each other (for example, a/a/a . . . z, b/b/b . . . z). This rhyming pattern appears only marginally in Sa'adyah's liturgical poems but he uses it more extensively in his anti-Karaite polemical composition *Esa meshali* (I Take up My Parable), the structure of which is extremely complex and unusual.[23]

Sa'adyah's creative approach to Hebrew is clearly expressed in poetic works that abound in linguistic and stylistic innovations (see pp. 92–6). Some of his *piyutim*, particularly the *azharot*, exhibit an unusual concentration of syntactical features characteristic of biblical Hebrew, such as the *vav* conversive, parallelism, and negative imperatives introduced by words such as *pen* (lest) and *al* (do not). A more common feature of his poetry is the creation of quasi-biblical forms based on the idea, explained above, that any structural pattern found in biblical Hebrew may be applied to any linguistic element attested there. He creates synonyms for existing nouns by applying other nominal patterns to their roots. In this regard Sa'adyah favours the formation of feminine nouns from existing masculine forms (as opposed to the usual practice in earlier *piyut* of forming masculine nouns from feminine ones) and makes frequent use of the *kitlon* pattern. He is also particularly fond of rare biblical constructions, especially verbal formations with extended endings. We find many words of the *ya'avorun*, *vetodi'ehu*, or *ḥokhmathu* type.[24] In addition, under certain circumstances, he allows the augmentation of the root through consonantal doubling, as, for example, in the formation of the infinitive *ledogeg* from *dug* (to fish).[25]

---

[23] A further remarkable achievement, amazing even to Sa'adyah, is his *seder avodah*; here we find an a/b/a/b scheme, where the two rhymes change at different rates, together with an alphabetical acrostic in which every letter appears at the beginning of the first and third lines of four consecutive strophes (after the linking word, the *shirshur* or anadiplosis; see following), and, in addition, a reverse form of *shirshur* is created, with each strophe beginning and ending with the same word (excluding the initial letter *beit* that opens each strophe). See Assaf et al., *Sa'adyah Gaon's Siddur* (Heb.), 280–8, discussed in Tobi, *Sa'adyah Gaon's Liturgical Poems* (Heb.), 118–19, 121–2.

[24] Tobi, *Sa'adyah Gaon's Liturgical Poems* (Heb.), i. 272.   [25] Ibid. 273.

Also worth mentioning is Sa'adyah's fondness for scriptural names, especially those that appear rarely and in obscure places in the Bible, such as the catalogue of settlements in the book of Joshua or the genealogical records in the book of Chronicles. He generally uses these names metonymically, for example, 'the young men of Ahishahar and Tarshish', two of the descendants of the tribe of Benjamin who in this context represent the entire nation of Israel.[26] Furthermore, Sa'adyah makes deliberate use of the semantic sense of the names he employs. Thus, for example, he writes: *katrah li be'amad / rishyonekha im benei Elad / li omedet la'ad* (Seal for me in Amad / your warrant with the sons of Elad / for me it stands forever), where Amad, literally 'eternal nation', serves both as a toponym (Josh. 19: 26) and an allusion to Israel as an everlasting nation. Elad, a proper name that means 'eternal God', (1 Chr. 7: 21) here signifies that the God of the children of Israel is eternal. In other cases Sa'adyah uses proper names paired with their homonyms, as in the couplet, 'Answer those who pray on the tenth [of Tishrei, i.e. Yom Kippur] and bring their merits to light, as you answered the prayer of Barak [and helped him in the battle that he led] on Mount Tabor' (Judg. 4), where the rhyme is provided by the word *tavor*, meaning 'you shall bring to light', and the proper noun Tavor.[27]

Stretching the Bounds of *Piyut* and the Question of Sa'adyah's Influence

In addition to *piyutim*, Sa'adyah also composed two types of 'secular' or non-liturgical poems, albeit decidedly 'religious' in content. The first type, which includes at least two long poems, is the polemical work that I shall address further on (see Chapter 8). Sa'adyah was not the first to use poetry as a vehicle for religious polemics, since, as we know, one of his poems was written in response to Hivi of Balkh's poetic criticism of the Bible and in imitation of it, but he may have been the first Rabbanite Jew to write such poems. The other type is represented by a curious work called 'The Song of the Alphabet', which uses a highly complex system to indicate the number of times each letter of the alphabet appears in the Bible. The Masoretes who preceded Sa'adyah had counted the occurrences of each letter and invented a double mnemonic device for remembering the number of their appearances. Sa'adyah's contribution was to turn the early list into an extremely abstruse poem with many structural constraints. Let us look at a small sample:

עומדים כמחלקותיהם
קציני עדה הם
באָרך וברחב להם
אברהם לזכרון פיהם

---

[26] Ibid. 281.   [27] Ibid. 281–2.

> They stand according to their divisions
> They are officers of the congregation
> Having length and width
> A remembrance of Abraham in their mouths.

The solution to this riddle is as follows: the number of times that the letter *ayin* (the initial letter of the first word in this stanza) appears in the Bible is 20,175. This number is hinted at twice: once through the numerical value of the first letters of all the words in the first two lines, other than the first word in the first line: *kaf* (20,000) + *kuf* (100) + *ayin* (70) + *heh* (5) = 20,175, and again with an allusion to two biblical verses, one (Ezek. 48: 18) that includes the word 'length' and in which the number 10,000 occurs twice, and another (Gen. 25: 7) that specifies Abraham's age at the time of his death as being 175, which, added to 10,000 + 10,000, equals 20,175.[28]

In a more accessible type of composition Sa'adyah stretches the bounds of *piyut* in yet another direction—these are the *bakashot*, intended for individuals who wish to add an optional supplication to the fixed obligatory prayers. Such prayers express deep religious feeling, using relatively simple prose, in a language closely resembling that of the standard liturgy, without the elaborately clever wordplay of the *paitanim*. In this case, too, Sa'adyah did not create the literary genre itself—which had probably been introduced by his elder contemporary R. Nisi al-Nahrawani—but rather developed and expanded it as was his wont. We do not know precisely how many optional prayers in prose form Sa'adyah composed and the attribution of some of them is questionable, but there is no doubt that his most important works of this type are the two *bakashot* included in his prayer book. These circulated very widely and enjoyed extraordinary status: some congregations treated them almost like standard prayers, many people learned them by heart, and some even wondered whether it might be proper to stand while reciting them as when reciting the Amidah.[29] Sa'adyah explains his motives in composing the *bakashot* as follows:

And anyone who wishes to add an optional prayer should recite the Eighteen Benedictions [i.e. the weekday Amidah] several times . . . and if he wishes to add an optional supplication let him recite it by night or by day. And because I have seen the paucity of understanding in this matter and feared that the suppliant, instead of drawing nearer to his Master, would be alienated from him because of some mistake in speech, I have composed two versions of a *bakashah*, which include praises and reverence offered to God and meekness on the part of man, and acknowledgment of his sinfulness and a plea for forgiveness and for success in worldly matters as well as for the comfort of the nation and

[28]   See Malter, *Saadia Gaon*, 154–7; Stein, 'Saadya's Piyyut on the Alphabet' (the quotation is from p. 213, translation on p. 218); cf. Zulay, *Sa'adyah Gaon's Poetical School* (Heb.), 280–8. This poem is discussed very briefly by Tobi in *Sa'adyah Gaon's Liturgical Poems* (Heb.), i. 41–2.

[29]   See Tobi, *Sa'adyah Gaon's Liturgical Poems* (Heb.), i. 17–21.

its redemption. And one version I made harder and stronger than the other, so that the lighter one would serve for sabbaths and festivals and days of rejoicing, and the harder and stronger one for fast days and the like.[30]

Examples of the two *bakashot* follow here, first a selection from the 'lighter' version, which mainly offers praise of the Creator and which ends with matters concerning the individual and the community:

You are the Lord God who gives life to all, for in You is the source of life. The Lord who rules the world in his might, Your eyes are everywhere, no man can conceal himself where You will not see him, no person can escape Your spirit, and where can he run from You? Sovereign who loves justice, who establishes righteousness, and in whom there is no injustice, who will not show favour or accept bribery, what You imagine comes to pass, and what You counsel shall stand. Your voice hews out flames of fire, and Your spirit breaks the mountains and shatters the rocks, and Your word will not be in vain until it does what You have willed and performs Your behest. You who examine hearts, and inspect kidneys and reveal the innermost chambers of the abdomen . . .

You lead forth one generation and install another, dethroning kings and enthroning them, bringing low the mighty and raising up the lowly, taking life from the living and reviving the dead, impoverishing the rich and enriching the poor, raising the destitute from the dust, the wretched from the dungheap, sating the hungry and slaking those who thirst, clothing the naked and making upright those who are bowed down, and supporting the fallen and releasing the fettered, and causing the blind to see and the mute to sing, and fulfilling the needy and fecundating the barren and opening the womb, birthing after withholding, repairing after crushing, binding after breaking, near to those who are broken, salvation of the oppressed, lover of those who walk in humility, hater of the prideful, drawing nigh the distant and welcoming those who return.

Forgiver of iniquity and atoner of sins, remitter of offences, full of loving-kindness for the good and for evildoers, forbearing with the righteous, requiting the culpable with Your beneficence, and answering in any time of trouble those who go to sea in ships, or lose their way in the wilderness, prisoners of poverty and iron, invalids on their sick bed, those too weak to flee their pursuers, those facing the ferocity of beasts, those struck dumb in times of turmoil, strangers and foreigners in an alien land, those who live in a land where the sword shall strike them, those who tend the vineyards and fields when dew and rain cease to fall, the gazelle that yearns for streams of water, the ibex that crouches when it births its young, the raven when its chicks cry to God. And the cry of all will be heard at once, and in the twinkling of an eye You will save them all, for You are a gracious and merciful God, forbearing, full of loving-kindness, and repenting You of harshness.[31]

And now a section of the 'stronger' *bakashah*, which deals mainly with man's negligibility, his supplications and prayers for forgiveness, and his atonement:

---

[30] Assaf et al., *Sa'adyah Gaon's Siddur* (Heb.), 45–6.   [31] Ibid. 53–5.

If with repentance and confession You are appeased, I repent and confess and say before You: I have sinned to You O God, and I have sinned and transgressed and rebelled against You, and departed from Your ordinances and commandments, and distorted righteousness and I am unworthy.

And if my broken spirit will atone, I stand before You with broken heart and a spirit brought low with troubles and travail which I in my iniquity endured until I had no more healthy flesh, and what more can torment me, if for one brief moment Your hand should will it, I shall be no more. Or if You should desist from me I shall be as one fallen into a pit.

And if in my tears and crying out You shall forgive, lo my soul cries in hidden places over my many sins, and in chambers my spirit moans over all my iniquities. And if I had the strength my eyes would fill with unceasing tears until the tears destroy my eyes, because of this.

And if through prayer and supplication will You have mercy, I pray before You. And as the eyes of a slave implore his master, so do mine implore You.

And if I could stand thus I would stand before You all the days of my life. And You Lord know that the body You created is frail and its intelligence is feeble, and the leavening in the dough is evil.

Therefore O Lord our God, if I have acted according to my foolishness and sinfulness, do according to Your wisdom and absolve me, for Your wisdom is pure, and if I have requited good with evil, do requite my evil with good, for the righteous man is above others and how much more so the Creator.

And if I have sinned greatly, You are great in loving-kindness and great in forgiveness and frequently to be appeased, whose righteousness is greater than the mountains of the Lord, deeper than the great abyss, covering the firmament with Your glory and filling the earth with Your grandeur. God, I have heard of You that through one of these qualities You will grant forgiveness for one who has sinned before You, and more so through all of them. Forgive my sins and transgressions and the iniquities of Your people Israel and their sins, and cleanse me of my sins and purify me of my transgressions. And do not hold them against me forever, as You have said, 'For I am merciful says the Lord, I will not bear grudge forever' [Jer. 3: 12], and be not greatly angered with me and do not remember my iniquities forever.[32]

It is difficult to assess the extent of Sa'adyah's influence on poets who came after him and there are quite a few scholarly debates about this. In terms of his grammatical theories and return to the Bible, he may be viewed as heralding a revolution that would begin some time later on Spanish soil; yet his specific linguistic ideas never took root and the poets of Spain rejected on principle many of the morphological innovations that he was so fond of (in favour of more 'modern' linguistic theories). As concerns content, Sa'adyah deserves much credit for introducing philosophical and personal dimensions to certain genres of *piyut* (primarily the *bakashot* and several of the types of poetic expansion for Yom

---

[32] Assaf et al., *Sa'adyah Gaon's Siddur* (Heb.), 72–3.

Kippur). From a structural perspective, too, his influence in these genres was considerable. Some of his other compositions were widely imitated and had an important impact, particularly his *sidrei avodah* and *azharot*. A few of his innovations in the areas of rhyme and structure took root, but perhaps the most profound impact of his poetics was in the undermining of long-held conventions and the laying of a groundwork for future experimentation and innovation. From this point of view, the implications of dispensing with rhyme in his *tokhaḥah* were as far-reaching as the convoluted structure of *Esa meshali*. His endeavours in the field of poetry brought new life and originality to an area that had been on the verge of collapse under the yoke of a glorious past, and contributed to the dawn of a new era on Spanish soil.

CHAPTER SEVEN

༺ༀ༻

Sa'adyah, the Man of Halakhah

IN THE PREVIOUS CHAPTERS I explored Sa'adyah's activities in diverse fields which lay beyond the traditional purview of the geonim and the leading rabbinic sages of his day, where he showed a remarkable innovativeness in the very decision to pursue these subjects in a systematic way. Yet he also found ample room to leave his mark within the traditional domains of the Talmud and halakhah. My survey of Sa'adyah's writings and contributions to this field will be presented in two parts: first I examine the variety of genres and structures that he employed, and then their talmudic and halakhic contents. As we have seen, Sa'adyah frequently incorporated halakhic and aggadic elements drawn from the Talmud and midrash in different genres, particularly in his *piyutim* and biblical commentaries. The present chapter will examine those works that deal primarily with the Talmud and halakhah.

The Variety of Literary Genres

As far as we know, the only literary activity in which the Babylonian geonim before Sa'adyah's time engaged was the writing of responsa. In this particular field, the material that has come down to us from Sa'adyah himself is limited to about thirty or forty responsa—in contrast to more than 500 by the prominent mid-ninth-century gaon, Natronai ben Hilai, and over 1,000 by Hai ben Sherira Gaon in the early eleventh century. This disparity is most probably due to the waning of the Sura academy in the period before Sa'adyah's appointment and its weakening ties with the Jews of the diaspora. Another factor was the prolonged feud between Sa'adyah and the exilarch David ben Zakai that interfered with Sa'adyah's administration of the academy for much of his term.

No exceptional features distinguish the responsa of Sa'adyah Gaon from those of his predecessors, although in certain respects, such as his frequent references to biblical passages, they are somewhat innovative. This should not come as a surprise, since the centuries-old responsum tradition, unlike most of the genres that Sa'adyah engaged in, had its own set of literary conventions, and as a newly appointed gaon responsible for answering queries he had little leeway with regard to their structure. We should also bear in mind that the responsa were composed in the name of the senior scholars of the academy and with their consent, and this no doubt also contributed to the conservative style of the genre.

Many of Sa'adyah's responsa were originally written in Arabic, though most have come down to us in Hebrew translation. He was not the first gaon to answer enquiries in Arabic, since responsa were normally written in the language of the addressee. Sa'adyah's frequent use of Arabic was thus less a matter of personal choice than a reflection of cultural realities (on the other hand, there is no clear evidence in his responsa of a free use of Aramaic, which may well have been a matter of personal inclination).

Often, in Sa'adyah's responsa, we find him conducting a systematic analysis of principles in order to arrive at a practical solution for the specific case under discussion. Such an approach was not unprecedented among his predecessors in the geonate, but it is relatively more common in Sa'adyah's responsa, which in this respect are markedly similar to his writings in other areas. Beyond his analytical mindset in general, we find the familiar tendency to present numbered lists (of laws, considerations, and so forth) in his responsa. This was a stylistic feature that he seems to have introduced to the genre, a paradigm followed by some of his successors.

Let us take as an example one of Sa'adyah's responsa which has reached us in a Hebrew translation from the Arabic, and which is illustrative of his way of thinking and writing. The question in this case reflects the economic circumstances of the day, the flourishing of international trade and the many ventures undertaken in partnership, either ad hoc for a specific transaction limited in time, or long-term for a wide variety of financial enterprises. The long- or short-term nature of the partnership largely parallels the distinction between active partners, referred to in this case as Simon and Levi, and investors, like the Reuben and Judah of the case (actual names in enquiries addressed to the geonic academies were usually replaced with standard biblical names, particularly the names of the tribes of Israel). The discussion reflects an important halakhic development, known from a variety of geonic sources, involving the substitution of a kind of conditional curse called a *gezerah* for an oath in God's name. The questioner here asks about the status of such a *gezerah* relative to 'swearing by the Torah':

Reuben gave Simon and his partner Levi funds to use in a profitable business, and Judah also gave them funds. And Simon and Levi paid Reuben an appropriate amount of the profit on a regular basis. And later Reuben wished to withdraw his capital and Simon and Levi returned it to him and he was repaid in full. And subsequently the king confiscated all the assets of Simon and Levi together with Judah's funds which they had in their keeping. Judah then sued Reuben and told him: 'You are the partner of Simon and Levi, so return my funds for you are obligated to give them to me.' Reuben said: 'I was not their partner but had an investment [*iskah*] with them and have already been repaid by them and I have had no connection with them for some days,' and Simon and Levi acknowledge this. And nevertheless some people arranged a compromise between them, and Reuben swore to Judah by means of a *gezerah* that he is not in possession of any funds belonging to Simon and Levi and they are not partners, and this was satisfactory to Judah. And later . . . he changed his mind and sued Reuben a second time, saying, 'Swear to me by the Torah because I have heard that you do not consider a *gezerah* to be a binding oath.' Would it please our master to instruct us as to whether Reuben is obligated or not.[1]

Sa'adyah responded as follows:

If what transpired between Reuben and Simon and Levi and Judah is as described in this question, Judah has no claim on Reuben on account of Simon and Levi, inasmuch as the two partners who handled the funds are Simon and Levi, but Reuben and Judah are the investors, and no connection is created between them because of this . . . for, according to the law, both Reuben and Judah are lenders and depositors only, not partners . . . and since it is known that half the funds of an *iskah* are treated as a loan and half as a deposit . . . the investor of the money is exempt from any claims against the one who handles the funds, because one who deposits funds with another is not liable for the debts of the one who holds the funds and a lender is not liable for the debts of his debtor . . . it is clear that Judah was legally in the wrong to claim from Reuben the debts that Simon and Levi owed him. Moreover, it was not fitting for those who arranged a compromise to mediate between them when they knew that they were not parties to a case, as is written in the Torah: 'And I charged your judges at the time saying: Hear the causes between your brethren and judge righteously between a man and his brother' [Deut. 1: 16]. In other words, hear [the causes] from the parties themselves and not from the mouths of others, and, as it is said, 'Let us choose judgment for us; Let us know among ourselves what is good' [Job 34: 4]. And furthermore, not content to hear what they said, they imposed a *gezerah* on Reuben wrongly and unjustly . . .

And as for Judah who arraigned Reuben once again, after he had accepted a *gezerah* that was not required of him, and who said, 'Swear to me by the Torah for I have heard that you do not consider a *gezerah* to be an oath,' his words are flawed in many ways: for one, he had already received from him more than his due, and he was entitled only to pronounce an anonymous ban against anyone who is in partnership with Simon and Levi and does not acknowledge this, yet he imposed a *gezerah*; and secondly, in wanting to make him swear on the Torah and failing to realize that the *gezerah* was on the Book; and thirdly, he imagines that the *gezerah* is only effective against a person who considers it an oath, whereas it is indeed effective against anyone who lies, whether he considers it an oath or not, which is comparable to the fire that burns both one who believes it burns and one who does not, or iron that cuts both one who believes it cuts and one who does not, as it is written, 'Is not my word like as fire? Saith the Lord, and like a hammer that breaketh the rock in pieces' [Jer. 23: 29]. Be that as it may, it is most assuredly incumbent as an oath upon any son of Israel who accepts a *gezerah*, because a *gezerah* is an imprecation . . . and in many places an imprecation is called an oath . . . thus it is clear that

---

[1] *Sha'arei tsedek* (ed. Modai), book 4, sect. 2, no. 38.

Scripture calls an imprecation an oath; and therefore anyone who acknowledges that he is a Jew is constrained by the *gezerah* and is obliged by it when he accepts it or when it is imposed on him, just as an oath constrains him when he swears it or when he is forsworn. And this is the answer to the question.

Sa'adyah concludes that Reuben is not responsible for the deeds of Simon and Levi because he was not a full partner in their business but merely an investor of funds for the purpose of a certain transaction. Consequently, Reuben is not a party to the litigation between Judah and Simon and Levi, and he should not have been required to swear an oath. All the same, when an oath is required by law, swearing by a *gezerah* is sufficient and it is binding on a person who swears by it regardless of his personal beliefs as long as he 'acknowledges that he is a Jew'.

Although he more or less adhered to the formulaic style of the tradition in his responsa, in other, related, areas Sa'adyah broke new ground. I shall consider his works on exegesis and the classification of the *mitsvot* before returning to his revolutionary contribution to the more narrowly defined field of halakhic literature.

There is insufficient reason to suppose that Sa'adyah wrote systematic commentaries on sections of the Talmud. On the other hand, we know from various testimonies that he wrote a commentary on the six orders of the Mishnah, which was primarily a kind of lexicon. This commentary included, according to one source, 'an explanation of difficult words in all six orders of the Mishnah'.[2] In effect, it straddled the boundary between exegesis and lexicography, and he would only have had to alphabetize the entries to turn the book into a (selective) dictionary of mishnaic language. There are many other such works in the Cairo Genizah, glossaries or lexical commentaries on certain writings, mainly Arabic commentaries on Hebrew texts, especially on parts of Scripture. The commentaries are arranged in the order of the explicated text and are meant to guide and assist readers or students to overcome the obstacles that they were likely to encounter at a lexical level.

Over fifty years ago some Genizah fragments of lexical commentary on the Mishnah were published and, on the basis of manuscript evidence, identified as parts of Sa'adyah's work. Although the attribution was disputed by scholars on several grounds, especially because the fragments included words considered 'too easy' to require explanation, Sa'adyah's authorship has now been virtually established in light of other, as yet unpublished, Genizah discoveries.[3] Based on this identification, we are able to describe the general style of Sa'adyah's commentary on the Mishnah. It is principally a translation of words and phrases into Arabic, typically in one or two words or, more rarely, by means of slightly longer glosses. Sometimes alternative explanations are offered in anonymous fashion with

---

[2] See Brody, *The Geonim of Babylonia*, 268, and the sources cited in n. 4 ad loc.

[3] Ibid. 269 and nn. 6–7.

expressions such as the Arabic term *wa-yuqal* (and it is said). Sa'adyah avoids discussing the subject matter beyond what is required to clarify words and phrases in the explicated text, and cites no references to support his proposed definitions. Notwithstanding the relative dearth of commentary, his endeavour to compose a systematic and comprehensive explanation of a rabbinic work was a remarkable innovation that cleared the way for the geonim who came after him to expand and develop the genre. Prior to this time numerous exegetical responsa had been issued by various geonim, but they were answers to specific queries rather than continuous self-initiated commentaries (albeit the large number of expressions that people enquired about would sometimes result in a commentary of sorts).

In addition to his commentary on the Mishnah, which constitutes an independent and sizable treatise, Sa'adyah produced a commentary on another work of more limited scope: the well-known *Baraita derabi yishma'el*, a listing of the thirteen principles of biblical exegesis. This *baraita* was copied at the beginning of the *Sifra*, the tannaitic commentary on Leviticus, though it does not form part of it. Sa'adyah consequently comments on it within the framework of his commentary on Leviticus, and this unit was later copied and even translated into Hebrew as a separate entity. In addition to pithy definitions of each of the thirteen principles, the text provides examples (taken largely from rabbinic literature) of the application of these principles.[4]

Another work which strictly speaking does not belong to Sa'adyah's talmudic and halakhic writings is his *Sefer hamitsvot* (Book of the Commandments).[5] This is one of the first compositions in a genre that flourished in the Middle Ages in the wake of Rabbi Simlai's famous statement (BT *Mak.* 23*b*) that the biblical commandments number 613, of which 365 are negative and 248 positive. Many writers attempted to identify the *taryag* or 613 *mitsvot* and to classify them according to various systems, usually with allusions to their biblical sources, and some writers added considerable information about the traditions associated with each particular commandment. Sa'adyah wrote a preface to the monograph in which he set forth his principles—familiar from other writings, particularly the third chapter of *The Book of Beliefs and Opinions*—on the need for the commandments, the division between rational and non-rational commandments, the relationship between Divine *mitsvot* and the moral sensibility imprinted in human intelligence, and so forth. In the body of the monograph, he divided the commandments into twenty-six categories with a special chapter devoted to each, delineating them and briefly summarizing their biblical sources. Here, for example, is a short chapter in its entirety:

The fourth chapter consists of obligations incumbent on [a certain] place, and these are five, two of which pertain to every individual of the nation—one, he must enclose his

---

[4] Brody, *The Geonim of Babylonia*, 277 and nn. 40–2. Zucker has pointed out that this text is part of Sa'adyah's commentary on Leviticus; see Zucker, 'Fragments' (Heb.), 374 and n. 12.

rooftop [with a parapet] and keep his home free from danger, and of this it is said, 'When thou buildest a new house, then thou shalt make a parapet for thy roof' [Deut. 22: 8]; and the second, to write a portion of the Torah and affix it to the top third of the doorway of his home as it is written: 'And thou shalt write them upon the door-posts of thy house and upon thy gates' [Deut. 6: 9]. And the other three pertain to the nation as a whole, and these include giving the Levites forty-eight cities throughout the land in which to live, as it is written, 'All the cities which ye shall give to the Levites [shall be forty-eight cities]' [Num. 35: 7]; and to dedicate six of them as cities of refuge so that manslayers who have killed unintentionally might flee there and remain for a time, as it is written, 'And the cities which ye shall give unto the Levites they shall be six [cities of refuge]' [Deut. 35: 6]; and that no fields belonging to the Levites shall be sold although it is permitted for them to sell their houses, as it is written, 'But the fields of the open land about their cities may not [be sold for that is their perpetual possession]' [Lev. 25: 34].[6]

Halakhic Monographs

Sa'adyah's aptitude in the realm of halakhah found its principal expression in a new type of work: systematic monographs on selected legal topics, which represent a revolutionary departure in the history of rabbinic literature. Before Sa'adyah's time we find three main models: the central works of the classical rabbinic corpus (Mishnah, Talmud, midrash, etc.) are collective in nature and were composed by a number of sages, some well known and others anonymous.

In this respect there is much in common between the classical corpus and the few works dealing with talmudic and halakhic subjects which were composed during the geonic era before Sa'adyah, most notably the three books, *She'iltot*, *Halakhot pesukot*, and *Halakhot gedolot*. The *She'iltot* is a collection of homilies, most probably composed by a number of preachers according to a traditional paradigm. The two halakhic books (and other similar but lesser-known works) follow the order of the Babylonian Talmud for the most part, selecting some of its principal traditions and combining them with post-talmudic formulations based on the Mishnah and the Talmud. *Halakhot pesukot* is indeed a collective work and even *Halakhot gedolot*, the creation of an identifiable but essentially unknown writer named Shimon Kayara, sticks so closely to earlier sources (particularly the Talmud, the *She'iltot*, and the *Halakhot pesukot*) that it is difficult to view it as the work of an individual in the fullest sense.[7]

The most 'individual' form of writing produced during these centuries was the responsa, which occupied a sort of no-man's-land between literature and adminis-

---

[5] The most important discussion to date is Scheiber, 'Book of Commandments' (Heb.). A nearly complete edition of the text, by H. Sabato and N. Sabato, is in an advanced stage of preparation.   [6] Scheiber, 'Book of Commandments' (Heb.), 332–3.

[7] See Brody, *The Geonim of Babylonia*, 202–30.

trative documentation—although, as mentioned above, this was not an individual activity, strictly speaking, either. Not only were the topics dictated by the enquirer, but the responding gaon answered in the name of the scholars of his academy, who did in fact participate in the preparation of responsa, though to what extent is difficult to determine.

In the new monographs we find, for the first time, systematic writing initiated by an individual author, who assumes responsibility not merely for the content of the text (which was largely determined by talmudic sources) but for its structure and organization. He selected the contents to be included and in some cases had to decide between various interpretations of talmudic sources, or different possibilities raised in the Talmud.

These monographs share a number of structural features, most prominently, their language of composition, Judaeo-Arabic (other than citations in Hebrew and Aramaic from rabbinic and biblical sources, and to a lesser degree, as required by the text, from prayers, legal documents and so forth). There may be two complementary reasons for this: the desire to reach a relatively broad audience that included readers less than fluent in Hebrew and Aramaic, and the fact that the genre had been developed in a Muslim cultural milieu against a background of scientific writing in Arabic (although Sa'adyah improved and developed the existing models of his day).

The influence of Arabic and Islamic culture on these monographs is evident with respect to other structural elements as well, beginning with the titles—the names of earlier works of rabbinic literature had come from their readers and not from their authors or editors. Each monograph contains an introduction, also a departure from Jewish literary convention; with the possible exception of *Halakhot gedolot*, no other work of rabbinic literature before Sa'adyah's time had been provided with an introduction. Following the Arabic model, the introductions open with the praises of God before proceeding to prefatory remarks on the subject of the work. The transition is signalled by the Arabic words *amma ba'du* (literally 'but afterwards') in the sense of 'and now to the matter at hand.' The writer's main challenge was to select praises relevant to the content of the work as a whole and to segue as smoothly as possible from the first to the second part of his introduction. Below, for example, is how Sa'adyah begins his *Book of Testimony and Legal Documents*:

The collector said ... praised be the God of Israel, Truth in clarity, creator of truth as the noblest form of knowledge. But afterwards: truth is what is established in minds that are free of defect, and affirmed by those who behave in accordance with it. And of this definition, well known among scholars, it is written, 'They are all plain to him that understandeth' [Prov. 8: 9] and so forth. And I have found that the first thing required by truth is the belief that the compass of the universe and its centre have a Creator ... and then that His rational commandments and rational prohibitions and the approval of the good and the prevention of what is evil are also truth, and therefore it is said, 'The beginning of Thy word is truth' [Ps. 119: 160]. And then, that His non-rational commandments that are transmitted to us by the prophets are all truth, and thus it is written, 'Thou art nigh, O Lord, and all Thy commandments are truth' [Ps. 119: 151]. And from the non-rational commandments I proceed to the civil laws, for I have discovered that Scriptures speak of 'truth' more often with regard to them than to the other commandments, as is written: 'Thus hath the Lord of Hosts spoken, saying "Execute true judgement"' [Zekh. 7: 9] and so forth.

And I say, too, that those who examine this book will be greatly amazed that it [judgment] is called 'truth', and will ask: how so—for it is based on the words of the parties and revolves around the testimony of witnesses, and what party will claim something or answer a claim without the possibility arising that he will not find the words to express what he intended to say? And likewise, is any witness able to testify to what took place in his presence without the possibility arising that he has condensed or expanded his story . . . and if these two things form the root [of judgment], in what way should its branches be considered truth? Moreover, as to the question of witnesses there is an even greater flaw than the inability to relate [a story in words] and that is that witnesses may be prepared to express outwardly the opposite of what they conceal [in their hearts], and the judge will believe them to be speaking the truth while they are in fact lying to him, and this removes the judgment even further from truth.

[In view of that] I must, in the introduction of this section, resolve any doubts that may lodge in the reader's heart, and say to him: the Lord, may He be praised and magnified, requires the judge not to believe that what the witnesses say is [necessarily] true, but to decide in accordance with the testimony of two witnesses, while being aware that the two may be lying, just as they may be speaking the truth. But [he must believe] that the Lord would not have commanded [i.e. sanctioned] the judgment of the law on the basis of two [witnesses] unless the party being condemned was guaranteed compensation for any money which he should be wrongly penalized on the basis of their testimony, and the pleasures of the world to come to anyone who might be put to death in this world, if such a thing is caused by the two [witnesses]. And it is the judge's obligation to carry out the laws of God as He commanded, and to believe in the principle that He who commanded them did so in His wisdom. But it is necessary that the law should be decided on the basis of [the testimony of] witnesses.[8]

The last part of the introduction sets forth the contents of the book and, in the fully developed monographic model, includes a detailed table of contents in the form of a numbered list of chapters and headings. As we shall presently see, this technique developed gradually and Sa'adyah may well have been the first writer in human history to make use of it! But even his introductions to earlier monographs, which are arranged less systematically, include at least a general survey of the book's contents and of the manner of its division.

The internal organization of the halakhic monographs clearly distinguishes them from the talmudic model. The style of talmudic literature is associative,

[8] For the Arabic text see Ben Sasson, 'Fragments' (Heb.), 163–7.

dealing with topics in varied and unpredictable contexts. The authors of such works as *Halakhot pesukot* and *Halakhot gedolot* saw fit to improve on the talmudic organization and increase the concentration of material focusing on a given topic, but their order of presentation was still largely determined by the Talmud. In contrast, Sa'adyah and his successors freed themselves entirely from the talmudic style and order of presentation, and aimed at organizing halakhic material in a logical and 'scientific' manner, proceeding from basic terms to a consideration of the most complex cases. This analytical mode of division was also applied to individual chapters or sections, and often included numbered lists of cases or categories.

The inclination to structure material in a 'scientific' manner was consonant with Sa'adyah's thinking and writing in all genres, and finds a particularly interesting expression in his *Book of Testimony and Legal Documents*. Here the type of material—legal documents—would seem to require a separate discussion for each document, as was the practice among later generations of compilers. But Sa'adyah chose a different mode of procedure: he broke each document down into its components, and since the first and last clauses in almost all legal documents are repeated with comparatively minor variations, he concentrated their discussion in the general chapters at the beginning of the book. In his treatment of the individual legal documents, he presented only the distinctive middle sections, referring the reader to the standard beginning and ending sections found earlier in the book.

Sa'adyah's Method of Citation

In contrast to the far-reaching formal innovations stimulated by the surrounding non-Jewish culture which I have described, the influence of this culture on the contents of Sa'adyah's halakhic writings (unlike on his writings in the realms of philosophy, exegesis, and linguistics) is negligible. These monographs rely explicitly on rabbinic sources and frequently quote them. Having said that, Sa'adyah does not always cite his sources, and alongside statements supported by rabbinic quotations he sometimes introduces others without a reference, even though they, too, are based on rabbinic literature. Perhaps he did not quote his sources when this would have obliged him to expand his discussion beyond what he deemed appropriate for the nature of the monograph.

An illustration of this, and of Sa'adyah's general style in his halakhic writings, can be found in the following section from *The Laws of Succession*, where Sa'adyah lists five potential circumstances in which a firstborn son forfeits the right of primogeniture:

The firstborn's right [to a double portion] is revoked under five circumstances—under four of them completely, and under the fifth to some extent. The explanation of the four circumstances under which it is revoked completely is as follows:

The first is that if the sons are born after their father's decease, the firstborn has no advantage over his brothers, as the Talmud says: 'Mar, the son of Yosef, said in the name of Rava: a firstborn son who is born after the death of his father does not receive a double portion. What is the reason for this? We need "he shall recognize him" and there is none.' [BT *BB* 142*b*; the reference is to Deut. 21: 17, which establishes the firstborn's right to a double portion, adding that the father must recognize him as his firstborn, which would be impossible in this case.] And the explanation is this: if a person dies and leaves three wives with child and one of them gives birth in the month of Nisan and the second in the month of Iyar and the third in the month of Sivan, or if each gives birth one day earlier than the others, if so, the one born first has no advantage over his brothers—this is the first exception.

And the second is that if the inheritance is from the mother, again, the firstborn has no advantage over the others, and if a woman dies and leaves children and one of them is the firstborn, he does not receive a double portion of the inheritance, as the Sages say: 'The firstborn receives a double portion of his father's possessions and does not inherit a double portion of his mother's possessions, for it is written, "for he is the first-fruits of his strength" [Deut 21: 17] and not "her strength"' (see pp. 136–7).

And the third: if the inheritance comes from the grandfather or another relative of the father from whom he would inherit, the firstborn has no advantage, and the explanation is this: if the father dies during the grandfather's lifetime and the grandfather dies after him and the inheritance falls to the grandsons and there is a firstborn among them, they divide it equally among themselves. And likewise, if an uncle dies . . . or if one of the kin of the father from whom he is qualified to inherit dies after the father's death, then his sons inherit him equally, and the firstborn has no advantage in this.

And the fourth: if he has already divided up the inheritance and taken only one portion of something belonging to his father's possessions, if he did this without making a claim [pertaining to his birthright] and without saying, 'In this I have relinquished [my share] to you,' then he has forgone the birthright portion with respect to all the property and will have no advantage in it.[9]

Sa'adyah cites authorities for three of the above four cases but not for the third,[10] which relates to property inherited from a relative of the father after the father's death. The reason for this omission is that the ruling is impossible to derive from an isolated talmudic source. It is based on the principle that 'the firstborn does not

---

[9] See Müller, *The Book of Inheritance* (Heb.), 15–16 (where the talmudic sources are lacking); a corrected edition will be included in Brody, *Sa'adyah Gaon's Halakhic Works* (Heb.).

[10] I have not cited the third source here (that relating to Sa'adyah's fourth point) as it is more complex and would have required a lengthy chunk of the text to be copied in.

receive property that will accrue to the estate but only the estate as it is [at the time of the owner's death]', together with the clarification that property inherited 'through' the father from a more distant relative falls in the category of property that will accrue to the estate, and Sa'adyah preferred to dispense with such an argument.

The exceptions to this style of writing—in which most halakhic statements, though not all, are supported by citations—are few within the genre. At least one represents a real departure, but the other that we know of is only an 'optical illusion', that is, an impression based on an abridged version which omitted the citations of sources found in the original. The most conspicuous exception is Sa'adyah's prayer book, where he himself explains almost apologetically that he intended it as a practical guide rather than a theoretical text:

> And concerning everything under this heading, I shall not undertake to present evidence in its support from Scripture nor any proof from the masters of tradition, that is, from what is in the Mishnah and the Talmud, but will state everything in simple but precise terms, because I have not composed this work to serve as proof but [merely] as an aid to learning and understanding.[11]

The Laws of Succession

The 'optical illusion' that I have mentioned above refers to Sa'adyah's *Laws of Succession*, the first of his halakhic monographs to receive scholarly attention: the famous bibliographer M. Steinschneider discovered a manuscript of this work in the Bodleian Library, and an edition based on it was published towards the end of the nineteenth century. That version contained no talmudic references. Today, however, in light of the fragments discovered in the Cairo Genizah, it is clear that this is merely the abridged version of an original text that provided biblical and rabbinic citations as do Sa'adyah's other monographs (as exemplified by the quotation given above).[12]

Our knowledge of the extent of Sa'adyah's halakhic oeuvre comes from a fairly wide range of sources that include book lists found in the Genizah, citations in the works of later writers (starting with the last geonim and ending with medieval European authors), and cross-references found in Sa'adyah's own writings. Hundreds of fragments belonging to these have survived in the Genizah and the work of cataloguing them and preparing them for print is still in progress. Following is an overview list of the works known to us at present.

Although *The Laws of Succession* was first published in an abridged form, it is now possible to reconstruct most of the original text, including the author's talmudic and biblical sources, on the basis of the Genizah fragments. Moreover, quite a few fragments of a medieval Hebrew translation have been discovered

---

11 Assaf et al., *Sa'adyah Gaon's Siddur* (Heb.), 11–12.

12 See Abramson, *Topics in Geonic Literature* (Heb.), 232–3.

in the Genizah and here, too, we find the talmudic sources cited (although the translator abridged the text in other ways). The first and main part of the work deals with the basic laws of succession. Following the model of the biblical and mishnaic passages concerning this subject,[13] it is carefully organized into four numbered sections and further subsections according to the degree of kinship between the heir and the deceased. The second part of the book discusses the rights of heirs under various circumstances as well as doubtful cases in the division of property. It also contains a kind of appendix devoted to the manner of apportioning the possessions of the deceased (including detailed but not always accurate calculations of the areas of different geometric figures).

Sa'adyah begins his book with the statement that property may be transferred from one person to another in one of three ways: through inheritance, gift, or sale. This already suggests that he will not limit the discussion to the laws of succession but will broaden his canvas to include the laws of sales and gifts. One medieval author does indeed refer to a composition by Sa'adyah on the laws of gifts, and a Hebrew work by another medieval author based on this book appears to have been preserved.[14] However, no fragments of the original composition have as yet been discovered in the Genizah—possibly because the subject was seldom studied, and those who copied such works preferred the more comprehensive monograph on gifts by the Gaon Samuel ben Hofni. Sa'adyah's book on the laws of sales was not known at all from the writings of European sages, but it is mentioned in the preface to Hai ben Sherira Gaon's famous monograph on the laws of sales, *The Book of Buying and Selling*, in which he explains, somewhat apologetically, why he has seen fit to return to a subject already treated by his predecessor:

And the Fayyumite head of the academy [Sa'adyah Gaon], may God have mercy on him, appended to his book on the laws of succession fair words about sales and especially about the sale of land, and it might have been left [at that], making what I write about this [matter] superfluous; but I saw many things to which he refers without explaining them fully and I wished to clarify them further, seeing that such an arrangement would be of benefit to people in our day.[15]

Judging by the few surviving fragments of Sa'adyah's monograph in the Genizah, it seems that in this case, too, copyists (and translators) preferred the later and more comprehensive treatment to Sa'adyah's pioneering work.

The Book of Bailments and *The Book of Testimony and Legal Documents*

In addition to the above trilogy, segments of two other works by Sa'adyah on civil law have been published: *The Book of Bailments* and *The Book of Testimony and*

---

[13] Num. 27: 8–11 and Mishnah *Bava Batra*, which adds the category of the father's inheritance.
[14] See Brody, *The Geonim of Babylonia*, 256–7 and n. 30.
[15] Abramson, 'From the Arabic Original' (Heb.), 297.

Legal Documents. Only a few fragments of *The Book of Bailments* have been published so far by researchers, but I have succeeded in reconstructing it almost entirely and it is due to be published soon.

The first section of *The Book of Bailments* deals with disputes between a bailor and a bailee concerning the nature of their association. The various cases are divided into five categories in descending order, from outright denial on the part of the 'bailee' that he received goods from the bailor in trust to conflicting assertions about the amount entrusted. In this section of the book there is hardly any material specific to the laws of bailment, and consequently Sa'adyah refers the reader to a previous discussion of his on claims in general. He writes as follows: 'As we have explained in *The Laws of Claims and Oaths*, and provided evidence for each of the categories with proof from Scripture and from tradition which we need not mention here'. The book to which he is alluding here was previously unknown; thus, based on *The Book of Bailments*, it is now also possible to ascertain the existence of an earlier work on civil law by Sa'adyah.

The second part of the book treats disputes arising between two parties concerning the way in which a bailment has been lost. This is the halakhic essence of the book and many times longer than the preceding section. On the other hand, its overall structure is far looser than that of the first part: it is not divided systematically into numbered subsections, and the level of organization in the various sections is uneven. For example, in one instance Sa'adyah presents a numbered list of ten different ways in which a person may enter the category of 'paid bailee'; but when he itemizes the different types of negligence for which even the unpaid bailee is liable, he does not organize them in a carefully constructed or numbered list. He introduces all but the first with the words 'and another case of negligence', apparently in the order in which they occurred to him, without having decided in advance how many cases he would include in the list and in what order. Another noteworthy phenomenon is his inclusion in this part of the book of a discussion of biblical exegesis meant both to validate the position of the Sages about the relationship between two biblical pericopes dealing with bailees and to refute a conflicting interpretation, most probably by a Karaite author (see pp. 148–9 below).

Portions of *The Book of Testimony and Legal Documents* have been published by scholars over the years;[16] Menachem Ben-Sasson and I have recently prepared a comprehensive edition of the book, now in print,[17] which includes 85–90 per cent of the original monograph together with a Hebrew translation, preface, and notes. The book itself comprises an introduction and eight chapters, the first four dealing with testimony in general and the last four with legal documents, which may be viewed as a form of written testimony. The eighth chapter makes up the bulk of the book. After a brief introduction it is subdivided into fifty-four parts, each

[16] See Ben-Sasson, 'Fragments' (Heb.), 142–4.

[17] Ben-Sasson and Brody, *Saadia Gaon's Book of Testimony* (Heb.).

devoted to a specific document. The documents are arranged in three groups, eighteen documents in each, organized according to the principle that the most commonly used among them are in the first section, followed by a second section of less common documents, and a third and final section of even rarer ones—though in fact all of these are common, Sa'adyah explains, but some are more common than others.

It is worth noting that Sa'adyah presents the texts of these legal documents in Aramaic—one might say, almost pure Aramaic: an ancient tradition known to us from citations scattered throughout tannaitic literature and legal documents from the Bar Kokhba period discovered around the Dead Sea, as well as from other sources. Some aspects of this tradition go back even further and certain formulations in Sa'adyah's texts are reminiscent of Aramaic documents found in the Aswan region of Egypt dating from the fourth and fifth centuries BCE. Sa'adyah takes it for granted that documents in which witnesses record their testimony are always written in Aramaic, although the parties normally express themselves in Arabic. (Interestingly enough, there is no mention in this work of a class of scribes or professional witnesses, even though this was the accepted norm of his age, at least in Muslim society. Sa'adyah assumes that anyone might be asked to give evidence about legal actions at some point and should therefore know how to do so in writing.)

The third chapter of the monograph begins with the following words:

It goes without saying that a witness is required to understand what is included in each term [in the case] because this is the essence of his role, especially when translating from one language to another, as our nation does at this time, when many people testify in the Arabic language and [the witnesses] translate it into Aramaic, the language of the Targum.

Further on he provides several illustrations of this. Even though there is no halakhic imperative to write documents in a specific language, and despite the practical difficulties of doing so, Sa'adyah resolutely maintains the ancient tradition in this area (the only one in which he actually wrote in Aramaic). It should be noted in this regard that we have in our possession copies of judgments issued by Sa'adyah's rabbinical court and formulated as legal documents, and these, too, are written in fluent Aramaic.[18]

The Book of Testimony and Legal Documents appears to be the only one of Sa'adyah's halakhic monographs that can be dated. He illustrates the manner in which documents are dated using the publication date of his own work, 926 CE—two years before his appointment to the geonate of Sura. Being innovative in the genre of halakhic writing may have been necessary for the rabbinic scholar who was not yet a gaon, and therefore virtually prohibited from writing responsa, in

---

[18] Harkavy, *Responsa*, nos. 555–6; repr. in Müller, *The Book of Inheritance* (Heb.), 119–22.

order to have a say in halakhic matters. It is also possible that Sa'adyah's achievement as the author of monographs was a contributing factor in his subsequent appointment to the geonate. In his preface to the monograph he writes the following: 'This will form part of the *Book of Religious Law* that I intend to write, but I saw fit to give it precedence because I had become aware of the nation's great need for it, and saw how great its utility would be.' This statement has been interpreted by certain scholars as signifying that the work in question was Sa'adyah's earliest halakhic monograph. We know, however, that this trope was commonly used by writers of the period, and it should not be taken to mean that it was actually Sa'adyah's first book in the field, only that he gave it precedence over others that he planned to write in the future.

Judging by the fragments in our possession, *The Book of Testimony and Legal Documents* surpasses Sa'adyah's other halakhic monographs both in scope and in the highly developed organization of its material. It is hardly conceivable that after writing such a comprehensive and elaborate work, Sa'adyah would take a step backwards from his earlier achievements and devote himself to far less ambitious monographs in other realms of halakhah. The book thus appears to be Sa'adyah's last, or at least one of his last, halakhic books. The idea of writing a comprehensive work on halakhah may have developed gradually over time, gaining its full expression only in this late piece.

In the *Book of Testimony and Legal Documents* there are a number of allusions to a 'Book of Religious Law'. Sa'adyah sometimes refers the reader to it for a discussion of certain points of a more general nature; elsewhere he contents himself with noting that a given topic is beyond the scope of the present work. He may have intended to expand on these topics in *The Book of Religious Law*, but he apparently did not live to complete this book.

In addition to works on civil law, we know of other monographs by Sa'adyah that deal with three further areas of halakhah. Let us first mention a topic that falls between civil law and the laws of the permitted and the prohibited, namely, the prohibition against usury. The opening page of a composition attributed to Sa'adyah has been discovered in the Genizah, along with a number of other fragments possibly belonging to it, although the actual scope and character of the book still have to be ascertained. There are several references to a work by Sa'adyah on the laws of purity and impurity or menstruation. At least one unpublished fragment of a monograph by Sa'adyah on the laws of purity and impurity has been identified in the Genizah, apparently distinct from another monograph dealing specifically with the laws of menstruation, though this is yet to be confirmed.[19]

Perhaps Sa'adyah's most popular monographs in the area of halakhah concern the laws of preparing kosher meat, and two widely circulated compositions in this

---

[19] See Brody, *The Geonim of Babylonia*, 259 and n. 37; cf. Malter, *Saadia Gaon*, 348–9.

field are attributed to him. It was a subject of pressing concern in an era when there were no means of storing meat for extended periods or transporting it over long distances without spoilage, and its importance is reflected in numerous writings found in the Genizah that concern these laws. The large number of anonymous fragments dealing with ritual slaughter and the liberties taken by copyists and adapters of these compositions make it difficult to identify the fragments that belong to Sa'adyah's writings or to determine their original form. In any event, it is possible to reconstruct a large portion of at least one composition divided into five chapters: the first of these identifies permitted (kosher) species and those that are prohibited; the second deals with the laws of ritual slaughter; the third with the examination of an animal after slaughter for signs of disease which would render it *terefah* or prohibited; the fourth with the removal from the meat of certain fats, prohibited for consumption; the fifth with techniques of salting meat in order to purge it of remaining blood. The popularity enjoyed by this composition is manifest in a remarkable phenomenon: an anonymous writer took the trouble to compile an Arabic glossary of the Hebrew and Aramaic terms found in the book.[20]

Sa'adyah's Prayer Book

Finally, I will discuss one of Sa'adyah's most important and widely read works, the prayer book, which in some ways is a borderline halakhic monograph. Here again, we find evidence of his penchant for the fullest possible analytical division of the contents, as illustrated in his preface to the book:

The prayers, as I have said previously, are of two categories, one for the usual run of time [normal weekdays] and one for special times; and each of these is of two categories, one for individual prayer and one for communal prayer. And since all public prayers, whether at normal times or at special times, are expansions of individual prayers, we must first establish the simpler of the two categories, namely, the individual prayer; and similarly, since the prayer for special times is an expansion of the prayer for normal times, we must first establish the simpler of them, namely, the prayer used at normal times. In light of these premises we must begin from the prayer of the individual at normal times, because these two [conditions] are the simple ones. We begin by saying: the times when prayer is required are the morning, the afternoon, and the beginning of the night.[21]

The category of 'special times' is further divided into four categories: sabbath, Rosh Hodesh, festivals, and fast days—each of the latter two branching off into subcategories that correspond to the number of festivals and fasts. Sa'adyah's desire to organize material as logically and economically as possible (as in his treatment of legal documents) outweighs considerations of utility: he does not repeat anew in each of the categories the prayers that he has set down under the

---

20 A fragment of this glossary is found in MS Cambridge, T-S Ar. 25.56.
21 Assaf et al., *Sa'adyah Gaon's Siddur* (Heb.), 12.

previous headings, but limits himself to those phrases that are to be added or changed in the prayers in the special circumstances under discussion. Thus, a person engaged in communal prayer or praying on special days will be unable to find a continuous version of the appropriate prayers anywhere in the book and will be forced to skip from place to place in order to piece together the complete prayer that he is supposed to recite.

The liturgical texts are interwoven with halakhic formulations that deal not only with the prayers themselves but with other aspects of the special days (the kinds of work prohibited on the sabbath, regulations concerning leaven and matzah during Passover, and so forth). A noteworthy aspect of the prayer book is Sa'adyah's frequent critiquing of customs, as he emphasizes already in the preface. After expounding on his theory of the great antiquity of the standard prayer service and its transmission by the prophets in two versions, one suitable for the period of the monarchy and the other for the period of the exile (see p. 35), he writes:

[Therefore] it is necessary to collect the prayers and praises of the canon of our day, that is to say, the period of exile, and to set them down, especially in view of what has happened in our time in three respects: neglect, addition, and deletion. On account of this I am fearful that they may be lost from memory and changes will take root, for I have witnessed the severity of what happens in these three ways in the lands where I have journeyed and felt compelled to halt it . . . And thus I saw [fit] to assemble in this book the most important prayers and praises and blessings according to their ancient formulation as their foundations were before the exile and after it, and to canonize them. And after this I will add what I know to have been added or deleted by individuals acting on their own judgment, in villages or cities or regions or countries, and I have forbidden the recitation of that which negates the [basic] intention, and where it does not negate it I have nevertheless stated that it is not part of the essential tradition.[22]

Despite Sa'adyah's attainments as a liturgical poet discussed in the previous chapter, in his prayer book he adheres almost exclusively to the prosaic prayers and includes *piyutim* in only a few contexts, where their recitation had become standard. In these cases Sa'adyah shows a preference for the works of several classical poets that he held in high esteem rather than the works of more contemporary *paitanim*. In addition to these few *piyutim*, Sa'adyah introduces two particularly beautiful *bakashot* of his own composition in an elevated prose style, one for weekdays and one for sabbaths and festivals. These highly popular and greatly admired *bakashot* were translated into Judaeo-Arabic for the sake of those worshippers who had trouble understanding the original language. Aside from the relatively short preface to the prayer book, a number of copyists added a separate composition by Sa'adyah on the obligations relating to prayer, to which he refers in the preface to the prayer book itself.[23] This composition deals extensively with more

---

[22] Assaf et al., *Sa'adyah Gaon's Siddur* (Heb.), 10–11.

[23] Ibid. 1*–4*, 1–10; cf. the reference to this work, ibid. 12.

general questions relating to obligatory prayer, most notably his attempts to prove that the biblical book of Psalms is unsuitable for use as a prayer book (see pp. 64–5) and to establish various principles related to the rabbinic version of the prayers, such as the list of blessings included in the Amidah, frequently relying on scriptural passages.

Sa'adyah's Use of Halakhic Sources

The full explication of Sa'adyah's works remains a distant goal. Much of what he wrote has yet to be published, and what has been published so far demands a great deal more study and in-depth research. Hence, what follows here is only a preliminary attempt to describe some fundamental aspects of Sa'adyah's halakhic writings.

Legitimizing the Palestinian Talmud

A glance at Sa'adyah's 'bookshelf' reveals one particularly significant departure from precedent: he was the first to introduce the Palestinian Talmud and aggadic midrashim to the literary world of rabbinic Babylonia. Among the geonim who preceded Sa'adyah we find references to Palestinian tannaitic sources from the Mishnah, Tosefta, and halakhic midrash, but no amoraic sources from Palestine. Moreover, there are fairly clear indications that these rabbinic sages were not closely acquainted with the Palestinian literature of the amoraic period and beyond, or simply chose to disregard it. For instance, they give halakhic rulings on a question for which there is no apparent answer in the Babylonian Talmud but an unequivocal one exists in the Palestinian Talmud, and decide against the solution of the latter. In other words, even when not constrained by Babylonian sources, these sages do not regard the Palestinian Talmud as an authoritative source of guidance in their rulings.[24] The most substantive reference to the Palestinian Talmud by a Babylonian sage in the period before Sa'adyah Gaon appears in the polemical writing of Pirkoi ben Baboi, who disparages the Palestinian Talmud for not dealing with the orders of *Kodashim* and *Taharot* in the Mishnah: 'They have not a single talmudic halakhah on ritual slaughter or the entire order of *Kodashim*, and they have forgotten the order of *Kodashim* and the order of *Taharot* in their entirety',[25] while ignoring the fact that the Babylonian Talmud has two missing orders as well, *Zera'im* and *Taharot*.

In contrast to his predecessors in the Babylonian sphere, Sa'adyah legitimized the Palestinian Talmud, citing it in the same vague terms that he used when citing the Babylonian Talmud, such as 'the sages said'.[26] This is easily understandable

---

[24] See Brody, *The Geonim of Babylonia*, 168–9, and the sources cited in the notes ad loc.

[25] Ginzberg, *Ginzei Schechter*, ii. 560.   [26] See e.g. Assaf, *The Geonic Era*, 39 and n. 1.

in view of Sa'adyah's atypical background: his upbringing in Egypt, where Palestinian influence was decisive, and his long sojourn in Palestine before settling in Babylonia and being appointed gaon. Subsequently, the wheel could not be turned back, and even geonim who had been educated in the Babylonian academies—particularly Hai ben Sherira Gaon—used the Palestinian Talmud alongside the Babylonian, although they preferred their own when it came into conflict with the Palestinian Talmud. Moreover, they formulated the principle that 'Whatever in the Palestinian Talmud is not contradicted in our Talmud, or whenever it gives a helpful explanation of its words, we rely on it [the Palestinian Talmud] and hold to it, since it is no worse than the explanations of early sages, but whatever contradicts our Talmud we reject.'[27] From the Middle Ages onwards, under the sway of these geonim influenced by Sa'adyah, the Palestinian Talmud was incorporated as an authoritative text within the mainstream of halakhic rulings, albeit in a subordinate capacity.

Sa'adyah's Use of the Babylonian Legacy

While Sa'adyah took pioneering steps to include the Palestinian Talmud in the halakhic canon, the Babylonian Talmud (and related sections of the Mishnah) nevertheless continued to be his main source for halakhic rulings, as it had been for the Babylonian geonim who preceded him.[28] I shall now consider Sa'adyah's use of this source, particularly in his monographs. To begin with, as we have seen, the citations in his monographs are generally succinct, sometimes extremely so. They follow Sa'adyah's own formulations and are offered in their support, using vague formulas such as 'they say' or 'in the words of the ancients' and the like. Normally, he cites a single source, an amoraic or tannaitic saying or story, or alludes briefly to a talmudic exchange without noting its particulars. In some cases, he is content to present his own formulation even when there is an obvious talmudic source; or he refers to a talmudic source in a general way, without providing details of its content; at other times he might choose to combine direct quotations with paraphrases rather than cite the talmudic discussion in its entirety.

Sa'adyah's habit of adapting citations to fit their new literary settings is particularly noteworthy. In places, he prefers not to quote the actual language of the source, but to pour its contents from one vessel into another, as it were, in order to present it in a more succinct and simplified manner. This had been the occasional practice of earlier geonim, but it seems especially pronounced in Sa'adyah's writings—understandably so, given the nature of his monographs and the function that he intended for his talmudic citations in their framework. For example, in *The Laws of Succession* he cites the following as a 'saying of the Sages': 'The firstborn

---

[27] For this and similar formulations see ibid. 244.

[28] For the contents of this section see Brody, *Sa'adyah Gaon's Halakhic Works*.

receives a double portion of his father's possessions and does not inherit a double portion of his mother's possessions, for it is written, "for he is the first-fruits of his strength" [Deut. 21: 17] and not "her strength".' This is really the conflation of a mishnaic source (*BB* 8: 4) with one of the explanations offered by the *amora'im* for this rule (BT *BB* 111*b*). Moreover, Sa'adyah chooses to adopt the suggestion of Nahman ben Yitshak here rather than that of Rava, which, in the context of the talmudic discussion, appears to be the more authoritative one. He evidently did this in order to make the material more easily understandable, seeing that Nahman's explanation was closer to the straightforward meaning of the verse than Rava's construal of it.

Another example, taken from the same monograph, is the following quotation: 'And what is plentiful [property]? R. Judah said in the name of Samuel: "Enough to sustain these and those [i.e. sons and daughters] until they are of age." And if there is not enough for these and those until they are of age, sustenance for the daughters until they come of age is to be set aside and the rest goes to the sons as an inheritance.' When we examine the source of this citation we find that what Sa'adyah quotes in the name of 'R. Judah in the name of Samuel' is presented quite differently in *Bava Batra* 139*b*: 'And what is plentiful [property]? R. Judah said in the name of Rav: "Enough for these and those to be fed for twelve months." When I [Judah] reported this before Samuel, he said: "This is what Rabban Gamliel, the son of Rabbi [Judah the Prince] says, but the Sages say: enough so that both these and those may be fed until they are of age."' It is hard to imagine that Sa'adyah is quoting here from a version of the Talmud that was so dramatically different from the versions that we know, and he is clearly not quoting from corresponding passages in the Palestinian Talmud. Evidently, he understood from the words 'This is what Rabban Gamliel son of Rabbi [Judah the Prince] said, but the Sages say' that Samuel supported the position that he attributes to the 'Sages'. Therefore, Sa'adyah allowed himself to put these words into Samuel's mouth as though he himself had said them, and formulated the chain of transmission in the normal straightforward way as 'R. Judah said in the name of Samuel', without entering into the complexities of the disagreement between Rav and Samuel, R. Judah's wandering from one teacher to another, and the differences of opinion which Samuel reports between Rabban Gamliel, son of Judah the Prince, and 'the Sages'.

In addition to Sa'adyah's free use of citations, this case reflects another characteristic phenomenon: here as elsewhere we must learn indirectly how the author understands his sources and how he reaches his own conclusions, because these elements are not made explicit in his writings. To some extent, the same can be said about the responsa of the geonim, but it is more prevalent in monographic writings—especially in Sa'adyah's. In this case, we may deduce that Sa'adyah (in keeping with prevailing but not universal opinion) understands the expression 'this is what so and so said but the Sages say' to signify that the author of the saying is siding with the position attributed to the Sages rather than merely engaging in academic source-critical analysis. On the whole, it would be correct to say that Sa'adyah does not disclose the reasoning behind his halakhic judgments, particularly in his monographs. Often it would not occur to the reader that there are other options unless he examined the talmudic sources. For instance, in the *Book of Bailments* we find Sa'adyah quoting only one opinion in an amoraic dispute, the only hint that a dispute exists being the added phrase 'and the ruling is thus'. In a nearby passage he simply quotes the dictum that 'If one deposits [something] with his friend for safe keeping [and records this] in a document, the return [of the objects deposited] must also be [recorded] in a document' from one talmudic source (BT *Shevu.* 45*b*), never explaining why he follows it in his ruling or even intimating that there is another talmudic discussion (BT *BB* 70*a–b*) which contradicts it. There is an obvious tension between the two talmudic passages and the Babylonian geonim had disagreed in their rulings on the question before Sa'adyah's day, yet he finds it unnecessary to hint at the problem, let alone to explain his line of reasoning.

In this context we may mention a halakhic principle to which Sa'adyah alludes in a number of places. In the *Book of Testimony and Legal Documents* he states that a halakhah is determined in accordance with a ruling by R. Ashi (BT *BB* 57*a*), which is cited by an expression that literally means 'what they said at the end of the story'. Sa'adyah uses R. Ashi's words, quoted at the end of a short talmudic discussion, and refers to their location 'at the end of the story' to stress that their placement at the end gives them the status of a 'conclusion', which was generally accorded decisive weight by halakhic authorities of the geonic period and later. The same approach is reflected in an even more extreme case in Sa'adyah's *Laws of Succession*, where he rules that the firstborn son receives a double share of any loan repaid to the estate, based on a general statement in BT *Bava Batra* 126*b* that 'the law is that the firstborn has [rights] before the division of the inheritance', as opposed to R. Papa's ruling, quoted at the end of the previous page. In this case it is interesting that Sa'adyah prefers the general statement even though it can be interpreted in a more restrictive way that does not contradict R. Papa's statement, and even though it appears at the conclusion of a separate discussion and does not immediately follow the discussion in which R. Papa participated.

Sa'adyah's approach to the post-talmudic legacy of Babylonia has a number of distinctive features. Nowhere in his writings, to the best of my knowledge, does he quote a specific predecessor in the geonate. This might be seen as a departure from custom, since other geonim did cite their predecessors, albeit in relatively rare and clearly delineated circumstances. However, such a departure need not surprise us in Sa'adyah's case: after all, he had been raised outside Babylonia and had not formed early ties with previous geonim. On the other hand, his writings clearly reflect the collective influence of the geonic academies, even with respect to the new traditions that emerged during this period in opposition to talmudic law, whether through official enactments (such as the well-known ruling from the mid-seventh century expediting cases in which 'rebellious' wives sought a divorce from their husbands) or in the gradual developments which occurred in the system of oaths and bans. It may be that Sa'adyah was the first to cite explicitly from the repository of fixed traditions transmitted—orally, it would seem—in the geonic academies. In one place, where he deals with the famous dispute between the academies of Sura and Pumbedita about whether it is preferable for the levir to marry the wife of a deceased brother who has died without issue (*yibum*) or to undergo *ḥalitsah* (the ritual of releasing the widow from the obligation to marry him), Sa'adyah is faithful to the Suran tradition of preferring *yibum*, but, as is to be expected, he did not always agree with the previous geonim of Sura.

In summary, it is not easy to discern anything strikingly original in Sa'adyah's halakhic works with respect to his use of the Babylonian tradition. His main innovations in the realms of halakhah and Talmud consist of his introduction of post-tannaitic Palestinian literature into the scholarly sphere of the Babylonian geonim and of his development of new literary genres—above all, the halakhic monograph. In these respects, he blazed a trail not only for the last of the Babylonian geonim but for leading rabbinic authors in the generations that followed.

※

CHAPTER EIGHT

Sa'adyah, Polemicist and Publicist

POLEMICS and the propagation of doctrines constitute an important area of Sa'adyah's wide-ranging literary activity. Although he was not the first to engage in polemical writing in the geonic era, he certainly enlarged the scope of polemics and elaborated various literary models for this purpose. Quite a few of Sa'adyah's works were intended primarily as polemics, but in keeping with his usual practice he did not restrict them to a single topic and often incorporated a wide range of subjects, even when these contributed little to his polemical argument or did so only indirectly. Conversely, he introduced polemical motifs, both explicit and implicit, into works in other genres, even where a modern reader might consider them irrelevant.

Sa'adyah began composing polemical works as a young man and continued for many decades. He was certainly well suited to this line of activity, which demanded intellectual and rhetorical vigour and a powerful and combative personality. We should also bear in mind his sense of mission, his image of himself as the member of his generation chosen to fulfil the promise that God never leaves the nation without a leader 'to counsel and instruct her and cause her condition to improve'.[1] Seeing the circumstances of the Jews and Judaism in his day, and realizing that his people were faced with challenges that no one else could help them meet, Sa'adyah took the role on himself in accordance with the proverb, 'Where there are no [worthy] men, strive to be a man.' Only in one instance (*Sefer hagalui*) does a personal note dominate his polemic, and here, too, he writes out of a deep conviction that his personal good is synonymous with the public good, as we shall presently see.

Sa'adyah's polemics may be viewed as a series of concentric circles. In this chapter, I will survey them moving from the outermost—his debates with members of other religions—to the innermost circle: his struggles over the leadership of Rabbanite Jewry in Babylonia.

Religious Debates

To the best of our knowledge, Sa'adyah did not devote any separate work to the criticism of other religions or to the refutation of criticisms levelled at Judaism by

---

[1] Harkavy, *Fugitive Remnants*, 155 (Arab. text), 154 (Heb. trans.).

adherents of other religions. The reason for this is unclear, but it most probably had to do with his sense that criticism from without posed no threat to the integrity of the Jewish community. We know about cases of Jews who converted to Christianity or Islam during this period, but Sa'adyah must have viewed this as a rare phenomenon, marginal enough for him to focus instead on internal threats. At the same time, he did not avoid engaging in polemics with the positions and arguments of other religions, especially Christianity and Islam, only he did so by incorporating such polemics in works devoted mainly to other purposes, particularly in his exegetical writings and in his theological magnum opus, *The Book of Beliefs and Opinions*.

Christians and Muslims alike believed that God had transmitted the Hebrew Bible to the children of Israel through his prophet Moses, but they also believed that its authority had lapsed long ago. Christians held that Jesus had fulfilled the biblical promises of the coming of the messiah, ushering in a new era in which 'Israel of the flesh' was replaced by the 'true Israel', the Christian Church, because most of the Jews in Jesus' time had refused to recognize his mission. The 'Old Testament' had likewise been replaced by a 'New Testament' based not on the observance of practical commandments but on faith as the means of salvation. Although Christians sanctified the Hebrew Bible, they held that it had been intended for a limited stage of human history and that it contained many intimations of its supersession by the more spiritual message of Jesus. At the heart of the controversies that raged among Christians over many centuries was the question of the nature of Jesus: was he a person (prophet or messiah) or the human embodiment of God on earth; and what was his relation to 'his father in heaven'? The view that eventually gained acceptance was the concept of a Divine unity in three persons—the Father, the Son (Jesus), and the Holy Ghost—'three that are one', in a manner surpassing human comprehension.

As opposed to the Christians, Muslims were little concerned with the study and interpretation of the Bible. Although they, too, sought hints here and there of Muhammad's future mission, they claimed that the Jews had corrupted the text of the Bible in order to hide the fact that Moses himself had heralded the future coming of Muhammad, the prophet of Islam. They believed in principle that God had revealed himself a number of times in the course of history, and each revelation could in turn cancel or amend aspects of previous revelations. This principle of abrogation and replacement of doctrinal truths that had once been valid, called *naskh* in Arabic, was probably developed in order to resolve various contradictions in the prophecies of Muhammad as they appear in the Qur'an by asserting that the most recent revelation was the one in force at any given time. This principle was then applied to earlier religions as well: God had sent various true prophets over the generations, among them Moses and Jesus, but the last and greatest of them all was Muhammad. And since the message transmitted to believers through each of these prophets abrogated earlier ones, Islam had emerged as the ultimate religion even though the 'religions of the Book', led by Judaism and Christianity, could lay claim to a certain legitimacy as opposed to other religions defined as idolatrous.

Jewish responses to these principles, including Sa'adyah's, focused on a number of points: a denial of Christian and Muslim interpretations of the Bible as presaging the future emergence of their religions; attempts to prove that the messianic prophecies had not yet been fulfilled; criticism of Christian faith in the divinity of Jesus; and an effort to demonstrate that the messages of revelation are eternal. God does not 'change his mind', nor does he alter his commandments from time to time, and therefore anyone who acknowledges that God revealed himself to Moses and gave him the Torah (which, as we have seen, includes both Christians and Muslims) must also acknowledge the eternal truth of Judaism.

An explicit example of negation of the Christian reading of Scriptures is found in Sa'adyah's commentary on Genesis 1: 26, 'And God said, "Let us make man in our image and after our likeness"':

He said 'Let us make man' in the plural, by way of the royal 'we', which is used in the Hebrew language to express greatness and glory, as when a king or minister or nobleman says, 'We commanded, we said, we did'; and thus Laban said, 'And we will give you this one as well' [Gen. 29: 26] and Amazia said, 'Have we made thee of the king's counsel?' [2 Chr. 25: 16] And later on He says, 'In our image, after our likeness' [Gen. 1: 26], also in the plural, in the manner that we have explained before. And the Christians present this verse to prove their system of the trinity, [claiming] that if the Creator had been one without hypostases or 'persons', He would have said 'In my image, after my likeness'. And we say to them: 'Do you believe that some of the words in this chapter are metaphorical or that every word has a straightforward meaning?' And if they say every word has a straightforward meaning, they must say that man is truly in the form of God, and therefore, God must have a body of flesh and blood and bones and so forth, [though in fact] not one of them believes this; and similarly, they must say that God is male and female as man is, for it is [also] written: 'In the image of God He created him' [Gen. 1: 27], and further, 'Male and female He created them'. And in the same way they must say that all the [three] persons created man, for it is said, 'Let us make man', but only one of them created Eve, for it is said 'I will make a helpmeet for him' [Gen. 2: 18]. Since Christians accept none of these [hypothetical positions], they must admit that there are words in this chapter that are said metaphorically, and it is not a real form or real likeness that is meant but a form of action and a likeness of action. And if so, in the matter of the trinity they must admit that 'Let us make man in our image, after our likeness' is said metaphorically, just as a person will say, 'We have done, we have made', even though he did it alone. And however hard they try to convert the singular into the plural, our grounds for converting the plural into the singular are stronger.[2]

---

[2] Zucker, *Sa'adyah's Commentary on Genesis*, 51 (Arab. text), 252 (Heb. trans.). On Sa'adyah's treatment of the 'suffering servant' in Isaiah 52–3, see Ch. 4 n. 28.

Sa'adyah's main attempts to prove that the messianic prophecies in the Bible have not yet been fulfilled and that God does not abrogate or alter his commandments appear in *The Book of Beliefs and Opinions* (where we also find a discussion in which he distinguishes four Christian opinions concerning the precise nature of Jesus and argues against them all).[3]

As an example of the nature of these discussions I will cite a section where Sa'adyah polemicizes against those who claim that the messianic promises were fulfilled during the Second Temple period. He first refutes the claim at a theoretical level and then presents fifteen different proofs based on prophecies that had not yet been fulfilled at that time.

After these interpretations I shall discuss what I have learned, that some who are called Jews imagine that all of these promises and consolations refer to the Second Temple, and that they have passed and nothing at all remains of them; and they do this by building their arguments on a false premise, namely, that all assurances that we see concerning redemption ... depend on whether or not the nation heeds the word of God. They say that this resembles what Moses our Rabbi said to Israel, 'That your days may be multiplied and the days of your children' [Deut. 11: 21], and when they sinned they were deprived of governance and their monarchy came to an end. Similarly, in the time of the Second Temple some of these promises were fulfilled and then departed ... And I took the basis of what these people say, namely, that the promises are conditional, and I analysed this closely and found it to be invalid for several reasons: one, that the promises of Moses our Rabbi, may he rest in peace, were explicitly conditional ... but these consolations are unconditional and absolute. And further, that Moses our Rabbi, may he rest in peace, did not content himself with the conditional 'if you keep' and 'if you hearken', leaving the alternative to their discernment ... but also turned the matter around and specified to them that if they did not keep their side of the promise, the opposite of the promise would befall them, as it is written, 'And it shall be if thou shalt forget the Lord thy God ... As the nations that the Lord maketh to perish before you, so shall ye perish' [Deut. 8: 19–20]; and in these consolations no condition was set, let alone its opposite ...

Having eradicated the basis of their structure, I shall provide fifteen responses, five with proof from Scriptures, and five with proof from tradition, and five obvious to the eye. The five proofs from Scriptures are as follows, beginning with the fact that these consolations require that all of Israel should assemble in the Temple and none remain in exile, as it is written, 'And [I] have gathered them unto their own land; and I will leave none of them any more there' [Ezek. 39: 28], and in the [time of the] Second Temple only 42,360 returned, as it is written, 'The whole congregation together was forty and two thousand three hundred and threescore' [Neh. 7: 66] ... And the five from tradition begin with [the prophecy that] for seven years the people shall use the wood of the weapons of Gog for kindling, as it is written: 'And they that dwell in the cities of Israel shall go forth and shall make fires of the weapons and use them as fuel, both the shields and the bucklers, the bows and the arrows' [Ezek. 39: 9] ... And the remaining five,

---

[3] *Book of Beliefs and Opinions*, ed. Landauer (Arab.), 90–1; ed. Rosenblatt, 109–10.

which are conspicuous to the eye, begin with [the prophecy that at that time] all created beings will believe in God and in Him alone, as it is written: 'And the Lord shall be King over all the earth; [on that day shall the Lord be One and His name one]' [Zekh. 14: 9], but we see their error and their heresy . . . These conditions provide absolute proof that these consolations have not yet come to pass.[4]

Polemic against Critics of the Bible

During the period of the geonim even Jews who rebelled against Rabbanite tradition normally accepted the authority of the Bible; but there were exceptions to this as well. This complex situation is strikingly reflected in a responsum of one of the geonim, probably Natronai ben Nehemiah Gaon, who headed the Pumbedita academy during the first half of the eighth century CE. Natronai was asked about a group of 'Israelite heretics who have abandoned the ways of Israel and observe neither the commandments nor the sabbath . . . nor the [prohibition of] forbidden fat and blood and the eighteen types of *terefot* . . . and do not practise *ḥalitsah* or *yibum*', some of whom expressed the wish to return to the fold of normative Judaism. At the beginning of his responsum he voices his surprise at the situation described by the enquirers:

For these heretics are different from all the heretics in the world—for all heretics scoff at the words of the Sages, such as *terefot* and the second day of festivals [which is] of rabbinic origin and *sheniyot* [rabbinically prohibited marriages], which are of the words of the scribes, but as for the words of Torah and Scripture, they keep and observe them like genuine Israelites, whereas those whom you describe scoffed at the essence of the Torah.[5]

It is unclear precisely which group is being described here and what its fate was, but we do know that one man, Hivi of Balkh, had devoted an entire work to disparaging the Bible and Sa'adyah felt duty-bound to refute his arguments. Hivi's Hebrew poem contained 200 hostile questions about the Bible. The poem was divided into rhyming quatrains, one stanza per question, arranged in biblical order and also displaying an alphabetical or counter-alphabetical acrostic (apparently in alternating sequence). Hivi may thus be considered the first systematic 'Bible critic', at least among the Jews, though his criticism is not directed at the textual integrity or accuracy of the Bible but rather at questions of biblical faith, more particularly, the belief in Divine justice (theodicy). Sa'adyah states that sixty years after the publication of this destructive work—which, according to one source, had achieved so much popularity that it was used as a school text—he had undertaken to write a defence of the Bible.[6] Sa'adyah's composition follows the basic

⁴ *Book of Beliefs and Opinions*, ed. Landauer, 247–8; ed. Rosenblatt, 312–19.
⁵ See Brody, *The Geonim of Babylonia*, 84–5 and n. 5.
⁶ See Harkavy, *Fugitive Remnants* (Heb.), 147 and n. 1; 177 (Arab. text), 176 (Heb. trans.).

form of Hivi's poem—an acrostic divided into rhyming quatrains alphabetically and counter-alphabetically arranged—though in other respects, such as rhyme scheme, he departs from Hivi's structure.

Only a few short fragments of Hivi's poem have survived in their original form, but we may learn about many of his questions from the poem that Sa'adyah devoted to its refutation, about a third of which has come down to us. The few sections that I have chosen here to demonstrate Hivi's critical style and Sa'adyah's method of responding are relatively clear. In these, Sa'adyah addresses Hivi in the second person and presents the questions that he will address, although not necessarily in Hivi's own words. It is worth mentioning that in other sections he uses a different style and we can only surmise from his occasionally opaque answers which arguments he is refuting.

The section below opens with the presentation of Hivi's question: why did God fail to prevent Cain from killing Abel, thus depriving his progeny of their life as well? Sa'adyah's answer is that reward and punishment should not be calculated solely on the basis of how a person fares in this world but also (in fact primarily) according to the requital that awaits, for good or evil, in the world to come. He elaborates on this principle and indicates the moral lesson to be learned: evildoers should not rejoice too much over success in this world because punishment awaits them in the world to come, nor should the righteous regret a bitter fate in this world because their reward will be received in the world to come.

> I shall answer your question with a resounding reply
> When you said: why did He not preserve him and save his progeny?
> A fitting query if there were one world, one abode only,
> But as there is a second, it is no way blameworthy.
>
> Let not oppressors here rejoice in their oppression
> For when their legs falter there will be retribution
> And the oppressed and harried should not bemoan their situation
> For the Lord can reverse this, and they will not be forsaken.
>
> For God stays not the hand of the cruel
> Nor always spares the oppressed from tyranny
> Since one day justice will be meted duly
> To those who serve God and those who do not.[7]

In the following section Sa'adyah addresses two fundamental questions posed by Hivi which appear to have no clear correlation with a specific verse: why human beings suffer and why they are mortal. His main answer—consistent with the positions he takes in other works, particularly *The Book of Beliefs and Opinions*—is that God created the world in order to benefit his creatures, but the true and

---

[7] Davidson, *Saadia's Polemic*, 40–2 (Heb. text), 41–3 (Eng. trans.).

transcendent Good is the Good that is earned in the world to come as a reward for good deeds performed in this world. The purpose of suffering is to bring home the punishment in store for evildoers and thus to guide human beings towards the path of the Good. Here, as elsewhere in his polemical writings, Sa'adyah mingles harsh personal insults with principled replies to his antagonist:

> You go on to ask about different forms of suffering
> Wherefore hunger and disease, fear and theft and devastation
> And heat and cold, why is man not spared them
> All these are one question, but you go on at length!
>
> See and know that God chastens His creatures for their good
> That they may learn the pain and bitterness of punishments
> And cease from evil-doing which condemns them to them
> Which they would never recognize if He took them away.
>
> You wonder mightily and ask critically:
> Why should man not live forever and not descend to Sheol?
> Would he had been formed from the beginning, saved, in the next world!
> Yet you would leave him here in dire straits and woe.
>
> Despite His doing all of this many still rebel
> And despite His scaring them with travails some are traitors to His faith
> How much more so if they had not been afraid
> Then all as one would not have served [Him].
> Would it be wise to preserve your form forever?
> Or to spare it affliction, trouble, and fear?
> What intelligence would judge [it right] to save you from faltering?
> For you have spoken falsely against the Eternal One.
>
> Chastisements and blows are in store for the wicked
> Hell is wrathfully set before them of old
> Reserved for a time of distress, a day of battle and war
> And you among them [face] the anger of the avenging Lord.[8]

Sa'adyah then responds to two more of Hivi's questions: why were animals killed during the Flood and why did God spare Noah and his sons? Beyond his specific answers, Sa'adyah observes that the perversity of Hivi's questions betrays his tainted motives, and shows that he is only looking for excuses to attack the Bible.

> You ask: why was the world destroyed along with man,
> With the birds and crawling creatures, wild and domestic animals?
> They were all created in his honour and shared pleasantness with him
> And [so] they follow him in destruction and devastation.

---

[8] Davidson, *Saadia's Polemic*, 42–4 (Heb.), 41–3 (Eng.).

You grumbled: why did he leave a remnant of the seed of evil?
Why shouldn't Noah survive, since he did not sin?!
If He had destroyed him, you would have spoken thus:
Does He slay the righteous with the wicked man?!

Worse yet: you regret [the destruction of] chattel and possessions,
How much more would you have complained about [the death of]
    the righteous and innocent!
Now every wise man will understand from your words
That you tell tales and speak in vain.[9]

Polemic against the Karaites

Although Sa'adyah engaged in numerous debates with non-Jews and sectarians who denied the religious and moral authority of the Bible, there is no doubt that the main targets of his polemics were Anan and the Karaites, who upheld the Bible but rejected the Oral Law. Sa'adyah was apparently convinced that Karaism represented the greatest threat to the faithful adherents of traditional Judaism and the only real alternative for most worshippers who adhered to Rabbanite tradition. He was not the first exponent of Rabbanite Judaism to defend the tradition and attack dissenters, but he was undoubtedly the most important one in his day and later, as may be inferred from the many Karaite works written over a period of centuries in response to his writings.[10]

Sa'adyah devoted a considerable number of works to this controversy—ten or more in all—although none of these seem to have survived in anything like their original form. Many bibliographical questions are still unresolved, such as whether a certain composition is known by two or more different names, or the identity of some of Sa'adyah's disputants. Moreover, sections from several polemics found in the Genizah are possibly attributable to Sa'adyah, but the works they come from have not yet been determined. It is clear, at any rate, that Sa'adyah was the author of two distinct types of anti-Karaite polemics: those written against a particular individual, bearing the standard title 'Refutation of So-and-So' (*al-radd 'ala fulan*), and those which take issue with common Karaite positions rather than focusing on a specific personality. Among Sa'adyah's works in the first of these categories we find *The Refutation of Anan* (only the ending of which has been published, while its precise contents remain unclear), *The Refutation of Ibn Saqawayh* (whose identity is unknown), and *The Refutation of an Overbearing Aggressor* (again, unidentified). A unique case in point is *The Refutation of Ben Asher*, which I shall discuss at length. His more general works include *The Book of Distinction*, *The Book Collecting the Proofs for the Lamps*, in which he proves that the

---

[9] Ibid. 52 (Heb.), 53 (Eng.).   [10] See Poznanski, *Karaite Literary Opponents*.

lighting of sabbath candles is permitted, and *The Book of the Source of the Non-Rational Commandments.*

As we have seen throughout, polemics both overt and implied are also found in many of Sa'adyah's writings that are not predominantly polemical in character. This is true especially with regard to his biblical commentaries—Sa'adyah himself, as we recall, asserts that his polemics against various heresies are a key element in his commentary on the Pentateuch, in contrast to the translation which he published separately—and *The Book of Beliefs and Opinions*, in which he frequently classifies and criticizes various theories relating to the central issues that he wishes to address. Polemics against those who rejected Rabbanite tradition even find their way into more surprising places, such as Sa'adyah's prayer book and its 'preface' or *Explanation of the Seventy Isolated Biblical Words*, his short monograph on cases of hapax legomena in the Bible (see pp. 84–5, 134–5). Another discussion worth mentioning may be found in a halakhic work on the laws of bailment. The biblical basis for these laws is spelled out in Exodus 22: 6–12, where the verses are divided into two groups (6–8 and 9–12) with legal distinctions between them. In the first section, beginning with the words 'If a man deliver unto his neighbour money or chattel to keep', the bailee is not held liable for property stolen from him. In the second section, which opens with 'If a man deliver unto his neighbour an ass or an ox or a sheep or any beast to keep', the bailee is held liable for an animal that is stolen from him. Rabbinic interpretation holds that the descriptions of the two sets of circumstances are not to be taken literally; rather, the first section concerns an unpaid bailee, and the second a paid bailee, who is held more strictly accountable. Before approaching the special laws regarding the two types of bailee, which form the bulk of this work, Sa'adyah finds it necessary to justify the rabbinic interpretation and to refute the competing one offered by Karaite authors:

And these two passages recorded in the Bible, 'If a man deliver unto his neighbour money' and 'if a man deliver unto his neighbour an ass', are distinguished from one another because, as the Sages say, the first one deals with an unpaid bailee and the second with a paid bailee . . . And lest anyone should distinguish between them in a way that is not in line with this and say that the second was held liable for theft because he was looking after a live creature, whereas the first was not held liable because he was looking after utensils, and both are unpaid . . . this is an erroneous distinction, because if even the second were unpaid and he were liable for the theft he would not deserve it, since the theft was not preventable . . . and if he were liable although unpaid that would be clearly unjust . . . And another proof of the erroneousness of this distinction lies in this: if the distinction were made and the verses were divided because the first bailment is not of an animal and the second one is, an animal could not possibly be linked together with the earlier passage at the end of the account where it says [verse 8] 'of every sort that is a trespass, whether it be an ox' etc. And because the ox and ass and sheep, being animals, are joined with the cloak and [other] lost property, we learn that the distinction between the passages is not that one speaks of animals while the other does not ... but that it depends on the bailee involved, whether he is an unpaid bailee or a paid bailee.

After this we say: but in the passage about the unpaid bailee why are money and chattel the main object with the animals added on, while in the passage about the paid bailee the animals are the main object? We say: it is customary for people to pay a fee for the care of an animal since animals have mobility and can remove themselves from one place to another, and this is why the passage concerning the paid bailee begins with it. And it is not customary to pay a fee for the care of utensils and [inanimate] movables because they have no mobility and cannot remove themselves, which is why the passage concerning the unpaid bailee begins with them. And since the erroneousness of this statement [i.e. interpretation] has been demonstrated, the distinction that we have drawn is the correct one, namely, that the first passage deals with the unpaid bailee and the second passage deals with the paid bailee.[11]

The topics treated in Sa'adyah's anti-Karaite polemics are both general and specific. We have already seen examples of the general arguments found at many points in his writings, where he tries to demonstrate the impossibility of a Judaism based solely on the Bible without the accompanying rabbinic tradition. His main line of argument is that the Torah omits important details concerning many of the commandments, and without rabbinic tradition it would be impossible to ascertain such matters as how to build a *sukkah* (booth used on Sukkot), or on which day the sabbath falls. In his *Explanation of the Seventy Isolated Biblical Words*, Sa'adyah goes a step further: the very language of the Bible cannot be understood solely in its context but only as part of a historical continuum of which rabbinic Hebrew forms a later stage.

The other side of the coin, as Sa'adyah himself points out, is the refutation of *hekesh*, the doctrine of analogy or inference, by means of which the Karaites tried to supply details omitted from the biblical commandments, and to this Sa'adyah devoted a special monograph called *The Book of the Source of the Non-Rational Commandments*. In addition to his specific criticisms of *hekesh* as used by Karaite sages, he puts forward a more fundamental argument: the commandments according to his doctrine are divisible into two classes, rational commandments and non-rational or revealed commandments. The rational commandments (e.g. to be truthful and honest and to avoid wrongdoing and iniquity) are imprinted in human intelligence by God, and because all the commandments that fall into this category are rational, their details can likewise be inferred on a rational basis. Non-rational or revealed commandments, on the other hand, such as the sanctification of certain times (the sabbath and the festivals) and certain places, or distinctions between foods that are permitted and those that are prohibited, are not similarly imprinted but are known to us only as a result of Divine fiat, hence their

---

[11] Zucker, *Sa'adyah's Translation of the Torah* (Heb.), 165–7 n. 657.

details cannot be discerned by rational means: 'And thus it follows that every detail of the second type is to be known by way of tradition, since the entire class consists of commandments that are not accessible through the intellect.'[12] Further on in this monograph, Sa'adyah claims—among other things—that *hekesh* in this category leads to dubious and arbitrary conclusions: for if the Karaites concede that there is an objective truth regarding the details of the commandments, in accordance with the will of God, and that they must abide by them, one person's analogy leads him to one conclusion, and another person's to another: 'For in this they allow division and dissension and sectarianism, all in defiance of the will of God in the matter of the commandments. And if they ascribe this to Him and say that He allows it to them, and, even more so, if they say that He commands it of them, this is worse indeed and more bitter still.'[13] At the end of the book Sa'adyah turns to a defence of rabbinic tradition, enumerating fifteen arguments raised by the Karaites against the Mishnah (i.e. the Oral Law) and refuting them one by one.[14]

The specific points that Sa'adyah addresses in his polemics against the Karaites are familiar to us as central issues of the Rabbanite–Karaite dispute frequently addressed by authors from both camps. Especially prominent are the calendar controversies: Sa'adyah takes issue with the well-known Karaite claims that sanctification of the new month depends on actually seeing the new moon and that the decision to add an intercalary month should be based on certain considerations, such as the ripeness of crops, rather than on the fixed astronomical calendar of Rabbanite Judaism. He rejects the Karaite claim that Shavuot should always fall on a Sunday, and vindicates the rabbinical interpretation of the words 'the morrow after the day of rest' (Lev. 23: 15) as indicating the day that follows the first day of Passover. He also supports the law which adds a 'second festival day for the diaspora' beyond the borders of Palestine for each of the festivals. Other matters that he discusses include the requirement to light sabbath candles, as opposed to the Karaite belief that it is forbidden to light a flame on the eve of the sabbath that continues to burn on the sabbath (this point was debated, as we recall, not only in the context of monographs covering assorted topics but also in a separate book devoted specifically to proving the permissibility of lighting sabbath candles); points on which Rabbanite Judaism is more lenient than Karaite tradition concerning *tumat nidah* (separation during menstrual impurity); and the permissibility of eating the fat of a sheep's tail, contrary to Karaite belief. Let us look at a sampling of Sa'adyah's arguments from the eighth and final chapter of his *Book of Distinction*:

On this matter there are no distinct schools, and no one who has opposed the rabbis has said anything about it beyond its negation . . . And the people say: 'We have heard from

---

[12] Zucker, 'Fragments' (Heb.), 388–9 (the quotation is from p. 389).
[13] Ibid. 393.   [14] Ibid. 404–7.

the prophets that when we are outside the special land [i.e. the Land of Israel] it is incumbent on us to add a second day to each of the days of holy convocation, and we have also seen them act in this way, except for the Day of Atonement.' And I examined the Scriptures lest I find them transgressing the commandment 'Thou shalt not add thereto nor diminish from it' [Deut. 13: 1], and I studied the beginning of the verse and it does not contain the words 'everything that I write to you' but rather [everything that I] 'command you', and I have found that what is passed down in our tradition is called commandment as if written ... Then I said: perhaps there are divisions among them concerning this. And when I examined this I found that the people of Palestine and the Diaspora say: 'We agree that the people of our nation who are in the Holy Land should keep one day [of the festival], and those who depart beyond its borders should keep two days' ... and there is no disagreement on this matter whatsoever ... Is this then rejected by our laws, that there should be a distinction between different members of the nation—that some of them add and some do not? I have enquired about this and the laws of the Torah and I have found that there are those who do not offer the Passover [sacrifice] and are punishable by *karet* [extirpation], namely, those who are near ... and there are those who do not offer it but are not punishable by *karet*, namely, those who are far away.[15]

A composition that stands out as unique among Sa'adyah's polemical works is the poem known by its opening line as *Esa meshali* (I Shall Relate My Parable). About a hundred years ago, centuries after its disappearance, fragments of the poem began to surface among the Genizah collections and we are now in possession of a little less than half of it.[16] This is a lengthy poem with a complicated and quite remarkable structure of twenty-two sections, all but the last (apparently) made up of twenty-six strophes each and ending in an alphabetical monorhyme: the first rhymes *-ah*, the second *-bah*, and so forth. The other lines in each strophe rhyme with each other in a scheme that alternates from strophe to strophe.[17]

A considerable amount of research has gone into this composition and there is still no consensus about a question with several major implications: should the poem be identified with *The Refutation of Ben Asher* known from the testimony of

---

[15] Hirschfeld, 'Arabic Portion of the Cairo Genizah', 103–4.

[16] The most important publication concerning this poem is Lewin, '*Esa Meshali*' (Heb.); more recent treatments are listed in Elizur, '*Esa meshali*' (Heb.).

[17] There is a fixed number of lines for each strophe, but not for the poem as a whole. In the fragments discovered so far this number is between three and five. The twenty-six verses in each section are arranged acrostically according to their initial letters. The verses that rhyme with *-ḥaḥ*, for example, begin with the letter *ḥet*, and when the acrostic reaches the end of the alphabet it goes back to *alef*. Though it ends with a repetition of the letter *ḥet*, the penultimate letter *zayin* appears at the start of each of three strophes, and the preceding letter *vav* at the start of two strophes. In this way, twenty-six strophes are created in each section rather than twenty-two, the number of letters in the Hebrew alphabet (the *-tah* section in our possession is structured differently, but for this reason it is not quite certain that it belongs to this poem).

Dunash ben Labrat, and should the opponent that Sa'adyah addresses in it be identified with Aaron Ben Asher, the best known of the Masoretic scholars, whose rulings on biblical texts have remained standard to this day? I shall not go into the details of the arguments for and against these identifications, but what is clear is that *Esa meshali* attacks Karaites who take pride in biblical and Masoretic knowledge but deny the oral tradition and criticize the rabbinic sages.

At the beginning of the composition Sa'adyah addresses 'every mortal creature', entreating man to fear God and to devote himself to serving Him, stressing the oneness and omnipotence of the Creator and the principle of reward and punishment. Towards the end of the *-ah* rhymes, he focuses on the demand to serve God specifically through the study of Torah. From there he goes on to attack the Masoretes, who are knowledgeable in every detail of the biblical text—the open and closed pericopes, plene or defective spelling, specially formed letters, and so forth—but who have no understanding of the contents because they rely on the sages of 'Gomer and Geter' (presumably sages from other nations, though the precise meaning of these words is unclear) and scorn the rabbinic sages:

> 'Open' and 'closed' [paragraphs] are in their mouths
> 'Full' and 'deficient' [spellings] in their speech
> And if reversed they will put them in their [proper] place
> But they don't know whence it derives and whither it goes
>
> Marking majuscular letters
> Suspended, dotted and inverted . . .
>
> He disparages the tradition of the one who sees hidden things
> And prefers to it Gomer and Geter
> And says: there is nothing hidden in its law.
> Its God and Master will contend against you.[18]

Sa'adyah devotes a large portion of what follows to the praises of the *tana'im* and *amora'im* both in general terms and in stories that emphasize their greatness and, above all, the integrity on which his opponent cast doubts, claiming that they had 'betrayed the awesome nation to gain profit through deceit'. Some of the stories are recounted according to the Talmud and some are extra-talmudic, for example, the one (merely alluded to in the Talmud) about R. Safra, who fulfilled the requirement of the verse to be one who 'speaketh truth in his heart' (Ps. 15: 2) when merchants came to buy certain goods from him while he was occupied in prayer. Though he had intended to sell the goods to them at the price they had offered to begin with, he refrained from answering because he was deep in prayer. They, however, understood from his silence that the price that they had offered was too

---

[18] Lewin, '*Esa Meshali*' (Heb.), 509–10.

low and continued to offer higher and higher prices, and yet when he finished praying, he would accept only the initial price that they had offered.

Sa'adyah then proceeds to attack opponents who do not observe a number of commandments specified in the Bible or generally acknowledged by Jews, but invent laws not based on the Torah:

> They dissent, there are no fringes, no *mezuzah*,
> No phylacteries attached to their biceps
> And no speech [of Torah learning] in the night ...
>
> They no longer recite the unity [i.e. the Shema] morning and evening
> Their lips do not utter sweetly, 'Holy' and 'Blessed'
> Of bread and drink they partake without blessing ...
>
> The husband of the wife of a stepfather
> And the wife of the husband of a stepmother
> They say is forbidden, [which is] not as said by Him who dwells on high
>
> And the wife of a deceased brother they allow to marry outside
> And her firstborn son of his inheritance they would deprive
> And God's pure Torah they desecrate.
>
> The religion of our God they circumvent
> The permitted they forbid, the forbidden permit
> Devoid of awe and fear.[19]

After some further words of tribute to the Sages, Sa'adyah presents his favourite argument: without the rabbinic tradition there would be no way of implementing the Torah commandments since many are insufficiently explicated:

> What is the sukkah's length
> And how many cubits its breadth
> And its height ...
>
> How many grains is the *peret*[20]
> Is any of these incised with a chisel
> Or hidden in Scripture?
>
> How do we know how to attach the fringes,
> The number of threads and knots,
> Whether ten or eight ...
>
> All these and many of their kind
> I ask all readers of Scriptures:
> Do they contain the details of any?

[19] Ibid. 522–3.   [20] Lev. 19:10.

> If not for the Mishnah and Talmud
> In which all of this is taught
> And sundry other things.[21]

The Calendar Dispute

As I mentioned in my brief biography in Chapter 2, the first point in Sa'adyah's life about which we have relatively detailed information was the great Hebrew calendar controversy that erupted in 921–3 CE between the sages of Babylonia and Palestine. Sa'adyah played an important role in this dispute on the side of the Babylonians, and his contribution to the struggle most probably paved the way for his appointment as gaon of the academy of Sura a few years later, in 928. Many of the details connected with this fateful controversy—both its substance (particularly the motives and theories of the Palestinian gaon Ben Me'ir) and its trajectory—are insufficiently clear. What is clear is that although Sa'adyah was not educated among the sages of Babylonia, he played a central role in the failed attempt of the Babylonians to dissuade Ben Me'ir from launching his calendar and in the far more successful campaign to persuade the Jews of the world to accept Babylonian authority and adopt the Babylonian calendar.

The importance of Sa'adyah's role in the above is attested by a letter from the Palestinian gaon listing his main opponents: 'And in recent days we received an epistle written by David . . . ben Zakai [the Exilarch] . . . from him and his sons and a priest [Kohen Tsedek, the priestly gaon of Pumbedita] and his accomplice Sa'id ben Yosef, the Dilasi [i.e. Sa'adyah Gaon; *al-Dilasi* is a reference to the village in Egypt from which he came].'[22]

Even stronger evidence is found in another letter by the same author, accusing his followers of betraying him and claiming that all the evils that they describe had come upon them 'when you abandoned truth and turned away from the straight path to the path of obstruction and heeded the words of the Dilazi ben Fayumi and his plea . . . You said that you were shamed among the Gentiles and disgraced among the sectarians, and this is the wish and desire of the Fayumi'.[23] We learn a great deal about Sa'adyah's involvement in the first stages of the controversy from an epistle that he sent to his former students in Egypt:

Know that while I was still in Aleppo some of the students from Ba'al Gad came and told me that Ben Me'ir intends to declare the months of Heshvan and Kislev [in the year 921] defective [meaning that each of them would have 29 days] and I did not believe this but . . . I wrote to him . . . and thus the exilarch and the heads of the academies and all the

---

[21]   Lewin, '*Esa Meshali*' (Heb.), 526–7.

[22]   Bornstein, *The Controversy Between Sa'adyah Gaon and Ben Me'ir* (Heb.), 50.

[23]   Ibid. 90–1.

alufim and sages, masters, and students have agreed and declared Marheshvan and Kislev full and Passover on the third day of the week [i.e. Tuesday], and I too [sent what I] had written with their epistles to most of the great communities in fulfilment of my duty.[24]

In addition to his epistles, Sa'adyah wrote a special book called *Sefer hamo'adim* (The Book of Appointed Times), to which he alludes in his *Sefer hagalui*: 'As when in Iraq, and with the approval of those who were there, I wrote a book in Hebrew on the subject of what had befallen the nation as a result of the sin [or error] of Ben Me'ir, [called] *Sefer hamo'adim*, divided into sections and provided with cantillation marks'.[25]

Quite a few fragments of this composition have survived. Some of them deal with technical details of calendar regulation which I will not enter into here, but I will cite a few fragments that illustrate the course of events from the point of view of the Babylonian sages. Notice how Sa'adyah derisively distorts the name of his opponent—in this case, the Palestinian gaon Ben Me'ir, whom he sometimes designates *mahshikh* (benighter) and sometimes *mamir* (malignant), both puns on the name Me'ir, literally meaning 'the enlightener'.

. . . The Benighter, who was Aaron . . . shun the receiver of bribery and flee those who fawn . . . open your eyes, I entreat you . . . look upon all these and let his words not ensnare you . . . And those whose hearts prompt them will read about his deeds at the appropriate time, in Elul, the sixth month, before the festivals . . . And when the ignorant are informed they will no longer act wickedly after all that he has done, for who would not be fearful of having his lot cursed in every generation, and who would not wish to improve his reputation? For his righteousness remains forever, and the tribes of God will be blessed in him and be praised on his account. This is the sign of the covenant which our fathers gave us in inheritance from ancient times, for it is not found in Scripture . . . And he sent his son in the fourth month . . . and made a proclamation . . . Marheshvan and Kislev are incomplete months . . . and the nation did not ascend with him [seeing] that this was so,[26] while all of Israel in every land thought otherwise.[27]

The exilarch and the sages of the academies were aghast when they heard about these deeds. They sent Ben Me'ir three letters, one after another, in an effort to prove that he had miscalculated, but instead of being convinced he 'persisted in his deception and refused to recant' and even 'answered them vehemently'. At this stage the Babylonian sages realized that there was no chance of settling the controversy by peaceful means; instead they excommunicated Ben Me'ir and sent an

---

[24] Ibid. 68–9.   [25] Harkavy, *Fugitive Remnants*, 151–3 (Arab. text), 150–2 (Heb. trans.).
[26] Sa'adyah is reusing the language of Exod. 24: 2 with a new meaning, namely, that the people did not follow Aaron's lead; see e.g. Gen. 50: 9 and cf. Exod. 19: 24.
[27] Bornstein, *The Controversy Between Sa'adyah Gaon and Ben Me'ir* (Heb.), 58–61.

epistle to 'the rest of the people . . . to warn them lest they err by reason of the words of the Malignant [i.e. Ben Me'ir]'.[28] Sa'adyah describes the ensuing events as follows:

After this, the Benighter [still] did not repent his evil ways but again wrote untruthful things . . . and was concerned only to uphold his counsel and his scheme, to bring sin and error upon the people . . . And when the sages of religion read his epistles, they rent their clothes . . . And they ceased to answer him for they understood that all his deeds were done out of evil intent and perversity. And they left him to the day of vengeance and fury reserved for those who mislead the people and they did not deign to take epistles from the king to remove him . . . saying: 'we cannot destroy all his writings in public and private, but let us write a book to perpetuate the memory for the generations that follow us, lest his words lead some of them to folly and they stray in his paths'.[29]

Sefer Hagalui

One of the most remarkable and fascinating works by Sa'adyah Gaon, and apparently one of his last, was the *Sefer hagalui*, an open letter to the Jewish people in which he presents his point of view in the controversy that erupted between him and David ben Zakai, the exilarch who had appointed him to his position. The book was published in two editions, the original one written in the elevated style of Sa'adyah's Hebrew works (though, as we shall see, they are not always elevated in terms of content). He divided his book into verses provided with biblical cantillation marks, as he had done in previous works. When his opponents levelled harsh criticism at this composition and its author, Sa'adyah issued a much expanded second edition in Judaeo-Arabic. In addition to a long preface, this edition included the Hebrew text accompanied by a literal translation into Judaeo-Arabic, linguistic annotations, and other comments and supplementary polemical material. As usual, Sa'adyah did not limit himself to the main subject—the polemic against the exilarch and his allies—but took advantage of the opportunity to discuss other subjects that he considered pertinent, as we shall later see. Aside from its piquancy and some added details that shed light on the protracted controversy between the gaon and the exilarch, this composition is of particular importance for its contribution to our understanding of the author's self-consciousness, and it includes a quantity of autobiographical material rare in its day.

This book is not formally divided into sections or chapters but Sa'adyah explains in his preface to the Arabic edition that he has organized the monograph in seven topical sections, and that, in addition to discussing these seven specific topics, he aims to achieve three general objectives by setting the book as a paradigm of belletristic Hebrew writing.

---

[28] Bornstein, *The Controversy Between Sa'adyah Gaon and Ben Me'ir* (Heb.), 61–2.

[29] Ibid. 64–5.

The purposes of this book, all of which will greatly avail our people, are ten—of these seven have their own place, and the final three concern the book in its entirety. And I must review their subject matter and my motives for choosing them ...

The first [section] comprises a description of wisdom and how it is acquired, and the worthy attributes of those who love it and the flaws of those who hate it. And the reason for including this [subject matter] is that these people opposed me owing to their hatred of wisdom and to their intention that there should be no knowledge or integrity among the people of the nation. And the second section [includes] a reckoning of how long prophecy existed in our nation, wherein I explain that this [period] lasted a thousand years, and how many years later the Mishnah was completed, and I explain that it was five hundred years ...

The third section recounts what happens to a land which a tyrant tries to rule, and what led [me] to [write] this was the matter of Ben Zakai.

The fourth section will explain that God will not leave his people in any generation without a 'pupil' to teach them and to bring light to their eyes and to instruct and educate them and bring about their improvement; and the reason for this is that which I have realized about my soul, how [God] has granted grace to me and to the people.

The fifth section includes explanations of the commandments and of the times to come ... and the reason for this is that I perceived a great need among the people for such things.

The sixth section is an account of what has been done to me by people whose names I mention therein, the troubles and provocations and persecutions, and how I called upon God and prayed for His salvation ...

In the seventh section there are descriptions and likenesses of each of these evildoers—I had to include this as an admonition to anyone who might be inclined to do evil like them ... and this is the explanation of the matters of the seven specific chapters.

And the three general headings concern the book as a whole. The first is to teach the nation eloquence in Hebrew, for I have seen that [the influence of the] Arabic and Aramaic [languages] has overpowered it ... and the people have forgotten their eloquent and elevated language. And the second is to teach the nation the composition of speech ... and the third to teach combinations, for the knowledge of any [type of] speech is perfected only by means of the ways in which it is put together.[30]

In the continuation of the preface Sa'adyah explains the need for an expanded Arabic edition:

And having enumerated these ten headings and revealed their use from end to beginning, I must now explain the reason that led [me] to translate this book.[31] And I say that the evil ones, when they saw that I had written a book about them in Arabic, divided into verses with vowels and cantillation signs, spread libellous rumours [about me] and called

---

[30] Harkavy, *Fugitive Remnants* (Heb.), 152–7; Arab. text and flawed Heb. trans., to be corrected according to Tobi, 'A New Page' (Heb.), 56–8.

[31] The Arabic word may mean 'to translate' or 'to interpret', or both.

it a pretence of prophecy—and this shows how ignorant they are of what I stated at the beginning [of the book], for in two places I stated that prophecy has ended ... And anyone who admits that it has ended cannot claim to be a prophet. And they also said that this book would make the people faint of heart and cause them to doubt the twenty-four books [of the Bible] and to think that they, too, are [human] compositions. And this is also ignorance on their part ... for these deeds, that is, these verses, can be created by mortals, as Ben Sira and Ben Iri and the children of the Hasmoneans and the children of Africa have done, and none of these claimed the status of prophecy, for the criteria of prophecy are threefold: one, that they contain mentions of revelation or secret knowledge ... two, that the author of the book is known to be a prophet either through a miraculous sign or through another prophet's testimony about him; and three, that the nation should include this book among its sacred writings and transmit it together with them. And unless all three things appear together, if even one should be lacking, it is not a book of prophecy; let alone if none of the above appear, as in the case of this book![32]

Sa'adyah then proceeds to defend himself against further attacks by his opponents, and especially to justify the words of self-praise that are included in the fourth section mentioned above: 'And I will say that I have established this for two reasons: one, because the book will reach people who do not know me at all, and two, as a warning to those present to remember how I have benefited the nation'. He also provides an explanation for levelling abusive epithets at his adversaries—apparently in the seventh section—for this point he relies on biblical precedents.[33]

Among the polemical fragments that have survived from this book, we may note a passage from the Arabic translation, probably from the third section of the book, describing David ben Zakai's attempts to usurp power. The beginning of the description is missing, but according to Sa'adyah, David abused and impoverished the sages of the Sura academy, took control of the property of those who died, whether 'from the sages or from others among the people', perverted justice, and showed favour to evildoers. Afterwards he tried to win the recognition of the sages of Pumbedita, but they had learned from the experience of their brethren and refused to accept him. Despite this, he succeeded in persuading the government to appoint him exilarch, surrounded himself with worthless people, and continued to pervert justice, cheating the poor and robbing orphans and widows. The only thing that he truly cared about was food and drink, and he was a notorious glutton.[34]

We also have in our possession two passages castigating an important figure or figures from the world of the sages, presumably those sages from the academy of Pumbedita who supported Ben Zakai. One of these passages refers clearly to R. Kohen Tsedek ben Joseph, who had been appointed head of the academy of

[32]   Harkavy, *Fugitive Remnants*, 161–3 (Arab. text), 160–2 (Heb. trans.).
[33]   Harkavy, *Fugitive Remnants* (Heb.), 162–7; the quotation is from pp. 166–7.
[34]   For the text and translation see Tobi, 'A New Page' (Heb.), 65–8; for discussion see ibid. 63–4.

Pumbedita by the exilarch. In this fragment, which has survived partly in the Hebrew original and partly in its Arabic translation, Sa'adyah addresses him in the harshest terms:

Strive in the swamps against the flowing stream, or in the sound of your barley against the pleasantness of honey, as straw against grain, as a lump [of coal] against onyx, darkness against great light, fleeing like a soldier: for the day has come in which the Lord has spoken of you to bring an end to the blasphemies with which you lorded it over the people, for God has revealed your secrets . . . and you will be shamed: how you have said, 'the land was given unto me and my sons', and you are as a corpse defeated! . . . God has commanded an evil end for you, to feed you unending bitterness and bring your old age bloodily to Sheol.[35]

Only a fragment of the Arabic version of the second passage survives, and this does not include the name of the person under attack, but it is likely, once again, to be Kohen Tsedek. Here Sa'adyah claims that the man is ignorant of 'Scriptures, the Mishnah, and the Talmud, speculative learning [*nazar*] and culture [*adab*]', holding himself above others only because of his knowledge of the formulas used in ten kinds of common legal documents. But, he asks, would a Muslim scribe who knows the formulas of ten deeds by heart be considered a proper witness, let alone a teacher of tradition or a sage?! How terrible is the illness of the Jewish people, in which such a person can achieve such an eminent position![36]

[35] Ibid. 71.
[36] See Stern, 'A New Fragment', 141 (Arab. text), 137 (Heb. trans.); cf. Tobi, 'A New Page' (Heb.), 69–70.

Afterword

SA'ADYAH GAON was so multifaceted that it would be impossible for any one person to do him justice or to evaluate the full extent and variety of his life's work. Nevertheless, it is my hope that the reader will come to the end of this book with at least some understanding, however incomplete, of the man and his achievements. A number of factors undoubtedly combined to promote Sa'adyah's unique literary endeavour: his extraordinary intellect and forceful personality; his deep knowledge of Jewish traditions, Palestinian and Babylonian alike; and the crisis of the Babylonian academies, which made it possible for someone like him, having been raised far from geonic circles, to be appointed head of the Sura academy. We must also remember his sense of personal mission and his faith that the Creator had chosen him to lead and nurture the Jewish people in his generation. This feeling led him to redefine the role of the gaon, and the new conception powerfully affected the geonim who succeeded him.

Sa'adyah blazed many new literary trails. Some of these, such as his linguistic and halakhic works, represent a sharp departure from traditional Jewish activities in these fields. In other areas—for example, biblical exegesis, theology, and polemics—he brought new vigour and momentum to what had formerly been areas of modest activity. Even when working within ancient traditions like liturgical poetry he revolutionized the field. He wrote in genres cultivated by the Jews of North Africa, Palestine, and Babylonia, and in most, if not all, of these he was deeply influenced by the surrounding cultures, where Arabic was the spoken language and most of the leading thinkers were Christian or Muslim. Sa'adyah did not hesitate to adopt and adapt vital elements of the general culture, and a major part of his work stems from the challenge of integrating these elements into his Jewish heritage.

The geonic era was the last period in Jewish history, at least until the founding of the State of Israel, when the focus of power and creativity for the Jewish people resided in the Middle East, particularly in the two ancient centres of Palestine and Babylonia. The geonic era transmitted a new version of rabbinic Judaism to future generations. It combined a halakhic legacy based on the Babylonian Talmud, as mediated by the geonim, with several important aspects of the Palestinian tradition, including significant activity in the areas of biblical exegesis, Hebrew linguistics, and liturgical poetry. Sa'adyah played a crucial role in the defence of rabbinical Judaism against external and internal critics and adversaries, both in his championing of the Babylonian tradition throughout the Jewish world (particularly by the role that he played in the calendar controversy) and in his introduction of elements of the Palestinian legacy and of universal culture to the world of the Babylonian sages and to the integrated tradition that they were to bequeath to future generations. No one in the Middle Ages had a broader and deeper influence on the development of Jewish tradition than Sa'adyah Gaon.

Bibliography

❖

ABRAMSON, SHRAGA, 'From the Arabic Original of the Book of Buying and Selling by Rav Hai Gaon' (Heb.), *Tarbiz*, 20 (1949), 296–315.

—— *Topics in Geonic Literature: Researches in the Literature and Responsa of the Geonim in Print and Manuscripts* [Inyanot besifrut hageonim: meḥkarim besifrut hageonim uteshuvoteihem shebidfus uvekitvei yad] (Jerusalem, 1974).

ALLONY, NEHEMIAH, *The Egron: The Book of the Principles of Hebrew Poetry by Rav Sa'adyah Gaon* [Sefer ha'egron: kitab usul al-shiʿr al-ʿibrani me'et rav sa'adyah gaon] (Jerusalem, 1969).

—— *Studies in Medieval Philology and Literature: Collected Papers* [Meḥkerei lashon vesifrut], 6 vols. (Jerusalem, 1986–92).

ASSAF, SIMCHA, *The Geonic Era and its Literature* [Tekufat hageonim vesifrutah], (Jerusalem, 1955).

—— *Rabbinic Texts and Documents*, i: *Gaonica: Gaonic Responsa and Fragments of Halachic Literature from the Geniza and Other Sources* [Toratan shel geonim verishonim, i: Misifrut hageonim: teshuvot hageonim useridim misifrei hahalakhah mitokh kitvei yad shel hagenizah umekorot aḥerim] (Jerusalem, 1933).

—— ISRAEL DAVIDSON, and ISSACHAR JOEL, *Sa'adyah Gaon's Siddur: The Book Collecting Prayers and Benedictions* [Sidur rav sa'adyah gaon: kitab jamʿ al-salawat wa-al-tasabih] (Jerusalem, 1941).

BEERI, TOVA, 'The Beginning of Poetic Creativity in Babylonia: The Piyutim of R. Hayim al-Baradani', *Hebrew Union College Annual*, 68 (1997), Hebrew section, 1–33.

BEN-SASSON, MENACHEM, 'Fragments of Sa'adyah Gaon's *Book of Testimony and Legal Documents*' (Heb.), *Shenaton hamishpat ha'ivri*, 11–12 (1984–6), 135–278.

—— 'The Structure, Goal and Contents of the Story of Nathan Habavli' (Heb.), in *Tarbut veḥevrah betoledot yisra'el biyemei habeinayim: Kovets ma'amarim lezikhro shel ḥayim hilel ben-sason* [Culture and Society in Medieval Jewry: Studies Dedicated to the Memory of Haim Hillel Ben-Sasson], ed. M. Ben-Sasson, R. Bonfil, and J. R. Hacker (Jerusalem, 1989), 137–96.

—— and ROBERT BRODY, *Sa'adyah Gaon's Book of Testimony and Legal Documents* [Sefer ha'edut vehashetarot shel rav sa'adyah gaon] (forthcoming).

BEN-SHAMMAI, HAGGAI, 'A Double Find: R. Samuel b. Hofni's Commentary on *Ha'azinu* and Sa'adyah's Commentary on *Vayosha* in a Forgotten Manuscript' (Heb.), *Kiryat Sefer*, 61 (1986–7), 313–32.

—— 'An "East Wind" from the South: Environmental Realia as a Consideration in Rav Sa'adyah Gaon's Translations and Commentaries' (Heb.), in J. Ben Arye and E. Reiner (eds.), *Vezot liyehudah: Studies in the History of Erets Yisra'el, Presented to Yehudah Ben Porat* [Vezot liyehudah: meḥkarim betoledot erets yisra'el veyishuvah, mugashim liyehudah ben porat] (Jerusalem, 2003), 288–307.

BEN-SHAMMAI, HAGGAI, 'An Important Monograph on Rav Sa'adyah, the Conservative Revolutionary' (Heb.), *Pe'amim*, 117 (2008), 177–86.

—— 'Midrashic-Rabbinic Literature in Rav Sa'adyah Gaon's Commentaries: Continuity and Innovation' (Heb.), in J. Blau and D. Doron (eds.), *Traditions and Change in Medieval Judaeo-Arabic Culture* [Masoret veshinui batarbut ha'aravit-hayehudit biyemei habeinayim] (Ramat Gan, 2000), 33–69.

—— 'Old and New: The "Long Introduction" and the "Short Introduction" to Rav Sa'adyah Gaon's Translation of the Torah' (Heb.), *Tarbiz*, 69 (2000), 199–210.

—— 'Rav Sa'adyah Gaon's Introduction to Isaiah—An Introduction to the Prophets' (Heb.), *Tarbiz*, 60 (1991), 371–404.

—— 'Sa'adyah Gaon's Ten Articles of Faith' (Heb.), *Da'at*, 37 (1996), 11–26.

—— 'Sa'adyah's Introduction to Daniel: Prophetic calculation of the end of days vs. astrological and magical speculation' (Heb.), *Aleph*, 4 (2004), 11–87.

BLAU, JOSHUA, 'Investigations in Rav Sa'adyah Gaon's Translation of Genesis 11–12' (Heb.), in Z. Amar and H. Sari (eds.), *Joseph Kafih Memorial Volume* [Sefer zikaron lerav yosef ben david kafih] (Ramat Gan, 2001), 309–18.

—— 'On Rav Sa'adyah Gaon's Translation of the Pentateuch' (Heb.), in *Mordechai Breuer Jubilee Volume* [Sefer hayovel lerav mordekhai broier: asupat ma'amarim bemada'ei hayahadut] (1992), 633–8.

—— and SIMON HOPKINS, 'On Early Judaeo-Arabic Orthography', *Zeitschrift für Arabische Linguistik*, 12 (1984), 9–27.

—— *Corpus of Judaeo-Arabic Texts in Early Phonetic Spelling* (Heb., forthcoming).

The Book of Beliefs and Opinions of Rav Sa'adyah ben Joseph al-Fayyumi [Kitab al-amanat wa-al-i'tiqadat von saadja b. jusuf al-fajjumi], ed. S. Landauer (Leiden, 1880).

BORNSTEIN, HAYIM, *The Controversy Between Sa'adyah Gaon and Ben Me'ir* [Maḥloket rav sa'adyah gaon uven me'ir] (Warsaw, 1904).

BRODY, ROBERT, *The Geonim of Babylonia and the Shaping of Medieval Jewish Culture* (New Haven and London, 1998).

—— *The Responsa of Rav Natronai bar Hilai Gaon* [Teshuvot rav natronai bar hilai gaon] (Jerusalem, 1994; 2nd edn. 2011).

—— *Sa'adyah Gaon's Halakhic Works* [Sifrei halakhah shel rav sa'adyah gaon] (forthcoming).

DAN, JOSEPH, *History of Jewish Mysticism and Esotericism: Ancient Times* [Toledot torat hasod ha'ivrit: Ha'et ha'atikah], 3 vols. (Jerusalem, 2008).

DAVIDSON, HERBERT, 'Saadia's List of Theories of the Soul', in A. Altmann (ed.), *Jewish Medieval and Renaissance Studies* (Cambridge, Mass., 1967), 75–94.

DAVIDSON, ISRAEL, *Saadia's Polemic against Ḥiwi al-Balkhi: A Fragment Edited from a Genizah MS*, Texts and Studies of the Jewish Theological Seminary of America 5 (New York, 1915).

DERENBOURG, JOSEPH, *Œuvres complètes de R. Saadia b. Iosef al-Fayyoumi*, i: *Version Arabe du Pentateuque* (Paris, 1893).

DOTAN, ARON, *First Light in Linguistics: The Book of Hebrew Eloquence of Rav Sa'adyah Gaon, Introduction and Critical Edition* [Or rishon beḥokhmat halashon: sefer tsaḥut leshon ha'ivrim lerav sa'adyah gaon, mavo umahadurah mada'it], 2 vols. (Jerusalem, 1997).

ELIZUR, SHULAMIT, 'Towards the Completion of the First Two Sections of the Book *Esa meshali* by R. Sa'adyah Gaon' (Heb., forthcoming).

FLEISCHER, EZRA, *Hebrew Liturgical Poetry in the Middle Ages* [Shirat hakodesh ha'ivrit biyemei habeinayim] (Jerusalem, 1975; 2nd edn. Jerusalem, 2007).

GINZBERG, LOUIS, *Ginzei Schechter*, ii: *Fragments of Geonic Writings from the Egyptian Genizah* [Ginzei shekhter, ii: keta'im mikitvei hageonim min hagenizah shebemitsrayim] (New York, 1929).

HARKAVY, ABRAHAM E., *Fugitive Remnants of the* Egron *and* Sefer hagalui [Hasarid vehapalit misefer ha'egron umisefer hagalui] (St Petersburg, 1891).

—— *Responsa of the Geonim* [Zikhron kamah geonim uveyiḥud rav sherira verav hai beno veharav yitsḥak alfasi] (Berlin, 1887).

HIRSCHFELD, HARTWIG, 'The Arabic Portion of the Cairo Genizah at Cambridge (Third Article)', *Jewish Quarterly Review*, OS 16 (1904), 98–112.

KAFIH, YOSEF, *The Book of Creation (Kitab al-Mabadi') with the Translation and Commentary of the Gaon Rabbi Sa'adyah b. R. Joseph* [Sefer yetsirah (kitab al-mabadi') im targum uferush hagaon rabenu sa'adyah b. r. yosef fayumi] (Jerusalem, 1972).

—— *Daniel with the Translation and Commentary of our Rabbi Sa'adyah ben Joseph Fayyumi* [Dani'el im targum uferush rabenu sa'adyah ben yosef fayumi] (Jerusalem, 1981).

—— *Job with the Translation and Commentary of our Rabbi Sa'adyah ben Joseph Fayyumi* [Iyov im targum uferush rabenu sa'adyah ben yosef fayumi] (Jerusalem, 1973).

—— *Proverbs with the Translation and Commentary of our Rabbi Sa'adyah ben Joseph Fayyumi* [Mishlei im targum uferush rabenu sa'adyah ben yosef fayumi] (Jerusalem, 1976).

—— *Psalms with the Translation and Commentary of our Rabbi Sa'adyah ben Joseph Fayyumi* [Tehilim im targum uferush rabenu sa'adyah ben yosef fayumi] (Jerusalem, 1966).

KLAR, BENJAMIN, *Researches and Investigations in Language, Poetry, and Literature* [Meḥkarim ve'iyunim belashon, beshirah uvesifrut] (Tel Aviv, 1954).

LEWIN, BENJAMIN M., *The Epistle of Sherira Gaon* [Igeret rav sherira gaon] (Haifa, 1921).

—— '*Esa Meshali* by Rav Sa'adyah Gaon' (Heb.), in J. L. Fishman (ed.), *Rav Sa'adyah Gaon* [Rav sa'adyah gaon: kovets torani umada'i] (Jerusalem, 1943), 481–532.

—— *A Geonic Thesaurus: Responsa and Commentaries by the Geonim of Babylonia according to the Order of the Talmud* [Otsar hageonim: teshuvot geonei bavel uferusheihem al pi seder hatalmud], 13 vols. (Haifa and Jerusalem, 1928–44).

LIEBES, YEHUDA, *The Theory of Creation of the Book of Creation* [Torat hayetsirah shel sefer yetsirah] (Tel Aviv, 2000).

MALTER, HENRY, *Saadia Gaon: His Life and Works* (Philadelphia, 1921).

MANN, JACOB, 'A Fihrist of Sa'adya's Works', *Jewish Quarterly Review*, NS 11 (1920–1), 423–8.

MIRSKY, ABRAHAM, *The Poems of Yosi ben Yosi* [Piyutei yosi ben yosi] (Jerusalem, 1977).

MÜLLER, JOEL, *The Book of Inheritance together with the Remaining Halakhic Writings of Rav Sa'adyah Gaon in Arabic and Hebrew and Aramaic* [Sefer hayerushot im yeter hamikhtavim bedivrei hahalakhah be'aravit uve'ivrit uve'aramit lerabenu sa'adyah gaon ben yosef hafayumi] (Paris, 1897).

NEUBAUER, ADOLF, *Mediaeval Jewish Chronicles and Chronological Notes, Edited from Printed Books and Manuscripts*, 2 vols. (Oxford, 1887–95).

POZNANSKI, SAMUEL, *The Karaite Literary Opponents of Saadiah Gaon* (London, 1908).

RATZABY, YEHUDA, *Sa'adyah Gaon's Commentary on Exodus: Original and Translation* [Perushei rav sa'adyah gaon lesefer shemot: makor vetargum] (Jerusalem, 1998).

—— *Sa'adyah Gaon's Commentary on Isaiah (Kitab al-Istislah)* [Tafsir yeshaya lerav sa'adyah (kitab al-istislah)] (Kiryat Ono, 1993).

Saadia Gaon: The Book of Beliefs and Opinions, trans. Solomon Rosenblatt (New Haven, 1948).

SCHECHTER, SOLOMON, *Saadyana: Geniza Fragments of Writings of R. Saadya Gaon and Others* (Cambridge, 1903).

SCHEIBER, ALEXANDER, 'Chapters of Saadya Gaon's Book of Commandments from the Kaufman Genizah Collection', in *S. Federbush Jubilee Volume* [Sefer yovel likhvod harav dr shimon federbush] (Jerusalem, 1961), 330–5.

Sha'arei tsedek, ed. Hayim Modai (Salonika, 1792).

STEIN, SIEGFRIED, 'Saadya's Piyyut on the Alphabet', in E. I. J. Rosenthal (ed.), *Saadya Studies* (Manchester, 1943), 206–26.

STERN, SAMUEL M., 'A New Fragment of *Sefer hagalui* by Rav Sa'adyah Gaon' (Heb.), *Melila*, 5 (1955), 133–47.

STROUMSA, SARAH, *Sa'adyah Gaon—A Jewish Thinker in a Mediterranean Society* [Sa'adyah gaon—hogeh yehudi behevrah yam-tikhonit] (Tel Aviv, 2001).

TOBI, YOSEF, 'A New Page of Rav Sa'adyah Gaon's *Sefer hagalui*' (Heb.), in J. Dishon and E. Hazan (eds.), *Studies in Hebrew Literature and Yemenite Culture: Jubilee Volume Presented to Professor Yehuda Ratzaby* [Mehkarim besifrut am yisra'el uvetarbut teiman: sefer hayovel liprof. yehudah ratsabi] (Ramat Gan, 1991), 55–75.

—— *Sa'adyah Gaon's Liturgical Poems: A Critical Edition of the Yotserot and a General Introduction to his Oeuvre* [Piyutei rav sa'adyah gaon—mahadurah mada'it shel hayotserot umavo kelali liyetsirato], Ph.D. diss. (Jerusalem, 1985).

YAHALOM, YOSEF, *The Language of Early Palestinian Liturgical Poetry* [Sefat hashir shel hapiyut ha'erets yisra'eli hakadum] (Jerusalem, 1985).

ZUCKER, MOSHE, 'Fragments of Rav Sa'adyah Gaon's *Treatise on the Source of the Non-Rational Commandments*' (Heb.), *Tarbiz*, 41 (1972), 373–410.

—— *On Rav Sa'adyah Gaon's Translation of the Torah: Exegesis, Halakhah, and Polemics in the Torah Translation of Rav Sa'adyah Gaon* [Al targum rasag latorah: parshanut, halakhah ufolemikah betargum hatorah shel rav sa'adyah gaon] (New York, 1959).

—— *Sa'adyah Gaon's Commentary on Genesis* [Perushei rav sa'adyah gaon livereshit] (New York, 1984).

ZULAY, MENACHEM, *Rav Sa'adyah Gaon's Poetical School* [Ha'askolah hapaitanit shel rav sa'adyah gaon] (Jerusalem, 1964).

Index

The main attributes of Sa'adyah's life and work are listed under Sa'adyah; individual works are listed alphabetically.